W9-DDG-834

COUNTDOWN to SPANISH

Learn to Communicate in 24 Hours

GAIL STEIN

McGraw-Hill

New York   Chicago   San Francisco   Lisbon   London   Madrid   Mexico City
Milan   New Delhi   San Juan   Seoul   Singapore   Sydney   Toronto

The *McGraw·Hill* Companies

Library of Congress Cataloging-in-Publication Data

Stein, Gail.
      Countdown to Spanish : learn to communicate in 24 hours / Gail Stein.
          p.   cm. (Countdown series)
      Includes index.
      ISBN 0-07-141423-1 (alk. paper)
      1. Spanish language—Textbooks for foreign speakers—English.   I. Title.

PC4129.E5S73 2003
468.2'421—dc21
                                          2003045940

Copyright © 2004 by The McGraw-Hill Companies, Inc. All rights reserved. Printed in the United States of America. Except as permitted under the United States Copyright Act of 1976, no part of this publication may be reproduced or distributed in any form or by any means, or stored in a database or retrieval system, without the prior written permission of the publisher.

1 2 3 4 5 6 7 8 9 0   AGM/AGM   2 1 0 9 8 7 6 5 4 3

ISBN 0-07-141423-1

Interior design by Think Design Group LLC

McGraw-Hill books are available at special quantity discounts to use as premiums and sales promotions, or for use in corporate training programs. For more information, please write to the Director of Special Sales, Professional Publishing, McGraw-Hill, Two Penn Plaza, New York, NY 10121-2298. Or contact your local bookstore.

This book is printed on acid-free paper.

This book is dedicated to:

My wonderfully patient and supportive husband, Douglas
My incredibly loving, understanding, and proud sons, Eric and Michael
My proud parents, Jack and Sara Bernstein
My creative sister and her family, Susan, Jay, and Zachary Opperman
My superior consultant and advisor, Roger H. Herz
My good friend and supporter, Christina Levy

Contents

Introduction

The main premise of *Countdown to Spanish* is that you can learn this extremely useful and beautiful language quickly and effectively. If you are willing to spend just 24 hours of your time studying the grammar, vocabulary, and phrases presented in the lessons, you will find that you will be able to understand and communicate in Spanish in various types of everyday situations. You can immediately feel confident that you will meet this challenge and accomplish your goals effortlessly and rapidly.

To make the task of learning Spanish as time-efficient as possible, *Countdown to Spanish* is divided into 24 one-hour lessons. Each lesson is then subdivided into very logical and manageable parts, which will enable you to learn the material with ease and self-assurance. Just divide the lesson so that you allow an equal number of minutes for each major heading. Do not worry about memorizing all the words in every table. That would prove to be an impossible and frustrating task. Instead, use the lists for reference, along with the key phrases you memorize. Those words that are high-frequency in your vocabulary will quickly become a part of your own personal word list.

Countdown to Spanish is completely different from other language books. It is not a grammar text for students, yet it contains an in-depth study of all the major grammar inherent to Spanish. It is not a phrase book for travelers, yet it contains all the in-depth vocabulary you might want or need in every conceivable situation. It is, therefore, a unique combination of the two that gives you the essentials for an immediate jump start in speaking and understanding Spanish.

Unlike any other foreign language book on the market, *Countdown to Spanish* is organized into a series of tasks that speakers will find useful and adaptable in a wide variety of situations: socializing, giving and receiving information, persuasion, expressing feelings and emotions, and expressing needs. These are the elements that are necessary for anyone who wants to understand and be understood: that is, to communicate as effectively as possible. Remember that dictionaries just give you words without teaching you how to put them together to form logical, comprehensive thoughts. *Countdown to Spanish* will allow you to reach this goal.

Hours 24:00 to 19:00 present the grammar you will need to form complete, simple, and correct sentences in the past, present, or future tense. The differences between American and Spanish syntax and structure will be pinpointed to give you a greater understanding and command of the language. The rules you learn in these lessons can then be applied to accomplish any of the tasks in the lessons that follow. So feel free to skip around and use the knowledge you've acquired in any of the parts that follow, without being overly concerned about sequence.

Hours 18:00 to 16:00 give you the phrases and structures necessary to strike up a conversation and make the acquaintance of a Spanish-speaking person. You'll learn how to extend, accept, and graciously refuse an invitation and offer apologies and excuses using the correct Spanish vocabulary and structures.

Hours 15:00 and 14:00 enable you to get someone to follow a course of action at a mutually convenient time and place. These lessons allow you to make proposals, offer suggestions, and give commands that can be used for a variety of different activities and events.

Hours 13:00 to 11:00 teach you the most effective ways to ask yes/no and information questions. In the event of a lack of communication, you'll be prepared. You'll also be able to properly furnish any necessary information in a quick, efficient manner. There are sections teaching you how to make a phone call and how to obtain help in securing personal services at the post office, the hair salon, the dry cleaner's, the optician's, the camera shop, and the jeweler's. There's even vocabulary for those with special needs who require special services.

Hours 10:00 to 8:00 allow you to express your positive and negative reactions and emotions, as well as your indifference and indecision towards varying activities. You'll be using colloquial and idiomatic Spanish and grammatically correct structures to accomplish these tasks, as well as to make comparisons.

Hours 7:00 to 1:00 will help you with your hotel, food, medical, clothing, transportation, banking, and business needs by means of easy but clear-cut Spanish expressions.

The appendixes at the back of the book give essential words and phrases in Spanish, and verb charts.

The rest is up to you. If you're really committed, you can do this! *¡Buena suerte!* (boo-weh-nah soo-wehr-teh) Good luck!

Focusing on Pronunciation

MASTER THESE SKILLS

. . . .

- Pronunciation

- Stress

- Accents

- Vowels

- Diphthongs

- Consonants

. . . .

In this chapter you'll learn how to stress
Spanish syllables and how different accents
affect the sounds of the Spanish letters.
You'll also be given a key to help you
properly pronounce vowels, consonants,
and diphthongs.

PERFECTING YOUR PRONUNCIATION

Although your level of competence in pronouncing Spanish properly has very little bearing on your ability to be understood, you can follow some simple steps that should enable you to express yourself in a more acceptable manner. Some suggestions and tips for better pronunciation include the following:

- Relax and speak slowly. No one expects you to sound like a native.
- Slip and slide sounds together to get a more natural flow.
- Lose your inhibitions by reading aloud Spanish newspapers, magazines, and literature.
- Set aside the necessary time to practice different sounds.
- Don't be afraid to "ham up" your accent.
- Remember to pronounce letters with accents properly.

STRESS

The rules for stress in Spanish are straightforward, but they do require your concentration at first. In general, Spanish words are pronounced exactly as they are written. Follow these simple guidelines:

- If a word ends in a vowel, an *n*, or an *s*, place the stress on the next to the last syllable, for example: es**cue**la, inteli**gen**te, **cen**tro, **jo**ven, in**sec**tos.
- If the word ends in any letter besides those mentioned above, the stress is on the last syllable, for example: pa**pel**, comuni**car**, sa**lud**.
- All exceptions to the above two rules have an accent over the vowel of the stressed syllable, for example: ca**fé**, **lám**para, in**glés**, se**gún**.

The only exceptions to these rules are words of foreign origin, usually words taken from English, which keep their original spelling and pronounciation, for example: **san**dwich, **In**ternet.

ACCENTS

Accent marks are small pronunciation guides that help you speak more like a native. Spanish has three different accent marks that may change the sound or stress of the letter.

The most common accent in Spanish is the acute accent (´), which is used only on a vowel and indicates that you must put additional stress on the syllable containing it:

mamá	ma-MAH
café	ka-FEH
egoísta	eh-goh-EES-tah

opinión	oh-peen-YOHN
música	MOO-see-kah

The *tilde* (˜) is used only on the letter *n* (*ñ*), producing the sound *ny* as in the *nio* of union:

cabaña	kah-bah-NYAH
mañana	mah-NYAH-nah

The least common accent is known as a *diéresis* (¨) and is placed on a *u* when it is followed by another vowel. A diéresis indicates that each vowel sound is pronounced separately:

nicaragüense	nee-kah-rah-goo-WEHN-seh
lingüistico	leen-goo-WEES-tee-koh

VOWELS

Each vowel in Spanish is represented by one phonetic sound, and accent marks are used only to determine the amount of stress needed. After each of the following vowel explanations you will have the opportunity to practice repeating sentences that reinforce the sounds presented. Take advantage and practice your accent until you feel comfortable that you have mastered the material.

a

There is only one sound for *a*. Just open your mouth and say *ahhh*.

VOWEL	SYMBOL	PRONUNCIATION
a, á	ah	a as in *ma*

Mariana is going home now with Susana's mother.

Mariana va a su casa ahora con la mamá de Susana.

mah-ree-yah-nah bah ah soo kah-sah ah-oh-rah kohn lah mah-MAH deh soo-sah-nah.

e

There is one sound for the vowel *e*:

VOWEL	SYMBOL	PRONUNCIATION
e, é	eh	e as in *gate*

Enrique Estevez is the man from Chile.

Enrique Estevez es el hombre de Chile.

ehn-ree-keh ehs-teh-behs ehs ehl ohm-breh deh chee-leh

i

The *i* is pretty straightforward and easy to pronounce as an *ee* sound:

VOWEL	SYMBOL	PRONUNCIATION
i, í	ee	*i* as in *magazine*

Isidro is an Italian individual.

Isidro es un individuo italiano.

ee-see-droh ehs oon een-dee-bee-doo-woh ee-tahl-ee-yah-noh

o

Round your lips to get the *o* sound:

VOWEL	SYMBOL	PRONUNCIATION
o, ó	oh	*o* as in *go*

I don't understand it.

Yo no lo comprendo.

yoh noh loh kohm-prehn-doh

u

Say the sound *oo* as in *moo* when pronouncing *u*:

VOWEL	SYMBOL	PRONUNCIATION
u, ú	oo	*oo* as in *too*

You use a pen in a university.

Tú usas una pluma en una universidad.

too oo-sahs oo-nah ploo-mah ehn oo-nah oo-nee-behr-see-dad.

DIPHTHONGS

A diphthong is the combination of a vowel sound and the consonant sound of *y* or *w* into a single syllable. The sound of *y* is represented in Spanish by *i* or *y*, and the sound of *w* is represented by *u*.

Diphthongs with Vowel Sounds First

DIPHTHONG	SYMBOL	PRONUNCIATION
ai, ay	ah-yee	*i* as in *light*
ei, ey	eh-yee	*e* as in *they*
oi, oy	oy	*o* as in *boy*
au	ow	*ow* as in *cow*
eu	eh-yoo	*eu* as in *reuse*

I hear that there are six kings and an author in Europe.

Oigo que hay seis reyes y un autor en Europa.

oy-goh keh ah-yee seh-yees rreh-yehs ee oon ow-tohr ehn eh-yoo-roh-pah

Diphthongs with Consonant Sounds First

DIPHTHONG	SYMBOL	PRONUNCIATION
ia, ya	ee-yah	*ya* as is *yarn*
ie, ye	ee-yeh	*ye* as in *yet*
ua	oo-wah	*wa* as in *watch*
ue	oo-weh	*we* as in *wet*
io, yo	ee-yoh	*yo* as in *yoke*
uo	oo-woh	*(w)uo* as in *quote*
iu, yu	ee-yoo	*you* as in *you*
ui, uy	oo-wee	*wee* as in *week*

I am serious and I study in the city when there is no noise.

Soy serio y estudio en la ciudad cuando no hay ruido.

soy seh-ree-yoh ee ehs-too-dee-yoh ehn lah see-yoo-dahd
kwahn-doh noh ah-yee rroo-wee-doh

CONSONANTS

The Spanish alphabet consists of twenty-eight letters, five of which are vowels. Three of the remaining twenty-three letters, *ch*, *ll*, and *ñ*, do not exist in the English alphabet. (*Ch* and *ll* are no longer commonly treated as separate letters, but they do have unique pronunciations.) The letter *w* is used only in words of foreign origin and is not considered part of the Spanish alphabet. The following Spanish consonants should pose no problem in pronunciation because they are the same in both Spanish and English: *b, d, f, k, l, m, n, p, s, t, y.*

c

The letter *c* may have a soft or hard sound depending on the letter that comes after it:

LETTER	SYMBOL	PRONUNCIATION
c before a, o, u (hard sound)	k	c as in *car*
c before i, e, y (soft sound)	s	s as in *sent*
ch	ch	ch as in *much*

Carlos Cepeda drives his car downtown with the check.

Carlos Cepeda conduce su coche al centro con el cheque.

kahr-lohs seh-peh-dah kohn-doo-seh soo koh-cheh ahl sehn-troh kohn ehl cheh-keh

g

The letter *g* may have a soft or hard sound depending on the vowel(s) that comes after it:

LETTER	SYMBOL	PRONUNCIATION
g before a, o, u, or consonant (hard sound)	g	g as in *good*
g before e, i (soft sound)	h	h as in *he*

Geraldo and Gabriela Gómez win in the gym.

Geraldo y Gabriela Gómez ganan en el gimnasio.

heh-rahl-doh ee gah-bree-yeh-lah goh-mehs gah-nahn ehn ehl heem-nah-see-yoh.

h

An *h* is always silent in Spanish:

Hector has a Hispanic ice cream.

Hector tiene un helado hispano.

ehk-tohr tee-yeh-neh oon eh-lah-doh ees-pah-noh

j

The letter *j* is pronounced like an English *h*:

LETTER	SYMBOL	PRONUNCIATION
j	h	*h* as in *he*

The big young boy plays with Julio and Gerald in the garden.

El joven grande juega con Julio y Geraldo en el jardín.

ehl hoh-behn grahn-deh hoo-weh-gah kohn hoo-lee-yoh ee heh-rahl-doh ehn ehl har-deen

ll

The Spanish *ll* has the sound of an English *y*:

LETTER	SYMBOL	PRONUNCIATION
ll	y	*y* as in *you*

The llama cries slowly.

La llama llora lentamente.

lah yah-mah yoh-rah lehn-tah-mehn-teh

ñ

The *ñ* has almost the equivalent sound of *ni* in *union*:

LETTER	SYMBOL	PRONUNCIATION
ñ	ny	*ni* as in *union*

The young girl doesn't add anything.

La niña no añade nada.

lah nee-nyah noh ah-nyah-deh nah-dah

q

The Spanish *q* has the sound of an English *k*:

LETTER	SYMBOL	PRONUNCIATION
q	k	*k* as in *key*

Perhaps you want fifteen cheeses.

Quizás quieras quince quesos.

kee-sahs kee-yeh-rahs keen-seh keh-sohs

r

The Spanish *r* is rolled or trilled. A single *r* receives a single tap of the tongue whereas the double *r (rr)*, an *r* at the beginning of a word, and an *r* preceded by *l*, *n*, or *s* are strongly trilled (two or three tongue rolls).

LETTER	SYMBOL	PRONUNCIATION
r	r	*r* as in *ray*
rr	rr	*r* as in *rrray*

Mr. Robert wants the honor of seeing Ramón and Carlota Ruiz.

El señor Roberto quiere la honra de ver a Ramón y Carlota Ruiz.

ehl seh-nyohr rroh-behr-toh kee-yeh-reh lah ohn-rrah deh behr ah rrah-mohn ee kahr-loh-tah rroo-ees

v

The Spanish *v* sounds like the English *b*.

LETTER	SYMBOL	PRONUNCIATION
v	b	*b* as in *boy*

It is true that Violet had a glass of wine.

Es verdad que Violeta tuvo un vaso de vino.

ehs behr-dahd keh bee-yoh-leh-tah too-boh oon bah-soh deh bee-noh

x

The letter *x* is pronounced one way before a consonant and a different way between two vowels. In some words, it has the sound of the English *s*:

LETTER	SYMBOL	PRONUNCIATION
x (before a consonant)	s	*s* as in *see*
x (between two vowels)	gs	*gs* as in *eggs*

Mrs. Màxima explains the sixth test.

La señora Máxima explica el sexto examen.

lah seh-nyoh-rah mag-see-mah ehs-plee-kah ehl sehs-toh ehg-sah-mehn

z

The Spanish *z* has a soft sound:

LETTER	SYMBOL	PRONUNCIATION
z	s	s as in see

The blue fox is in the zoo.

El zorro azul está en el zoológico.

ehl soh-roh ah-sool ehs-tah ehn ehl soh-oh-loh-hee-koh

HAVING THE RIGHT TOOLS

A tape recorder can be an indispensable tool for language study, but also make sure that you have on hand an up-to-date, modern, clear, easy-to-use bilingual dictionary. Don't make a hasty purchase. Ensure that you understand the abbreviations in the front of the book and that grammatical explanations are clear. Verify that modern, everyday technical and business terms are included. Check the date of publication—the world is changing so rapidly that you want to have a book that has been updated quite recently.

A FINAL SUGGESTION

Now that you are well on your way to excellent pronunciation habits, try singing along to your favorite Latin tunes. Whether you prefer oldies or something more contemporary, you will find that you can learn a lot of vocabulary and easily become accustomed to the rhythms used by native speakers.

TIME'S UP!

Now that you've had the opportunity to thoroughly acquaint yourself with and practice the sounds of Spanish, try reading these potentially useful phrases without the aid of any pronunciation clues. Try to avoid looking back for help.

1. **Buenos días. Me llamo José Silva. ¿Cómo se llama?**
   Hello. My name is José Silva. What's your name?

2. **Hablo español (un poco).**
   I speak (a little) Spanish.

3. **Perdóneme. Yo no comprendo. Hable más despacio por favor.**
   Excuse me. I don't understand. Please speak more slowly.

4. **¿Qué dijo? Repítalo por favor.**
   What did you say? Please repeat it.

5. **Quisiera cambiar mis dólares en euros por favor.**
   I would like to change my American dollars to euros please.

6. **Perdóneme. ¿Dónde está la embajada americana?**
   Excuse me. Where's the American Embassy?

7. **No me siento bien. ¿Dónde está la oficina del médico más cercana?**
   I don't feel well. Where is the office of the nearest doctor?

8. **¿Podrías ayudarme, por favor? Perdí un documento importante.**
   Could you please help me? I've lost an important document.

9. **¿Cúanto cuestan estos pantalones negros y estas camisas rojas?**
   How much do these black pants and red shirts cost?

10. **Necesito una cuchara, un tenedor y un cuchillo. Gracias.**
    I need a spoon, a fork, and a knife. Thank you.

Recognizing and Using Nouns

MASTER THESE SKILLS

- Recognizing and using noun markers
- Using nouns properly
- Making nouns plural
- Recognizing and using cognates

In this chapter you'll learn how to differentiate between masculine and feminine nouns and how to form the plural of nouns. Cognates will be explained, and a useful, working list will be presented to allow for immediate communication.

GENDER

Like English, all Spanish nouns have a number: singular (one), as in *la familia*, or plural (more than one), as in *las familias*. Unlike English, however, all Spanish nouns also have a gender: masculine or feminine. In some instances, the gender of the noun is blatantly obvious: *un hombre* (a man) is masculine, whereas *una mujer* (a woman) is feminine. In other cases, the gender of a noun is not in the least bit apparent and defies all rules of common sense or logic: *una corbata* (a tie) is feminine, while *un vestido* (a dress) is masculine.

Spanish syntax and grammar require that all words in a sentence agree in number and gender with the noun or pronoun they modify. For this reason, you must learn the gender of each noun you need or deem important. Special noun endings and markers, either articles or adjectives, indicate the gender and number of Spanish nouns.

NOUN MARKERS

Noun markers are articles or adjectives that tell you whether a noun is singular (sing.) or plural (pl.), masculine (m.) or feminine (f.). Three of the most common markers, as shown in the following table, are definite articles expressing "the," indefinite articles expressing "a," "an," "one," or "some," and demonstrative adjectives expressing "this," "that," "these," and "those."

Singular Noun Markers

	MEANING	MASCULINE	FEMININE
definite article	the	el	la
indefinite article	a, an	un(o)	una
demonstrative adjectives	this	este	esta
	that	ese	esa
	that	aquel	aquella

Plural Noun Markers

	MEANING	MASCULINE	FEMININE
definite article	the	los	las
indefinite article	some	unos	unas
demonstrative adjectives	these	estos	estas
	those	esos	esas
	those	aquellos	aquellas

Definite Articles

The definite article *the* indicates a specific person or thing: the teacher, the house. The definite article precedes the noun that it modifies and, in Spanish, agrees with that noun in gender and number. The masculine or feminine gender of the noun is usually, but not always, easily recognizable by the noun ending: *-o* for masculine and *-a* for feminine. Plural nouns end in *-s*:

el muchach**o**	the boy	**la** muchach**a**	the girl
los muchach**os**	the boys	**las** muchach**as**	the girls

Use the definite article in the following instances:

- With nouns in a general or abstract sense: *El chocolate es delicioso.* (Chocolate is delicious.)
- With time of day:

Es la una.	It's one o'clock.
Son las siete.	It's seven o'clock.

- With names of languages, except immediately after *hablar, en,* and *de*:

El español es fácil.	Spanish is easy.

But:

Hablo español.	I speak Spanish.
El libro está escrito en español.	The book is written in Spanish.
Es un libro de español.	It's a Spanish book.

- With parts of the body when the possessor is clear: *Cierra los ojos.* (Close your eyes.)
- With titles of rank or profession except when addressing the person:

El doctor Rueda llega.	Dr. Rueda arrives.

But:

Buenos días, Doctor Rueda.	Good morning, Dr. Rueda.

- With days of the week in a plural sense to express something that takes place regularly, except after the verb *ser* (to be) when expressing dates:

Los domingos descanso.	On Sundays I rest.

But:

    Hoy es lunes.   Today is Monday.

- With seasons, except that it may be omitted after *en*:

    Me gusta la primavera   I like spring (summer, fall, winter).
    (el verano, el otoño,
    el invierno).

But:

    Voy a España en (el) otoño.   I am going to Spain in the fall.

- With most geographical names (rivers, mountains, oceans, countries, states, and cities):

    Vivo en los Estados Unidos.   I live in the United States.

    El Amazonas es un río.   The Amazon is a river.

- Before verb infinitives used as nouns (although when the infinitive is the subject of the sentence, the definite article may be omitted): *(El) llegar temprano es bueno.* (Arriving early is good.)
- Before nouns of weight or measure: *dos dólares la docena* (two dollars a dozen)

The definite article is omitted:

- Before nouns in apposition, except where there is a family or business relationship:

    Madrid, capital de España,   Madrid, the capital of Spain, is a
    es una ciudad maravillosa.   marvelous city.

But:

    Susana, la hermana de   Susan, Juan's sister, is very intelligent.
    Juan,es muy inteligente.

- Before numerals expressing the numerical order of rulers: *Carlos Segundo* (Charles the Second).

The neuter definite article *lo* is used as follows:

- The neuter *lo* (used for masculine or feminine, singular or plural) precedes a masculine adjective used as a noun to express an abstract idea or a quality:

Pienso lo mismo que ellos.	I think the same as they do.
Lo caro no es siempre mejor que lo barato.	Expensive is not always better than inexpensive.

- *Lo* + adjective (or adverb) + *que* = how

Ya veo lo peligroso que es.	I see how dangerous it is.
¿Escuchas lo rápidamente que él habla?	Do you hear how fast he speaks?

Indefinite Articles

The indefinite article refers to persons and objects not specifically identified: a dog, some cats. The indefinite article also precedes the noun that it modifies and must agree with that noun in gender and number:

un muchach**o**	a boy	un**a** muchach**a**	a girl
unos muchach**os**	some boys	un**as** muchach**as**	some girls

Omit the indefinite article in these situations:

- Before nouns showing a class or group (occupation, nationality, religion, etc.) unless the noun is modified:

Soy profesora.	I'm a teacher.
Es americana.	She's (an) American.

But:

Soy una buena profesora.	I'm a good teacher.
Es una americana importante.	She's an important American.

- Before or after certain words that generally have the article in English:

otro día	another day
cierto hombre	a certain man
cien libros	a hundred books
mil dólares	a thousand dollars
tal mujer	such a woman
¡Qué lástima!	What a pity!

Demonstrative Adjectives

Demonstrative adjectives indicate or point out the person, place, or thing referred to: this girl, that country, these people, those pens. A demonstrative adjective precedes the noun that it modifies and agrees with that noun in gender and number.

In Spanish, the demonstrative adjective is selected according to how near or directly concerned the noun is to the speaker and the person addressed in the conversation.

Este/esta (this) and *estos/estas* (these) refer to nouns that are close to and directly concern the speaker:

este muchacho	this boy	esta muchacha	this girl
estos muchachos	these boys	estas muchachas	these girls

Ese/esa (that) and *esos/esas* (those) refer to nouns that are not near or directly concerned with the speaker or the person being addressed:

ese muchacho	that boy	esa muchacha	that girl
esos muchachos	those boys	esas muchachas	those girls

Aquel/aquella (that) and *aquellos/aquellas* (those) refer to things that are quite far from or do not directly concern either the speaker or the person being addressed:

aquel muchacho	that boy	aquella muchacha	that girl
aquellos muchachos	those boys	aquellas muchachas	those girls

Demonstrative adjectives may be reinforced by using corresponding adverbs that show location:

DEMONSTRATIVE ADJECTIVE	ADVERB	MEANING
este, esta, estos, estas	aquí	here
ese, esa, esos, esas	ahí	there (but not too far)
aquel, aquella, aquellos, aquellas	allá	over there (rather far)
este libro aquí		this book here
esa pluma ahí		that pen there
aquellos lápices allá		those pencils over there

NOUNS

A noun is a word used to name a person, place, thing, idea, or quality. All Spanish nouns are either masculine or feminine and the gender of most of them can be determined by their meaning or ending. Most masculine nouns end in -o, while most feminine nouns end in -a. A few nouns must be learned on an individual basis.

Gender-Obvious Nouns

Nouns that refer to males are obviously masculine. Refer to this list for common nouns you'll see:

NOUN	PRONUNCIATION	MEANING
abuelo	ah-boo-weh-loh	grandfather
hijo	ee-hoh	son
hombre	ohm-breh	man
muchacho	moo-chah-choh	boy
niño	nee-nyoh	boy
padre	pah-dreh	father
sobrino	soh-bree-noh	nephew
tío	tee-yoh	uncle

Nouns that refer to females are obviously feminine. Refer to the table below for the female counterparts of the males listed above:

NOUN	PRONUNCIATION	MEANING
abuela	ah-boo-weh-lah	grandmother
chica	chee-kah	girl
hija	ee-hah	daughter
madre	mah-dreh	mother
muchacha	moo-chah-chah	girl
mujer	moo-hehr	woman
sobrina	soh-bree-nah	niece
tía	tee-yah	aunt

Some nouns can be either masculine or feminine depending upon whom you are speaking about. Make sure to use the gender marker that identifies the person correctly. The following list of words may be used to refer to both males and females.

NOUN	PRONUNCIATION	MEANING
artista	ahr-tees-tah	artist
dentista	dehn-tees-tah	dentist
estudiante	ehs-too-dee-yahn-teh	student
joven	hoh-behn	youth
turista	too-rees-tah	tourist

El artista es talentoso.	The (male) artist is gifted.
La artista es talentosa.	The (female) artist is gifted.

Some high-frequency words are always masculine or feminine despite the gender of the person referred to:

NOUN	PRONUNCIATION	MEANING
un bebé	oon beh-beh	an infant
una persona	oo-nah pehr-soh-nah	a person
una víctima	oo-nah beek-tee-mah	a victim

Gender-Changing Singular Nouns
Changing the gender of a noun can be as easy as removing the *o* ending for the masculine form and substituting an *a* to get the feminine form as shown here:

MASCULINE	FEMININE	MEANING
amigo (ah-mee-goh)	amiga (ah-mee-gah)	friend
maestro (mah-yehs-troh)	maestra (mah-yehs-trah)	teacher
nieto (nee-yeh-toh)	nieta (nee-yeh-tah)	grandchild
niño (nee-nyoh)	niña (nee-nyah)	child
primo (pree-moh)	prima (pree-mah)	cousin
vecino (beh-see-noh)	vecina (beh-see-nah)	neighbor

Some nouns may be masculine or feminine depending upon their meaning as shown below:

MASCULINE	FEMININE	PRONUNCIATION
el capital (money)	la capital (of a city)	kah-pee-tahl
el cura (priest)	la cura (cure)	koo-rah

| el guía (male guide) | la guía (guidebook/ female guide) | gee-yah |
| el policía (policeman) | la policía (police force/ woman) | poh-lee-see-yah |

Gender Endings

Some nouns that end in -o are feminine:

NOUN	PRONUNCIATION	MEANING
la mano	lah mah-noh	hand
la radio	lah rrah-dee-yo	radio

Some nouns that end in -a are masculine:

NOUN	PRONUNCIATION	MEANING
el clima	ehl klee-mah	climate
el día	ehl dee-yah	day
el drama	ehl drah-mah	drama
el idioma	ehl ee-dee-yoh-mah	language
el mapa	ehl mah-pah	map
el planeta	ehl plah-neh-tah	planet
el problema	ehl proh-bleh-mah	problem
el programa	ehl proh-grah-mah	program
el tema	ehl teh-mah	theme
el telegrama	ehl teh-leh-grah-mah	telegram

Some noun endings are normally feminine:

- -dad: la ciudad, city
- -tad: la dificultad, difficulty
- -tud: la juventud, youth
- -umbre: la costumbre, custom
- -ie: la serie, series
- -ión: la canción, song

Two exceptions to -ión are avión (ah-bee-yohn) airplane, and camión (kah-mee-yohn) truck.

For masculine nouns referring to people and ending in -or, -és, or -n, add an a for the feminine equivalents:

MASCULINE	FEMININE	MEANING
el profesor (ehl proh-feh-sohr)	la profesora (lah proh-feh-soh-rah)	teacher
el francés (ehl frahn-sehs)	la francesa (lah frahn-seh-sah)	French person
el alemán (ehl ah-leh-mahn)	la alemana (lah ah-leh-mah-nah)	German person

Note that if the masculine noun is accented on the last syllable, the accent is dropped for the feminine form. Two exceptions to this rule are:

el emperador (ehl ehm-peh-rah-dohr)	la emperatriz (lah ehm-peh-rah-trees)	emperor, empress
el actor (ehl ahk-tohr)	la actriz (lah ahk-trees)	actor, actress

Making Nouns Plural

Just as in English, when a Spanish noun refers to more than one person, place, thing, idea, or quality, the noun must be made plural. Unlike English, however, it is not enough to simply change the noun; the marker must be made plural as well.

Spanish nouns ending in a vowel add a pronounced -s to form the plural:

el muchacho (the boy)	los muchachos (the boys)	lohs moo-chah-chos
una amiga (a friend)	unas amigas (some friends)	oo-nahs ah-mee-gahs
este hombre (this man)	estos hombres (these men)	ehs-tohs ohm-brehs
esa niña (that girl)	esas niñas (those girls)	eh-sahs nee-nyahs
aquel libro (that book)	aquellos libros (those books)	ah-keh-yos lee-brohs

Spanish nouns ending in a consonant (including y) add pronounced -es (ehs) to form the plural:

el papel (paper)	los papeles	lohs pah-peh-lehs
el mes (month)	los meses	lohs meh-sehs
el actor (actor)	los actores	lohs ahk-toh-rehs
la ley (law)	las leyes	lahs leh-yehs

Spanish nouns undergo the following changes in the plural:

- Nouns ending in -z change -z to -ce before adding -es:

el lápiz (pencil)	los lápices	lohs lah-pee-sehs
la actriz (actress)	las actrices	lahs ahk-tree-sehs
el pez (fish)	los peces	lohs peh-sehs

- In order to preserve the original stress of the noun, you may need to add or delete an accent mark:

el joven (youth)	los jóvenes	lohs hoh-beh-nehs
el examen (test)	los exámenes	lohs ehg-sah-meh-nehs
el francés (Frenchman)	los franceses	lohs frahn-seh-sehs
la canción (song)	las canciones	lahs kahn-see-yoh-nehs

- Nouns ending in -s, except for those ending in és, do not change in the plural:

el (los) jueves	ehl (lohs) hoo-weh-behs	Thursday(s)
la (las) dosis	lah (lahs) doh-sees	dose(s)

- In cases where there is a group of nouns from both genders, the masculine plural form of the noun is used:

el padre y la madre = los padres (the parents)

el niño y la niña = los niños (the children)

el señor y la señora Ruiz = los señores Ruiz (the Ruizes)

Some nouns in Spanish are always plural:

ENGLISH	SPANISH	PRONUNCIATION
eyeglasses	las gafas	lahs gah-fahs
	los espejuelos	lohs ehs-peh-hoo-weh-lohs
mathematics	las matemáticas	lahs mah-teh-mah-tee-kahs
vacation	las vacaciones	lahs bah-kah-see-yoh-nehs

Some nouns are singular but refer to a group of people. Make sure to use a singular verb that agrees with these subjects:

SPANISH	PRONUNCIATION	ENGLISH
el equipo	ehl eh-kee-poh	team
la familia	lah fah-meel-yah	family
la gente	lah hehn-teh	people
el grupo	ehl groo-poh	group
la pareja	lah pah-reh-hah	couple
el público	ehl poo-blee-koh	audience
todo el mundo	toh-doh ehl moon-doh	everybody

A note about regionalisms: Do not be surprised when traveling in certain regions or countries that the final -s of a plural word is not pronounced. You can still tell that the noun is plural by paying careful attention to the marker that accompanies it. This marker will also tell you whether the noun is masculine or feminine.

COGNATES

A cognate is a Spanish word that is spelled exactly the same, or almost the same, as a word in English and that has the same meaning. Sometimes the English word may have been appropriated from Spanish, letter for letter, and have been incorporated into our own vocabulary. The only real difference between the two words is in the pronunciation. The meanings of the Spanish cognates should be quite obvious to anyone who speaks English.

Perfect Cognates

Following is a list of some cognates that are the same in Spanish and English. Take time to compare the different pronunciations.

Adjectives

ADJECTIVE	PRONUNCIATION	ADJECTIVE	PRONUNCIATION
artificial	ahr-tee-fee-see-yahl	sociable	soh-see-yah-bleh
cruel	kroo-ehl	tropical	troh-pee-kahl
popular	poh-poo-lahr	usual	oo-soo-wahl

Masculine Nouns

NOUN	PRONUNCIATION	NOUN	PRONUNCIATION
actor	ahk-tohr	chocolate	choh-koh-lah-teh
animal	ah-nee-mahl	mosquito	mohs-kee-toh
cereal	seh-reh-yahl	taxi	tahk-see

Feminine Nouns

NOUN	PRONUNCIATION	NOUN	PRONUNCIATION
alpaca	ahl-pah-kah	plaza	plah-sah
banana	bah-nah-nah	radio	rrah-dee-yoh
llama	yah-mah	soda	soh-dah

Near Perfect Cognates

The following table lists the cognates that are nearly the same in both Spanish and English.

Adjectives

ADJECTIVE	PRONUNCIATION	ADJECTIVE	PRONUNCIATION
americano	ah-meh-ree-kah-noh	imposible	eem-poh-see-bleh
delicioso	deh-lee-see-yoh-soh	inteligente	een-teh-lee-hehn-teh
diferente	dee-feh-rehn-teh	interesante	een-teh-reh-sahn-teh
excelente	eh-seh-lehn-teh	moderno	moh-der-noh
famoso	fah-moh-soh	necesario	neh-seh-sah-ree-yoh
grande	grahn-deh	posible	poh-see-bleh
importante	eem-pohr-tahn-teh		

Masculine Nouns

NOUN	PRONUNCIATION	NOUN	PRONUNCIATION
apartamento	ah-pahr-tah-mehn-toh	diccionario	deek-see-yoh-nah-ree-yoh
automóvil	ow-toh-moh-beel	garaje	gah-rah-heh
café	kah-feh	grupo	groo-poh
calendario	kah-lehn-dah-ree-yoh	insecto	een-sehk-toh

plato	plah-toh	restaurante	rrehs-tow-rahn-teh
profesor	proh-feh-sohr	tigre	tee-greh

Feminine Nouns

NOUN	PRONUNCIATION	NOUN	PRONUNCIATION
aspirina	ahs-pee-ree-nah	gasolina	gah-soh-lee-nah
bicicleta	bee-see-kleh-tah	hamburguesa	ahm-boor-geh-sah
blusa	bloo-sah	medicina	meh-dee-see-nah
computadora	kohm-poo-tah-doh-rah	música	moo-see-kah
dieta	dee-yeh-tah	persona	pehr-soh-nah
familia	fah-mee-lee-yah	rosa	rroh-sah

False Friends

False friends are words that are spelled exactly or almost the same in both languages but have very different meanings in Spanish and English. These words might even be different parts of speech. Do not allow yourself to become overconfident and think that every Spanish word that resembles an English one is automatically a cognate. The following table will give you some common false friends.

SPANISH	PRONUNCIATION	MEANING
asistir	ah-sees-teer	to attend
caro	kah-roh	expensive, dear
comer	koh-mehr	to eat
fábrica	fah-bree-kah	factory
flor	flohr	flower
hay	ah-yee	there is, are
librería	lee-breh-ree-yah	bookstore
joya	hoh-yah	jewel
mano	mah-noh	hand
pan	pahn	bread
sopa	soh-pah	soup
vaso	bah-soh	glass

When in doubt about the meaning of a word, always verify by using a bilingual dictionary. Make sure to look at the part of speech so that you don't confuse a noun with a verb, adjective, or adverb. Cross-check by looking up the word on both the Spanish and English sides of the dictionary.

You can easily guess the meaning of many Spanish words that begin with -e by simply dropping the initial e:

SPANISH	PRONUNCIATION	MEANING
escena	eh-seh-nah	scene
España	ehs-pah-nyah	Spain
especial	ehs-peh-see-yahl	special
espectáculo	ehs-pehk-tah-koo-loh	spectacle, show
espía	ehs-pee-yah	spy
esquí	ehs-kee	ski
estupendo	ehs-too-pehn-doh	stupendous

TIME'S UP!

Here is a two-part exercise to find out how you have assimilated what you've learned about nouns during the last hour. Try your best not to look back at the chapter to arrive at your answers.

Part I
Change the markers and plural nouns to their singular forms.

1. los bancos

2. esos platos

3. estas catedrales

4. las flores

5. aquellos hombres

Part II
Change the feminine markers and nouns to their masculine counterparts.

6. una amiga

7. esa francesa

8. la actriz

9. esta policía

10. aquella profesora

Working with Present-Tense Verbs

MASTER THESE SKILLS

- Subject nouns and pronouns
- Conjugating -ar verbs
- Conjugating -er and -ir verbs
- Using shoe verbs properly
- Conjugating spelling-change and irregular yo verbs
- Conjugating other irregular verbs
- Speaking in the present

In this chapter you will learn how to conjugate verbs in the present tense so that they agree with their subject noun or pronoun. By the end of the lesson you will be able to speak, read, and write entire sentences in Spanish.

SUBJECT NOUNS AND PRONOUNS

A pronoun is a word that is used to replace a noun (that is, a person, place, thing, idea, or quality). A subject pronoun replaces a subject noun (the noun performing the action of the verb). Pronouns are extremely useful because they allow for fluidity by eliminating the need to constantly repeat the noun when speaking or writing.

Just as in English, the Spanish subject pronouns in the following table are given a person and a number (singular or plural).

PERSON	SINGULAR	PLURAL
first	yo (yoh) I	nosotros(as) (noh-soh-trohs[ahs]) we
second	tú (too) you	vosotros(as) (boh-soh-trohs[ahs]) you
third	él (ehl) he	ellos (eh-yohs) they
	ella (eh-yah) she	ellas (eh-yahs) they
	Ud. (oo-stehd) you	Uds. (oo-steh-dehs) you

Note the following about Spanish subject pronouns:

- In Spanish, subject pronouns are used far less frequently than in English because the verb ending usually indicates the speaker. Spanish speakers, however, generally use the pronouns *usted* (abbreviated as *Ud.;* formal *you,* singular) and *ustedes* (abbreviated as *Uds.;* formal *you,* plural) to clarify that the subject is not *él* or *ella.* All other subject pronouns in Spanish are used mainly for clarity, emphasis, and politeness.
- Unlike the English pronoun *I,* the pronoun *yo* is capitalized only when it begins a sentence. In all other instances, it remains in lower case.
- The pronouns *nosotras, vosotras,* and *ellas* are used when the subjects are all females. When the subject consists of a mixed group, the masculine plural pronoun is always used.

Elena y Roberto salen.	Elena and Roberto are going out.
Ellos salen.	They are going out.

- The English pronoun *it* has no Spanish equivalent and is not expressed as a subject: *¿Dónde está?* (Where is it?)
- The subject pronoun *tú* is used to address one friend, relative, child, or pet. For this reason, it is referred to as the familiar or informal form of *you.* The subject pronoun *vosotros(as)* is used in Spain and a few countries in Latin America. It is used in the plural to show familiarity, and as such, is the plural of the *tú,* singular familiar (informal) form.

REGULAR VERBS

A verb expresses an action or state of being and is generally shown in its infinitive, the basic "to" form: to live, to laugh, to love. An infinitive is the form of the verb before it has been conjugated. Conjugation refers to changing the ending of the verb so that it agrees with the subject noun or pronoun. Although we do this automatically in English, it will take some thought and practice in Spanish until verb endings and patterns become second nature.

Here is an example of a verb conjugated in English:

to speak

	SINGULAR	PLURAL
First Person	I speak	We speak
Second Person	You speak	You speak
Third Person	He speaks	They speak
	She speaks	They speak

Notice that the verb is rather simple and is written in only two ways. In Spanish, you need to know more ways to write the verb and you need to memorize more verb endings.

Keep in mind that, as in English, you cannot mix and match subjects and verb forms; each subject has its own personalized matching verb form that never changes.

Conjugating Regular Verbs

Spanish has regular verbs that are grouped into three main families: *-ar*, *-er*, and *-ir* verbs. The families are so named because the verb infinitives end in *-ar*, *-er*, or *-ir*. Each verb within its respective family follows the same rules of conjugation. After you've learned the pattern for one family, you know all the verbs within that family. This rule applies regardless of the tense being used.

Tense refers to the time period when the action is taking place. This chapter concentrates on the present tense, that is, what happens here and now.

Conjugating -ar Verbs. The *-ar* family is, by far, the largest and most widely used of regular verb families. To form the present tense of *-ar* verbs, drop the *-ar* from the infinitive and add the following endings, indicated in bold, for the subject pronouns listed. The following table gives the conjugation for the verb *hablar* (to speak).

VERB	PRONUNCIATION	MEANING
yo hablo	yoh ah-bloh	I speak
tú hablas	too ah-blahs	you speak
él habla	ehl ah-blah	he speaks
ella habla	eh-yah ah-blah	she speaks
Ud. habla	oo-stehd ah-blah	you speak
nosotros hablamos	noh-soh-trohs ah-blah-mohs	we speak
vosotros habláis	boh-soh-trohs ah-blah-yees	you speak
ellos hablan	eh-yohs ah-blahn	they speak
ellas hablan	eh-yahs ah-blahn	they speak
Uds. hablan	oo-steh-dehs ah-blahn	you speak

Another possible meaning for all present tense verbs uses a form of the word *do* plus the verb: I do speak. She does speak.

You should now be able to conjugate the common -*ar* verbs given in the list below. Take note of all the cognates, marked with an asterisk (*), which will make communication in Spanish a much easier task.

VERB	PRONUNCIATION	MEANING
*acompañar	ah-kohm-pah-nyahr	to accompany
*adorar	ah-doh-rahr	to adore
alimentar	ah-lee-mehn-tahr	to feed
alquilar	ahl-kee-lahr	to rent
*anunciar	ah-noon-see-yahr	to announce
apagar	ah-pah-gahr	to turn off
arreglar	ah-rreh-glahr	to fix, adjust
aterrizar	ah-teh-rree-sahr	to land
avisar	ah-bee-sahr	to warn
ayudar	ah-yoo-dahr	to help
bailar	bah-yee-lahr	to dance
bajar	bah-hahr	to go down, get off
buscar	boos-kahr	to look for
cambiar	kahm-bee-yahr	to change

caminar	kah-mee-nahr	to walk
cantar	kahn-tahr	to sing
cobrar	koh-brahr	to cash, charge
comprar	kohm-prahr	to buy
contestar	kohn-tehs-tahr	to answer
cortar	kohr-tahr	to cut
cruzar	kroo-sahr	to cross
dejar	deh-hahr	to let, allow, leave
desear	deh-seh-yahr	to desire
durar	doo-rahr	to last
enseñar	ehn-seh-nyahr	to teach, show
*entrar	ehn-trahr	to enter
escuchar	ehs-koo-chahr	to listen (to)
esperar	ehs-peh-rahr	to hope, wait for
*estudiar	ehs-too-dee-yahr	to study
evitar	eh-bee-tahr	to avoid
*explicar	eh-splee-kahr	to explain
*expresar	eh-spreh-sahr	to express
firmar	feer-mahr	to sign
ganar	gah-nahr	to win, earn
gastar	gahs-tahr	to spend
guardar	gwahr-dahr	to watch, keep
hablar	ah-blahr	to speak, talk
hallar	ah-yahr	to find
*invitar	een-bee-tahr	to invite
lavar	lah-bahr	to wash
llegar	yeh-gahr	to arrive
llenar	yeh-nahr	to fill
llevar	yeh-bahr	to wear, carry

mandar	mahn-dahr	to order
mirar	mee-rahr	to look at
montar	mohn-tahr	to go up, ride
nadar	nah-dahr	to swim
necesitar	neh-seh-see-tahr	to need
olvidar	ohl-bee-dahr	to forget
pagar	pah-gahr	to pay
pasar	pah-sahr	to spend (time)
*practicar	prahk-tee-kahr	to practice
preguntar	preh-goon-tahr	to ask
*preparar	preh-pah-rahr	to prepare
*presentar	preh-sehn-tahr	to introduce
prestar	prehs-tahr	to lend
regresar	rreh-greh-sahr	to return
*reparar	rreh-pah-rahr	to repair
*reservar	rreh-sehr-bahr	to reserve
saludar	sah-loo-dahr	to greet
*telefonear	teh-leh-foh-neh-yahr	to phone
*terminar	tehr-mee-nahr	to end
tirar	tee-rahr	to throw
tocar	toh-kahr (an instrument)	to touch, play
tomar	toh-mahr	to drink, take
*usar	oo-sahr	to use, wear
viajar	bee-yah-hahr	to travel
*visitar	bee-see-tahr	to visit

Conjugating -er Verbs. The -er verb family is much smaller than the -ar verb family. To form the present tense of -er verbs, drop the -er from the infinitive and add the following endings, indicated in bold, for the subject pronouns listed. The following table shows you how the verb *comer* (to eat) looks when it is conjugated.

VERB	PRONUNCIATION	MEANING
yo com**o**	yoh koh-moh	I eat
tú com**es**	too koh-mehs	you eat
él com**e**	ehl koh-meh	he eats
ella com**e**	eh-yah koh-meh	she eats
Ud. com**e**	oo-stehd koh-meh	you eat
nosotros com**emos**	noh-soh-trohs koh-meh-mohs	we eat
vosotros com**éis**	boh-soh-trohs koh-meh-yees	you eat
ellos com**en**	eh-yohs koh-mehn	they eat
ellas com**en**	eh-yahs koh-mehn	they eat
Uds. com**en**	oo-steh-dehs koh-mehn	you eat

The following is a list of common -*er* verbs that you should know. Notice that this list is much smaller than the one for -*ar* verbs. The asterisk (*) indicates easily recognizable cognates.

VERB	PRONUNCIATION	MEANING
aprender	ah-prehn-dehr	to learn
beber	beh-behr	to drink
comer	koh-mehr	to eat
*comprender	kohm-prehn-dehr	to comprehend, understand
correr	koh-rrehr	to run
creer	kreh-yehr	to believe
deber	deh-behr	to have to, owe
leer	leh-yehr	to read
*prometer	proh-meh-tehr	to promise
*responder	rrehs-pohn-dehr	to respond
*vender	behn-dehr	to sell

Conjugating -*ir* Verbs. The -*ir* verb family is also quite small. To form the present tense of -*ir* verbs, drop the -*ir* from the infinitive and add the endings, indicated in bold, for the subject pronouns listed. The following table shows how the verb *abrir* (to open) looks when it is conjugated.

VERB	PRONUNCIATION	MEANING
yo abr**o**	yoh ah-broh	I open
tú abr**es**	too ah-brehs	you open
él abr**e**	ehl ah-breh	he opens
ella abr**e**	eh-yah ah-breh	she opens
Ud. abr**e**	oo-stehd ah-breh	you open
nosotros abr**imos**	noh-soh-trohs ah-bree-mohs	we open
vosotros abr**ís**	boh-soh-trohs ah-brees	you open
ellos abr**en**	eh-yohs ah-brehn	they open
ellas abr**en**	eh-yahs ah-brehn	they open
Uds. abr**en**	oo-steh-dehs ah-brehn	you open

See the list below for common -*ir* verbs.

VERB	PRONUNCIATION	MEANING
abrir	ah-breer	to open
asistir	ah-sees-teer	to attend
*aplaudir	ah-plow-deer	to applaud
cubrir	koo-breer	to cover
*decidir	deh-see-deer	to decide
*describir	dehs-kree-beer	to describe
escribir	ehs-kree-beer	to write
*omitir	oh-mee-teer	to omit
partir	pahr-teer	to divide, share
recibir	rreh-see-beer	to receive
subir	soo-beer	to go up, climb
sufrir	soo-freer	to suffer
vivir	bee-beer	to live

Notice that -*er* and -*ir* verbs have the same endings except for the *nosotros* and *vosotros* forms, where -*er* verbs use an *e* and -*ir* verbs use an *i*.

SHOE VERBS

Verbs with certain spelling changes and irregularities are referred to as shoe verbs because the subject pronouns that follow one set of rules can be placed inside the shoe, and the other subject pronouns remain outside the shoe. To make this clearer, look at the pronouns that go inside and outside of the shoe:

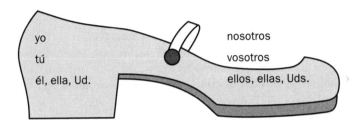

The infinitives of shoe verbs are often written with the type of change necessary in parentheses, as in *pensar (ie)*.

Verbs Ending in -*ar* and -*er*. The vowel within the stem of the verb changes as follows:

e to **ie** in all forms except for *nosotros* and *vosotros*

o to **ue** in all forms except for *nosotros* and *vosotros*

pensar (pehn-sahr)—to think

yo pienso	nosotros pensamos
tú piensas	vosotros pensáis
él, ella, Ud. piensa	ellos, ellas, Uds. piensan

Other verbs like *pensar* are *atravesar* (ah-trah-beh-sahr) to cross, *cerrar* (seh-rrahr) to close, **comenzar* (koh-mehn-sahr), **confesar* (kohn-feh-sahr), *empezar* (ehm-peh-sahr) to begin, and *recordar* (rreh-kohr-dahr) to remember.

querer (keh-rehr)—to wish, want

yo quiero	nosotros queremos
tú quieres	vosotros queréis
él, ella, Ud. quiere	ellos, ellas, Uds. quieren

Other verbs like *querer* are **ascender* (ah-sehn-dehr), **defender* (deh-fehn-dehr), **descender* (deh-sehn-dehr), *entender* (ehn-tehn-dehr) to understand, and *perder* (pehr-dehr) to lose.

encontrar (ehn-kohn-trahr)—to meet, find

yo encuentro	nosotros encontramos
tú encuentras	vosotros encontráis
él, ella, Ud. encuentra	ellos, ellas, Uds. encuentran

Other verbs like *encontrar* are *almorzar* (ahl-mohr-sahr) to eat lunch, *contar* (kohn-tahr) to tell or count, and *mostrar* (mohs-trahr) to show.

volver (bohl-behr)—to return, go back

yo vuelvo	nosotros volvemos
tú vuelves	vosotros volvéis
él, ella, Ud. vuelve	ellos, ellas, Uds. vuelven

Other verbs like *volver* are *devolver* (deh-bohl-behr) to return or give back, *poder* (poh-dehr) to be able to, and **resolver* (rreh-sohl-behr).

While we have studied verbs where o changes to *ue* within the shoe, there is one slightly irregular verb, the verb *jugar* (hoo-gahr) to play, where u changes to *ue* in all forms except *nosotros* and *vosotros*:

jugar (hoo-gahr)—to play

yo juego	nosotros jugamos
tú juegas	vosotros jugáis
él, ella, Ud. juega	ellos, ellas, Uds. juegan

Verbs Ending in -ir. The vowel within the stem of the verb changes as follows in all forms except *nosotros* and *vosotros*:

e to ie
o to ue
e to i

preferir (preh-feh-reer)—to prefer

yo prefiero	nosotros preferimos
tú prefieres	vosotros preferís
él, ella, Ud. prefiere	ellos, ellas, Uds. prefieren

Other verbs like *preferir* are *advertir* (ahd-behr-teer) to notify, *consentir* (kohn-sehn-teer), *mentir* (mehn-teer) to lie, *referir* (rreh-feh-reer), and *sentir* (sehn-teer) to feel, regret, or feel sorry.

dormir (dohr-meer)—to sleep

yo duermo	nosotros dormimos
tú duermes	vosotros dormís
él, ella, Ud. duerme	ellos, ellas, Uds. duermen

Another verb like *dormir* is *morir* (moh-reer) to die.

servir (sehr-beer)—to serve

yo sirvo	nosotros servimos
tú sirves	vosotros servís
él, ella, Ud. sirve	ellos, ellas, Uds. sirven

Other verbs like *servir* are *gemir* (heh-meer) to moan, *impedir* (eem-peh-deer), *medir* (meh-deer) to measure, *pedir* (peh-deer) to ask, and *repetir* (rreh-peh-teer).

Verbs Ending in -uir. For verbs ending in *-uir*, except those ending in *-guir*, insert a *y* after the *u* in all forms except *nosotros* and *vosotros*.

contribuir (kohn-tree-boo-weer)—to contribute

yo contribuyo	nosotros contribuimos
tú contribuyes	vosotros contribuís
él, ella, Ud. contribuye	ellos, ellas, Uds. contribuyen

Other verbs like *contribuir* include *concluir* (kohn-kloo-weer) to conclude, *construir* (kohn-stroo-weer) to construct, *destruir* (deh-stroo-weer) to destroy, *incluir* (een-kloo-weer) to include, and *sustituir* (soo-stee-too-weer) to substitute.

Verbs Ending in -iar and -uar. Some verbs ending in *-iar* and *-uar* require an accent on the *i* or *u* respectively, in all forms except *nosotros* and *vosotros*.

enviar (ehn-bee-yahr)—to send

yo envío	nosotros enviamos
tú envías	vosotros enviáis
él, ella, Ud. envía	ellos, ellas, Uds. envían

Other verbs like *enviar* are *confiar en* (kohn-fee-yahr ehn) to trust, *espiar* (ehs-pee-yahr) to spy, *guiar* (gee-yahr) to guide, and **variar* (bah-ree-yahr).

actuar (ahk-too-wahr)—to act

yo actúo	nosotros actuamos
tú actúas	vosotros actuáis
él, ella, Ud. actúa	ellos, ellas, Uds. actúan

Another verb like *actuar* is **continuar* (kohn-tee-noo-wahr).

Conjugating Spelling-Change and Irregular Yo Verbs

Some verbs in Spanish require a spelling change in order to preserve correct pronunciation according to the rules of the language. Note the changes that occur in verbs with these endings:

- Verbs ending in consonant + *-cer* or *-cir* change *c* to *z* before *o* or *a*:

  convencer (kohn-behn-sehr) to convince: yo convenzo

  esparcir (eh-spahr-seer) to spread: yo esparzo

- Verbs ending in vowel + *-cer* or *-cir* change *c* to *zc* before *o* or *a*:

  conocer (koh-noh-sehr) to know: yo conozco

  conducir (kohn-doo-seer) to drive: yo conduzco

- Verbs ending in *-ger* or *-gir* change *g* to *j* before *o* or *a*:

  coger (koh-hehr) to seize: yo cojo

  dirigir (dee-ree-heer) to direct: yo dirijo

  escoger (ehs-koh-hehr) to choose: yo escojo

  exigir (ehg-see-heer) to demand: yo exijo

  fingir (feen-heer) to pretend: yo finjo

  proteger (proh-teh-heer) to protect: yo protejo

  recoger (rreh-koh-hehr) to pick up: yo recojo

- Verbs ending in -*guir* change *gu* to *g* before *o* or *a*:

  distinguir (dees-teen-geer) to distinguish: yo distingo

The verb *seguir* (seh-geer) to follow or continue, is a common verb that has a stem change and a spelling change:

yo sigo	nosotros seguimos
tú sigues	vosotros seguís
él, ella, Ud. sigue	ellos, ellas, Uds. siguen

Other verbs like *seguir* are *conseguir* (kohn-seh-geer) to obtain, *perseguir* (pehr-seh-geer) to pursue, and *proseguir* (proh-seh-geer) to continue.

IRREGULAR VERBS

A good number of high-frequency Spanish verbs are irregular. Irregular means that they follow no specific rules of conjugation, and you must memorize them. Some of these verbs are used in idiomatic expressions that can help you speak the language more colloquially.

An idiom is a particular word or expression whose meaning cannot be readily understood by either its grammar or the words used. Idiomatic expressions cannot be translated word for word without causing confusion. Imagine trying to grammatically explain to a non-native English speaker the meaning of:

  It's raining cats and dogs.

  They fell for it hook, line, and sinker.

Verbs Only Irregular for Yo

The following high-frequency verbs have irregular *yo* forms only in the present tense. You should commit them to memory because you will use them often:

- *conocer* (koh-noh-sehr) to know: *yo conozco*. Other verbs like *conocer* are *agradecer* (ah-grah-deh-sehr) to thank, *crecer* (kreh-sehr) to grow, *merecer* (meh-reh-sehr) to deserve, *ofrecer* (oh-freh-sehr) to offer, *reconocer* (rreh-koh-noh-sehr) to recognize.
- *caer* (kah-yehr) to fall: *yo caigo*
- *dar* (dahr) to give: *yo doy*. The following list gives the most common idiomatic expressions that use the verb *dar*.

EXPRESSION	MEANING	EXAMPLE
dar a	to face	Mi casa da al mar.
		(My house faces the sea.)

dar las gracias (a)	to thank	Me dan las gracias. (They thank me.)
dar un paseo	to take a walk	¿Quieres dar un paseo? (Do you want to take a walk?)
dar una vuelta	to take a stroll	Vamos a dar una vuelta. (We are going to take a stroll.)
darse cuenta de	to realize	Me doy cuenta de mi error. (I realize my mistake.)
darse prisa	to hurry	Tengo que darme prisa. (I have to hurry.)

- *hacer* (ah-sehr) to make, do: yo hago. Below is a list of common idiomatic expressions that use the verb *hacer*.

EXPRESSION	MEANING	EXAMPLE
hacer buen (mal) tiempo	to be nice (bad) weather	Hace buen tiempo. (It's nice weather.)
hacer frío (calor)	to be cold (hot) weather	Hace calor. (It's hot.)
hacer una pregunta	to ask a question	Hágame una pregunta. (Ask me a question.)
hacer un viaje	to take a trip	Hago un viaje a Roma. (I'm taking a trip to Rome.)
hacerse + noun	to become	Nos hacemos amigos. (We're becoming friends.)

- *poner* (poh-nehr) to put: *yo pongo*
- *saber* (sah-behr) to know a fact, to know how to: *yo sé*
- *salir* (sah-leer) to go out: *yo salgo*
- *traducir* (trah-doo-seer) to translate: *yo traduzco*. Other verbs like *traducir* are *conducir* (kohn-doo-seer) to drive, conduct, or lead, *produir* (proh-doo-seer), *reducir* (rreh-doo-seer).
- *traer* (trah-yehr) to bring: *yo traigo*
- *ver* (behr) to see: *yo veo*

Other Irregular Verbs

The following verbs are irregular in all forms, and you should memorize them:

decir (deh-seer)—to say, tell

yo digo (dee-goh)	nosotros decimos (deh-see-mohs)
tú dices (dee-sehs)	vosotros decís (deh-sees)
él, ella, Ud. dice (dee-seh)	ellos, ellas, Uds. dicen (dee-sehn)

estar (eh-stahr)—to be

yo estoy (eh-stoy)	nosotros estamos (eh-stah-mohs)
tú estás (eh-stahs)	vosotros estáis (eh-stah-yees)
él, ella, Ud. está (eh-stah)	ellos, ellas, Uds. están (eh-stahn)

The following are the very common idiomatic expressions that use the verb *estar*:

EXPRESSION	MEANING	EXAMPLE
estar a punto de (+ infinitive)	to be just about to	Estoy a punto de salir. (I'm just about to leave.)
estar por (+ infinitive)	to be inclined to	Estoy por cocinar. (I'm inclined to cook.)
estar de acuerdo	to be in agreement	Estoy de acuerdo con Ud. (I agree with you.)

ir (eer)—to go

yo voy (boy)	nosotros vamos (bah-mohs)
tú vas (bahs)	vosotros vais (bah-yees)
él, ella, Ud. va (bah)	ellos, ellas, Uds. van (bahn)

oír (oh-eer)—to hear

yo oigo (oy-goh)	nosotros oímos (oh-ee-mohs)
tú oyes (oy-ehs)	vosotros oís (oh-ees)
él, ella, Ud. oye (oy-eh)	ellos, ellas, Uds. oyen (oy-ehn)

ser (sehr)—to be

yo soy (soy)	nosotros somos (soh-mohs)
tú eres (eh-rehs)	vosotros sois (soh-yees)
él, ella, Ud. es (ehs)	ellos, ellas, Uds. son (sohn)

tener (tehn-ehr)—to have

yo tengo (tehn-goh)	nosotros tenemos (teh-neh-mohs)
tú tienes (tee-yeh-nehs)	vosotros tenéis (teh-neh-yees)
él, ella, Ud. tiene (tee-yeh-neh)	ellos, ellas, Uds. tienen (tee-yeh-nehn)

In most instances, if a larger verb form contains an irregular verb you recognize, the chances are great that you may use the conjugation endings of the smaller verb. *Tener* is contained in *contener* (cohn-teh-nehr) to contain, *detener* (deh-teh-nehr) to detain, *entretener* (ehn-treh-teh-nehr) to entertain, *mantener* (mahn-teh-nehr) to maintain, *obtener* (ohb-teh-nehr) to obtain and *sostener* (soh-steh-nehr) to sustain. You conjugate these verbs as you would *tener*.

Although English speakers use the verb "to be" when speaking about certain physical conditions, Spanish speakers use the verb "to have" (*tener*) plus a noun to express the same thought.

The following list gives the very common idiomatic expressions that use the verb *tener*:

EXPRESSION	MEANING	EXAMPLE
tener . . . años	to be . . . years old	Yo tengo veinte años. (I'm twenty years old.)
tener calor (frío)	to be hot (cold)	Yo tengo calor. (I'm hot.)
tener cuidado	to be careful	Tenga cuidado. (Be careful.)
tener ganas de	to feel like	Tengo ganas de salir. (I feel like going out.)
tener hambre	to be hungry	Tenemos hambre. (We're hungry.)
tener sed	to be thirsty	Tienen sed. (They are thirsty.)
tener miedo de	to be afraid of	Tengo miedo de eso. (I'm afraid of that.)
tener prisa	to be in a hurry	Ella tiene prisa. (She's in a hurry.)
tener que	to have to	Tengo que estudiar. (I have to study.)
tener razón	to be right	Ud. tiene razón. (You're right.)
tener suerte	to be lucky	Tengo suerte. (I'm lucky.)

venir (beh-neer)—to come

. . . .

yo vengo (behn-goh)

tú vienes (bee-yeh-nehs)

él, ella, Ud. viene
(bee-yeh-neh)

nosotros venimos (beh-nee-mohs)

vosotros venís (beh-nees)

ellos, ellas, Uds. vienen (bee-yeh-nehn)

USES OF THE PRESENT TENSE

The present tense is customarily used instead of the future tense to ask
for instructions or to discuss an action that will take place in the immediate future:

Yo preparo la cena?

Yo te veo pronto.

Shall I prepare dinner?

I'll see you soon.

To express an event that began in the past and is continuing in the present,
use the following formulas for questions and answers. Questions containing *hace + que* must be answered with *hace + que*. Those questions
containing *desde* must be answered with *desde*.

¿Cuánto tiempo hace + que + present tense?

¿Cuánto tiempo hace que vives aquí?

How long have you been living here?

hace + an expression of time + que + present tense

Hace un año que vivo aquí.

I've been living here for a year.

¿Desde cuándo + present tense?

¿Desde cuándo vives aquí?

How long have you been living here?

present tense + *desde*

Vivo aquí desde hace un año.

I've been living here a year.

> **▽ NOTE**
>
> When it is necessary to use two verbs in succession, the first verb is conjugated and the second verb remains in the infinitive:
>
> Yo quiero salir.   I want to go out.
> Ellos pueden bailar.   They can dance.

THE PRESENT PROGRESSIVE

Whereas the present tense expresses what the subject generally does at any given time, the present progressive expresses what the subject is doing now. The present progressive is formed as follows: *estar* (conjugated) + present participle (gerund—the *-ing* form).

Gerunds are formed as follows:

- From *-ar* verb infinitives, drop *-ar* and add *-ando*: *Yo estoy cantando.* (I'm singing.)
- From *-er* and *-ir* verb infinitives, drop *-er* or *-ir* and add *-iendo*:

  Él no está comiendo.   He's not eating.

  Estamos escribiendo   We're writing a poem.
  un poema.

For *-er* and *-ir* verbs whose stems end in a vowel, add *-yendo*:

creer (to believe)   creyendo

leer (to read)   leyendo

oír (to hear)   oyendo

traer (to bring)   trayendo

- Stem-changing *-ir* verbs change the stem vowel from *e* to *i* and from *o* to *u*:

decir (to say, tell)   diciendo

dormir (to sleep)   durmiendo

morir (to die)   muriendo

pedir (to ask)   pidiendo

sentir (to feel)   sintiendo

venir (to come)   viniendo

- Note the following irregular gerunds:

  ir (to go)   yendo

  poder (to be able to)   pudiendo

TIME'S UP!

Without looking back, try to correctly complete this short story about a boy and his friend. Conjugate the verbs carefully.

Yo _____ (1. estar) en casa. Yo _____ (2. ser) un muchacho muy

aplicado. Yo _____ (3. tener) hambre. Yo _____ (4. querer) comer.

Yo _____ (5. poder) preparar una comida deliciosa. Yo _____

(6. buscar) los ingredientes. Yo _____ (7. medir) todo con cuidado.

Yo no _____ (8. sustituir) nada. Mi madre _____ (9. venir) a la

cocina. Nosotros _____ (10. ir) a comer mi excelente arroz con pollo.

45

The Past Tense

(The Preterit)

MASTER THESE SKILLS

- Using the preterit
- Using -*ir* stem-changing verbs and irregular verbs in the preterit
- Using the present and preterit perfect tenses
- Forming the imperfect and the pluperfect
- The preterit versus the imperfect

In this chapter you'll learn when to use the preterit and when to use the imperfect. You'll also learn how to recognize the present perfect tense (implying the past) and the past perfect tenses, and when to use each.

FORMING THE PRETERIT

The preterit, which expresses an action or event completed at a specific time in the past, is referred to in Spanish as *el pretérito*.

The preterit of regular verbs is formed by dropping the *-ar*, *-er*, or *-ir* infinitive endings and adding the following preterit endings as shown here.

PRONOUN	*-AR* VERBS	*-ER* AND *-IR* VERBS
yo	-é (eh)	-í (ee)
tú	-aste (ahs-teh)	-iste (ees-teh)
él, ella, Ud.	-ó (oh)	-ió (ee-yoh)
nosotros	-amos (ah-mohs)	-imos (ee-mohs)
vosotros	-asteis (ahs-teh-yees)	-isteis (ees-teh-yees)
ellos, ellas, Uds.	-aron (ah-rohn)	-ieron (ee-yeh-rohn)

Verbs That Change *i* to *y*

Except for the verb *traer* (to bring) and verbs ending in *-guir*, which are regular in the preterit, all *-er* and *-ir* verbs that end in a vowel when the infinitive ending is dropped, change *i* to *y* in the third person singular (*él, ella, Ud.*) and plural (*ellos, ellas, Uds.*) forms. The first and second person forms all have an accented *i*: *í*.

	STEM	YO	TÚ	ÉL	NOSOTROS	VOSOTROS	ELLOS
caer (to fall)	ca						
creer (to believe)	cre						
leer (to read)	le	-í	-íste	-yó	-ímos	-ísteis	-yeron
oír (to hear)	o						
poseer (to possess)	pose						

Verbs ending in *-uir* (*construir, distribuir, incluir,* and so on) follow the *i* to *y* change but do not accent the *i* in the *tú, nosotros,* or *vosotros* forms: *incluí, incluiste, incluyó, incluimos, incluisteis, incluyeron.*

Verbs Ending in *-car*, *-gar*, and *-zar*

Verbs ending in *-car*, *-gar*, and *-zar* have the following changes only in the *yo* form of the preterit:

c changes to *qu*	aplicar (to apply)	yo apliqué
g changes to *gu*	castigar (to punish)	yo castigué
z changes to c	avanzar (to advance)	yo avancé

Some common verbs ending in *-car* are listed here:

VERB	PRONUNCIATION	MEANING
buscar	boos-kahr	to look for
comunicar	koh-moo-nee-kahr	to communicate
explicar	eh-splee-kahr	to explain
significar	seeg-nee-fee-kahr	to mean
tocar	toh-kahr	to touch, to play (music)

Common *-gar* verbs are:

VERB	PRONUNCIATION	MEANING
apagar	ah-pah-gahr	to turn off
colgar (ue)	kohl-gahr	to hang
entregar	ehn-treh-gahr	to deliver
jugar (ue)	hoo-gahr	to play
llegar	yeh-gahr	to arrive

Common *-zar* verbs are:

VERB	PRONUNCIATION	MEANING
almorzar (ue)	ahl-mohr-sahr	to eat lunch
comenzar(ie)	koh-mehn-sahr	to begin
empezar (ie)	ehm-peh-sahr	to begin
gozar	goh-sahr	to enjoy

-ir Stem-Changing Verbs in the Preterit

Present-tense stem-changing (shoe) verbs ending in -ir also have a stem change in the preterit. In the third person forms, e changes to i, and o changes to u, as in the following examples:

preferir: preferí, preferiste, **prefirió**, preferimos, preferisteis, **prefirieron**

servir: serví, serviste, **sirvió**, servimos, servisteis, **sirvieron**

dormir: dormí, dormiste, **durmió**, dormimos, dormisteis, **durmieron**

Irregular Verbs in the Preterit

Most irregular verbs in the preterit have the following endings:

yo	-e	nosotros	-imos
tú	-iste	vosotros	-isteis
él, ella, Ud.	-o	ellos, ellas, Uds.	-ieron

The stems of high-frequency irregular verbs are listed below.

VERB	STEM	MEANING
estar	estuv-	to be
hacer	hic-	to do
poder	pud-	to be able to
poner	pus-	to put
querer	quis-	to want
saber	sup-	to know
tener	tuv-	to have
venir	vin-	to come
decir	dij-	to say, tell
traer	traj-	to bring

Other irregularities to which you must pay careful attention include:

- If the stem ends in a j, add only -eron in the third person plural: Ellos dijeron la verdad. (They told the truth.)
- The third person singular (él, ella, Ud.) form of hacer in the preterit is hizo (ee-soh). This change preserves the soft sound of the consonant: Ella hizo el trabajo. (She did the work.)
- Dar (to give) is conjugated as follows in the preterit: di, diste, dio, dimos, disteis, dieron.

- The verbs *ser* (to be) and *ir* (to go) have the same preterit forms: *fui, fuiste, fue, fuimos, fuisteis, fueron.*

Él fue abogado.	He was a lawyer.
Él fue al centro.	He went downtown.

- The accent mark is omitted in the preterit forms of *dar*, *ser*, *ver*, and *ir*:

  dar: di, diste, dio, dimos, disteis, dieron

  ir and *ser*: fui, fuiste, fue, fuimos, fuisteis, fueron

  ver: vi, viste, vio, vimos, visteis, vieron

- All verbs ending in *-ducir* are conjugated in the preterite like *producir*: *produje, produjiste, produjo, produjimos, produjisteis, produjeron.* Other common verbs ending in *-ducir* are *conducir* (to drive, to conduct); *deducir* (to deduce); and *reducir* (to reduce).
- All compounds of verbs (*tener, detener,* etc.) are conjugated in the preterit in the same manner as the basic verb.

THE PRESENT PERFECT TENSE

The present perfect tense describes an action that started in the past and continues to the present, or an action that happened in the past but is in some way connected to the present.

The present perfect tense is a compound tense. Compound is the key word because it implies that this tense is made up of more than one part. In fact, the present perfect, as well as other compound tenses, is made up of two elements. Observe how this works.

Formation of the Present Perfect

The present perfect of most Spanish verbs is formed by combining the present tense of *haber* and the past participle of the verb expressing the action.

The formula for the formation of the present perfect is: subject (noun or pronoun) + helping verb + past participle.

The Helping Verb *Haber*

Because *haber* means "to have," it serves well as the helping verb. First, it must be conjugated in the present tense:

yo he (eh)	nosotros hemos (eh-mohs)
tú has (ahs)	vosotros habéis (ah-beh-yees)
él, ella, Ud. ha (ah)	ellos, ellas, Uds. han (ahn)

After you have conjugated *haber* in the appropriate person, you must add a past participle.

Past Participles of Regular Verbs

The past participle of regular verbs is formed by dropping the *-ar*, *-er*, or *-ir* infinitive ending and adding *-ado* for *-ar* verbs and *-ido* for *-er* and *-ir* verbs:

habl~~ar~~	hablado	spoken
com~~er~~	comido	eaten
recib~~ir~~	recibido	received

When an *-er* or *-ir* stem ends in a vowel, add an accent mark on the *i* as follows:

caer	caído	fallen
creer	creído	believed
leer	leído	read
oír	oído	heard

English usage often omits the use of the helping verb, although it is implied. For example, "I prepared the dinner" is acceptable for "I have prepared the dinner." In Spanish, the helping verb is used: *He preparado la cena.*

The past participle remains the same for every subject. Only the helping verb changes:

Yo he comido.	Nosotros hemos comido.
Tú has comido.	Vosotros habéis comido.
Él, ella, Ud. ha comido.	Ellos, ellas, Uds. han comido.

Past Participles of Irregular Verbs

The verbs shown here, and their compounds (for example, *volver*, *devolver*, etc.), have irregular past participles.

INFINITIVE	PAST PARTICIPLE	PRONUNCIATION	MEANING
abrir (to open)	abierto	ah-bee-yehr-toh	opened
decir (to say)	dicho	dee-choh	said
escribir (to write)	escrito	ehs-kree-toh	written
hacer (to do)	hecho	eh-choh	done

morir (to die)	muerto	moo-wehr-toh	died
poner (to put)	puesto	poo-wehs-toh	put
romper (to break)	roto	rroh-toh	broken
ver (to see)	visto	bees-toh	seen
volver (to return)	vuelto	boo-wehl-toh	returned

THE PRETERIT PERFECT

The preterit perfect has limited use because it is employed primarily in formal, literary, and historical writings to express that an action or event had just ended. The preterit or the pluperfect is preferred in conversation and informal writing. Therefore, learn the preterit perfect only for recognition, as you will be seeing it primarily in literary works.

The preterit perfect is formed by using the preterit of the helping verb *haber* and the past participle. The preterit of *haber* is:

yo hube (oo-beh)	nosotros hubimos (oo-bee-mohs)
tú hubiste (oo-bees-teh)	vosotros hubistéis (oo-bee-steh-yees)
él hubo (oo-boh)	ellos hubieron (oo-bee-yeh-rohn)

Apenas hube llegado a casa cuando él me telefoneó.	Scarcely had I arrived home when he called me.
En cuanto hubimos entrado, todo el mundo aplaudió.	As soon as we had entered, everybody applauded.

THE IMPERFECT

The imperfect expresses a continuing state or an incomplete action in the past:

The door was open.

He was watching television.

Regular Verbs

The imperfect of regular verbs is formed by dropping the *-ar*, *-er*, or *-ir* infinitive ending and adding the imperfect endings:

PRONOUN	*-AR* VERBS	*-ER* AND *-IR* VERBS
yo	-aba (ah-bah)	-ía (ee-yah)
tú	-abas (ah-bahs)	-ías (ee-yahs)
él, ella, Ud.	-aba (ah-bah)	-ía (ee-yah)

nosotros	-ábamos (ah-bah-mohs)	-íamos (ee-yah-mohs)
vosotros	-abais (ah-bah-yees)	-íais (ee-yah-yees)
ellos, ellas, Uds.	-aban (ah-bahn)	-ían (ee-yahn)

Irregular Verbs
There are only three Spanish verbs that are irregular in the imperfect:

	YO	TÚ	ÉL	NOSOTROS	VOSOTROS	ELLOS
ir (to go)	iba	ibas	iba	íbamos	ibais	iban
ser (to be)	era	eras	era	éramos	érais	eran
ver (to see)	veía	veías	veía	veíamos	veíais	veían

THE PLUPERFECT

The pluperfect is used to describe an action that *had* been completed in the past before another past action took place:

I had lived there before.

They had eaten in that restaurant in the past.

The pluperfect is actually the compound form of the imperfect. The pluperfect is composed of two parts: the imperfect of the helping verb *haber* (which expresses "had") and the past participle of the verb indicating the action that took place. The imperfect of *haber* is:

yo había (ah-bee-yah)   nosotros habíamos (ah-bee-yah-mohs)

tú habías (ah-bee-yahs)   vosotros habíais (ah-bee-yah-ees)

él había (ah-bee-yah)   ellos habían (ah-bee-yahn)

Ella tenía hambre porque ella no había comido nada.

She was hungry because she hadn't eaten anything.

THE PRETERIT VERSUS THE IMPERFECT

The preterit expresses an action that was completed at a specific time in the past. Think of the action as one moment in time. Think, too, of a camera. The preterit represents an action that could be captured by an instamatic—the action happened and was completed.

The imperfect, on the other hand, expresses an action that continued in the past over an indefinite period of time. Think again of a camera. The imperfect represents an action that could be captured by a video camera—the action continued over a period of time, it *was* happening, *used to* happen, or *would* (meaning "used to") happen.

The basic uses of the preterit and the imperfect are summarized in the following table:

PRETERIT	IMPERFECT
1. Expresses specific actions or events that were started and completed at a definite time in the past (even if the time isn't mentioned).	1. Describes ongoing or continuous actions or events (what *was* happening) in the past (which may or may not have been completed).
Él preparó la cena. He prepared dinner.	Ella hablaba con su amiga. She was speaking to her friend.
2. Expresses a specific action or event that occurred at a specific point in past time.	2. Describes habitual or repeated actions in the past.
Él salió ayer. He went out yesterday.	Generalmente salía a menudo. He usually went out often.
3. Expresses a specific action or event that was repeated a stated number of times.	3. Describes a person, place, thing, or state of mind with the verbs *creer* (to believe), *pensar* (to think), *querer* (to want), and *saber* (to know).
Juan telefoneó dos veces. John called two times.	Ella estaba triste. She was unhappy.
	Queríamos salir. We wanted to go out.
	4. Expresses time of day.
	Era la una. It was one o'clock.

The imperfect is used to describe a situation that was going on in the past when another action or event took place. The action or event that took place is in the preterit: *Yo salía cuando el teléfono sonó.* (I was going out when the telephone rang.)

When *would* means "used to," use the imperfect: I would go to the beach every weekend with my friends.

When *would* states what the subject would do under specific conditions (I would go to the beach if the weather were nice), use the conditional, which is discussed in further detail in Chapter 20:00.

Clues to the Preterit and the Imperfect

The following words and expressions often require the use of the preterit because they specify a time period:

SPANISH	PRONUNCIATION	MEANING
ayer	ah-yehr	yesterday
ayer por la noche	ah-yehr pohr lah noh-cheh	last night
de repente	deh rreh-pehn-teh	suddenly
el año pasado	ehl ah-nyoh pah-sah-doh	last year
el otro día	ehl oh-troh dee-yah	the other day
la semana pasada	lah seh-mah-nah pah-sah-dah	last week
por fin	pohr feen	finally
primero	pree-meh-roh	at first
un día	oon dee-yah	one day
una vez	oo-nah behs	one time

The imperfect is used with the following expressions that generally imply repetition:

SPANISH	PRONUNCIATION	MEANING
a menudo	ah meh-noo-doh	often
a veces	ah beh-sehs	sometimes
cada día	kah-dah dee-yah	each/every day
de vez en cuando	deh behs ehn kwahn-doh	from time to time
en general	ehn heh-neh-rahl	generally
siempre	see-yehm-preh	always
todo el tiempo	toh-doh ehl tee-yehm-poh	all the time
todos los días	toh-dohs lohs dee-yahs	every day
usualmente	oo-soo-wahl-mehn-teh	usually

Sometimes you may be confused about which form of past tense to use. Do not be overly concerned about this. In many instances, either the preterit or the imperfect is acceptable depending upon the meaning the speaker is trying to convey:

Yo hablé con mis amigas.
I spoke with my friends.
(The action is completed.)

Yo hablaba con mis amigas.
I was speaking to my friends.
(The action was ongoing or continuous in the past.)

⏱ TIME'S UP!

Read this young girl's story about her past and fill in the correct form of the verb in the appropriate tense, the preterit or the imperfect:

Cuando yo _____ (1. tener) 14 años, yo _____ (2. ir) a la escuela

todos los días para ver a un muchacho en mi clase de español, Ramón.

Él _____ (3. ser) muy guapo. Desafortunadamente él no _____

(4. prestar) atención a las muchachas porque siempre _____

(5. jugar) a los deportes con sus amigos. Pero un día, después de las

clases, él me _____ (6. pedir) mi número de teléfono. Él _____

(7. querer) salir conmigo. Yo _____ (8. estar) muy contenta.

Nosotros _____ (9. ir) al cine para ver una historia de amor ridícula.

De esta manera yo _____ (10. conocer) a mi futuro marido.

Back to the Future

Speaking Conditionally

MASTER THESE SKILLS

. . . .

* Forming and using the future
* Forming and using the conditional

. . . .

In this chapter you'll learn how to form,
use, and differentiate between the future
tense and the conditional. You will need to
pay careful attention to the verb endings
and to what you are trying to express.

THE FUTURE

In Spanish, the future may be expressed in three possible ways: by using the present, by using *ir* + *a* + infinitive, and by using the future tense. You can expect to encounter any of these forms regularly in daily conversations.

Using the Present to Express the Future

The present tense may be used to imply the future when asking for instructions or referring to an action that will take place in the immediate future. You will instinctively know when the future is implied by the present through the context of the conversation.

¿Pongo el libro aquí?	Shall I put the book here?
Ella telefonea más tarde.	She will call later.

Ir + *a* + Infinitive

In Spanish, as in English, the near future may be expressed with a form of the present tense of the verb *ir* (to go) + *a* + the infinitive referring to the action that the speaker will perform. The near future is generally used for an action that is imminent, that is going to happen soon.

The irregular present tense of *ir* is conjugated as follows:

ir—to go

yo voy (boy)	nosotros vamos (bah-mohs)
tú vas (bahs)	vosotros vais (bah-yees)
él, ella, Ud. va (bah)	ellos, ellas, Uds. van (bahn)

Add *a* + an infinitive to get the near future:

Voy a ir a España.	I'm going to go to Spain.
Vamos a viajar en avión.	We're going to travel by plane.

THE FUTURE TENSE OF REGULAR VERBS

The future tense tells what the subject will do or what action will take place in future time. The future tense of all regular verbs is formed by adding the endings indicated in bold to the infinitive of the verb, as shown here.

-ar Verbs

hablar—to speak

yo hablar**é** (ah-blah-reh)	nosotros hablar**emos** (ah-blah-reh-mohs)

tú hablar**ás** (ah-blah-rahs) vosotros hablar**éis** (ah-blah-reh-yees)

él hablar**á** (ah-blah-rah) ellos hablar**án** (ah-blah-rahn)

-er Verbs

leer—to read

yo leer**é** (leh-yeh-reh) nosotros leer**emos** (leh-yeh-reh-mohs)

tú leer**ás** (leh-yeh-rahs) vosotros leer**éis** (leh-yeh-reh-yees)

él leer**á** (leh-yeh-rah) ellos leer**án** (leh-yeh-rahn)

-ir Verbs

abrir—to open

yo abrir**é** (ah-bree-reh) nosotros abrir**emos** (ah-bree-reh-mohs)

tú abrir**ás** (ah-bree-rahs) vosotros abrir**éis** (ah-bree-reh-yees)

él abrir**á** (ah-bree-rah) ellos abrir**án** (ah-bree-rahn)

It is important that you note the following idiosyncrasies about the formation of the future of regular verbs:

* All future endings except -*emos* have accent marks.
* Verbs that have an accent mark in the infinitive (such as *oír*) drop that accent in the future: *yo oiré*.

THE FUTURE TENSE OF IRREGULAR VERBS

The following verbs have irregular future stems, which always end in -*r* or -*rr*. Just add the future endings to these stems to get the correct future form:

* Verbs like *poder* drop the *e* from the infinitive ending before adding the future endings:

INFINITIVE	STEM
haber (to have)	habr-
poder (to be able to)	podr-
querer (to want)	querr-
saber (to know)	sabr-

* Verbs like *poner* substitute a *d* for the *e* or *i* in the infinitive ending before adding the future endings:

INFINITIVE	STEM
poner (to put)	pondr-
salir (to go out)	saldr-
tener (to have)	tendr-
venir (to come)	vendr-

- The verbs *decir* and *hacer* have irregular future stems:

INFINITIVE	STEM
decir (to say, tell)	dir-
hacer (to make, do)	har-

- Compounds of irregular verbs (such as *contener*, a compound of *tener*) are also irregular.

Uses of the Future

The future is used as follows:

- The future tense, as in English, is used to express what will happen:

Él llegará mañana.	He will arrive tomorrow.
Iremos a España.	We will go to Spain.

The future is used to express wonder and probability in the present:

¿Cuántos años tendrá?	I wonder how old he is.
Será la medianoche.	It's probably midnight.
Estarán viejos.	They must be old.

THE FUTURE PERFECT

You use the future perfect to describe an action or event that will happen in the future before another future action. Because you are expressing what will have happened, you need the future of the helping verb *haber* + the past participle of the verb that shows the action or event to have been completed. The future perfect of *haber* is:

haber—to have

yo habré (ah-breh)	nosotros habremos (ah-breh-mohs)
tú habrás (ah-brahs)	vosotros habréis (ah-breh-yees)
él habrá (ah-brah)	ellos habrán (ah-brahn)

Él habrá terminado el trabajo antes de que el día termine.

He will have finished the work before the end of the day.

You may also use the future perfect to express probability in the recent past:

¿Lo habrán hecho?	I wonder if they did it.
Ella habrá perdido su dinero.	She has probably lost her money.
Habré ganado.	I must have won.

THE CONDITIONAL

The conditional is not a tense, because it does not indicate a time period. It is, instead, a mood that expresses what the speaker would do or what would happen under certain circumstances or conditions.

You form the conditional with the same stem that you use to form the future, and by adding the endings indicated in bold. Note these are the same endings used to form the imperfect.

-ar Verbs

hablar—to speak

yo hablaría (ah-blah-ree-yah)	nosotros hablaríamos (ah-blah-ree-yah-mohs)
tú hablarías (ah-blah-ree-yahs)	vosotros hablaríais (ah-blah-ree-yah-ees)
él hablaría (ah-blah-ree-yah)	ellos hablarían (ah-blah-ree-yahn)

-er Verbs

leer—to read

yo leería (leh-yeh-ree-yah)	nosotros leeríamos (leh-yeh-ree-yah-mohs)
tú leerías (leh-yeh-ree-yahs)	vosotros leeríais (leh-yeh-ree-yah-ees)
él leería (leh-yeh-ree-yah)	ellos leerían (leh-yeh-ree-yahn)

-ir Verbs

abrir—to open

yo abriría (ah-bree-ree-yah)	nosotros abriríamos (ah-bree-ree-yah-mohs)
tú abrirías (ah-bree-ree-yahs)	vosotros abriríais (ah-bree-ree-yah-ees)
él abriría (ah-bree-ree-yah)	ellos abrirían (ah-bree-ree-yahn)

Uses of the Conditional

Use the conditional as follows:

- The conditional is used to express what would happen under certain conditions: *Si hiciera buen tiempo, yo no iría al cine. Yo montaría en bicicleta.* (If the weather were nice, I wouldn't go to the movies. I'd go bike riding.)

    When *would* has the sense of "used to," the imperfect is used: *Viajaba en Europa a menudo.* (I would (used to) travel to Europe often.)

    When *would* has the sense of "to be willing, to want," the preterit of *querer* is used: *Quise viajar a Europa.* (I wanted [was willing] to travel to Europe.)

- The conditional is used to express wonder and probability in the past:

¿Cuántos años tendría?	I wonder how old you were.
Sería la medianoche.	It was probably midnight.
Estarían viejos.	They must have been old.

THE PERFECT CONDITIONAL

Use the perfect conditional to describe an action or event that would have taken place in the past had something else happened.

Because you are expressing what would have happened, you need the conditional of the helping verb *haber* + the past participle of the verb that shows the action or event that would have been completed. The conditional of *haber* is:

haber—to have

yo habría (ah-bree-yah)	nosotros habríamos (ah-bree-yah-mohs)
tú habrías (ah-bree-yahs)	vosotros habríais (ah-bree-yah-ees)
él habría (ah-bree-yah)	ellos habrían (ah-bree-yan)
Con más tiempo, yo habría terminado el trabajo.	With more time, I would have finished the work.

⏰ TIME'S UP!

Part I

Complete the sentence with the correct form of the future:

En el año 2010 yo

1. (ser) _____ más inteligente.

2. (querer) _____ viajar.

3. (tener) _____ mucho dinero.

4. (vivir) _____ en una casa grande.

5. (conducir) _____ un automóvil deportivo.

Part II

Complete the sentence with the correct form of the conditional:

Con un millón de dólares yo

6. (poner) _____ mi dinero en el banco.

7. (dar) _____ mucho dinero a los pobres.

8. (hacer) _____ un viaje a través del mundo.

9. (comprar) _____ un castillo para mi familia.

10. (decir) _____ la verdad a todo el mundo.

Adding Adjectives and Adverbs

MASTER THESE SKILLS

- Making adjectives feminine and/or plural
- Positioning adjectives properly
- Using *ser* and *estar* with adjectives
- Forming and using adverbs properly

In this lesson you'll learn how to use adjectives, how to make them agree with the nouns they describe, and where to position them with respect to the noun.

MAKING ADJECTIVES FEMININE

Most Spanish adjectives form the feminine singular by changing the *o* of the masculine adjective to *a*, as shown in the table below. This table and the ones that follow will help you build a good, working adjective vocabulary.

MASCULINE	FEMININE	MEANING
aburrido (ah-boo-rree-doh)	aburrida	boring
alto (ahl-toh)	alta	tall
bajo (bah-hoh)	baja	short
bonito (boh-nee-toh)	bonita	pretty
bueno (boo-weh-noh)	buena	good
delgado (dehl-gah-doh)	delgada	thin
divertido (dee-behr-tee-doh)	divertida	fun
enfermo (ehn-fehr-moh)	enferma	sick
enojado (eh-noh-hah-doh)	enojada	angry
famoso (fah-moh-soh)	famosa	famous
feo (feh-yoh)	fea	ugly
flaco (flah-koh)	flaca	thin
generoso (heh-neh-roh-soh)	generosa	generous
gordo (gohr-doh)	gorda	fat
guapo (goo-wah-poh)	guapa	pretty
listo (lees-toh)	lista	smart, ready
malo (mah-loh)	mala	bad
necesario (neh-seh-sah-ree-yoh)	necesaria	necessary
nuevo (noo-weh-boh)	nueva	new
pequeño (peh-keh-nyoh)	pequeña	small
perezoso (peh-reh-soh-soh)	perezosa	lazy
perfecto (pehr-fehk-toh)	perfecta	perfect
rico (rree-koh)	rica	rich
romántico (rroh-mahn-tee-koh)	romántica	romantic
rubio (rroo-bee-yoh)	rubia	blond

serio (seh-ree-yoh)	seria	serious
simpático (seem-pah-tee-koh)	simpática	nice
tímido (tee-mee-doh)	tímida	shy
tonto (tohn-toh)	tonta	foolish
viejo (bee-yeh-hoh)	vieja	old

Past participles of verbs may be used as adjectives. In such cases, the past participle must agree in gender and number with the noun it describes:

La puerta está cerrada.	The door is closed.
Los libros están abiertos.	The books are open.

Masculine Adjectives Ending in Letters Other than O

If a masculine adjective ends in -a, -e, or a consonant, you don't have to make any changes to get the feminine form. Note that most adjectives ending in -a are feminine, but those on the list below can be both. The following table demonstrates that these adjectives are spelled and pronounced in the same manner.

ADJECTIVE	PRONUNCIATION	MEANING
alegre	ah-leh-greh	happy
amable	ah-mah-bleh	nice
cortés	kohr-tehs	courteous
difícil	dee-fee-seel	difficult
eficiente	eh-fee-syehn-teh	efficient
egoísta	eh-goh-ees-tah	selfish
excelente	ehg-seh-lehn-teh	excellent
fácil	fah-seel	easy
grande	grahn-deh	big
horrible	oh-rree-bleh	horrible
importante	eem-pohr-tahn-teh	important
inteligente	een-teh-lee-hen-teh	intelligent
interesante	een-teh-reh-sahn-teh	interesting
joven	hoh-behn	young
optimista	ohp-tee-mees-tah	optimistic

pesimista	peh-see-mees-tah	pessimistic
pobre	poh-breh	poor
popular	poh-poo-lahr	popular
realista	rreh-yah-lees-tah	realistic
triste	trees-teh	sad

Note the following irregularities to these rules:

- Some adjectives of nationality whose masculine form ends in a consonant add -a to form the feminine:

MASCULINE	FEMININE	MEANING
español	española	Spanish
francés	francesa	French
alemán	alemana	German

- Some adjectives whose masculine form ends in -or add -a to form the feminine:

MASCULINE	FEMININE	MEANING
hablador	habladora	talkative
encantador	encantadora	enchanting
trabajador	trabajadora	hard-working

MAKING ADJECTIVES PLURAL

The plural of adjectives ending in a vowel is formed by adding *s*:

SINGULAR	PLURAL	MEANING
pequeño	pequeños	small
alta	altas	tall
grande	grandes	big

The plural of adjectives ending in a consonant is formed by adding *-es*:

SINGULAR	PLURAL	MEANING
fácil	fáciles	easy
popular	populares	popular

Note the following exceptions to these rules:

- Singular adjectives ending in -z change -z to -c in the plural:

SINGULAR	PLURAL	MEANING
feliz	felices	happy
feroz	feroces	ferocious
sagaz	sagaces	shrewd, astute

- In order to maintain original stress, some adjectives add or drop an accent mark:

SINGULAR	PLURAL
joven (HOH-behn)	jóvenes (HOH-beh-nehs)
francés (frahn-SEHS)	franceses (frahn-SEH-sehs)
inglés (een-GLEHS)	ingleses (een-GLEH-sehs)

POSITION OF ADJECTIVES

The position of adjectives in Spanish follows different rules from those with which you may be accustomed in English:

- Unlike English, most descriptive adjectives in Spanish follow the noun they modify:

mis pantalones negros	my black pants
una casa nueva	a new house

- When an adjective is used to emphasize quality or inherent characteristics, it may be placed before the noun:

Admiro los árboles con sus verdes hojas.	I admire the trees with their green leaves.
Me trae buenos recuerdos.	It brings me good memories.

- Adjectives that impose limits (numbers, possessive adjectives, demonstrative adjectives, and adjectives of quantity) usually precede the noun:

dos vestidos blancos	two white dresses
mis hijos	my children
este hombre	this man
algún día	someday
tal cosa	such a thing

otro hombre   another man

el último viaje   the last trip

Common adjectives of quantity are:

ADJECTIVE	PRONUNCIATION	MEANING
algunos(-as)	ahl-goo-nohs	some
cada	kah-dah	each
cuanto(-a,-os,-as)	kwahn-toh	as much
más	mahs	more
menos	meh-nohs	less
ningunos(-as)	neen-goo-nohs	no, not any
poco(-a,-os, -as)	poh-koh	few, little
tanto(-a,-os,-as)	tahn-toh	so much, many
todo(-a,-os, -as)	toh-doh	all, very
unos(-as)	oo-nohs	some
varios(-as)	bah-ree-yohs	several

- When more than one adjective is used in a description, put each adjective in its proper place, either before or after the noun, according to the previously mentioned rules. Two adjectives in the same position are joined by *y* (and):

  dos casas rojas   two red houses

  un niño grande y flaco   a tall, thin boy

  mis malos recuerdos   my bad memories

- The masculine plural form of the adjective is used when it modifies two or more nouns of different gender: *El muchacho y la muchacha son ambiciosos.* (The boy and the girl are ambitious.)

Shortened Forms of Adjectives

Spanish adjectives may take on shortened forms. Follow these rules for shortening adjectives in certain situations.

Some adjectives drop the final -*o* before a masculine singular noun:

ADJECTIVE	EXAMPLE	MEANING
uno	un hombre	a man
bueno	un buen libro	a good book

malo	un mal año	a bad year
primero	el primer piso	the first floor
tercero	el tercer día	the third day
alguno	algún muchacho	some boy
ninguno	ningún amigo	no friend

▽ **NOTE**

An accent is added to the *u* of *alguno* and *ninguno* when the *-o* is dropped.

If the adjective is separated from the noun by a preposition, then the original adjective is used:

| uno de mis amigos | one of my friends |

When *grande* is placed before a singular masculine or feminine noun it becomes *gran* and means "important, famous." When it is placed after the noun it is not shortened and means "large":

| un gran actor | a great actor |
| una gran actriz | a great actress |

But:

| un apartamento grande | a large apartment |
| una casa grande | a large house |

(See page 74 for more adjectives that change meaning depending on placement.)

Ciento becomes *cien* before a masculine or feminine noun and before the numbers *mil* and *millones*:

cien muchachos	one hundred boys
cien muchachas	one hundred girls
cien mil personas	one hundred thousand people
cien millones de personas	one hundred million people

But:

| doscientas personas | two hundred people |
| ciento cincuenta libros | one hundred fifty books |

The masculine *Santo* becomes *San* before the name of a saint whose name does not begin with *To-* or *Do-*:

San Juan   Saint John

But:

Santo Domingo   Saint Dominick

Adjectives with Different Meanings

Some adjectives have different meanings depending on whether they are positioned before or after the noun they modify. Adjectives before the noun tend to have a more literal meaning. When these adjectives follow the noun, the meaning changes:

una costumbre antigua	an old (ancient) custom
una antigua costumbre	an old (former) custom
una cosa cierta	a sure thing
una cierta cosa	a certain thing
un hombre grande	a tall (large, big) man
un gran hombre	a great man (quality, not size)
el cuarto mismo	the room itself
el mismo cuarto	the same room
la gente pobre	the poor people (without money)
la pobre gente	the unfortunate people
una razón simple	a silly reason
una simple rázon	a simple reason
una mujer triste	a sad (unhappy) woman
una triste mujer	a sad (sorry, wretched) woman

USING *SER* AND *ESTAR* WITH ADJECTIVES

Because two verbs in Spanish express *to be,* it is important that you understand the differences in their usage, especially when you use them with adjectives.

Both *ser* and *estar* are irregular verbs and require that you memorize them.

	SER	ESTAR
yo	soy	estoy
tú	eres	estás
él, ella, Ud.	es	está
nosotros	somos	estamos
vosotros	sois	estáis
ellos, ellas, Uds.	son	están

Carefully study the uses of *ser* to ensure that you use it correctly. Then compare the uses of *ser* with those of *estar*. Naturally it is best to use each verb properly, but keep in mind that if you make a mistake, you will still be understood.

SER	ESTAR
1. Expresses a natural quality or inherent characteristic that will not change.	1. Expresses a temporary state, condition, or phase or the result of an action that may change.
Marta es colombiana. Martha is Colombian.	Marta está enferma. Martha is sick.
La puerta es de madera. The door is made of wood.	La puerta está abierta. The door is open.
2. Expresses traits that will probably not change soon.	2. Expresses a location or position of the subject.
Mi hermana es abogada. My sister is a lawyer.	Ella está en su oficina. She is in her office.
Juan es rubio. Juan is blond.	¿Dónde está Juan? Where is Juan?
3. Expresses time and dates.	3. Is used to form the progressive tenses with the gerund.
Es la una. It is one o'clock.	Está nevando. It is snowing.
Es el once de julio. It is July 11th.	Estamos jugando. We are playing.

4. Expresses possession.

> Es mi coche.
> It's my car.

5. Is used with impersonal expressions.

> Es necesario estudiar.
> It is necessary to study.

6. Expresses a passive action with the past participle and an adjective.

> La puerta fue abierta por Juan.
> The door was opened by Juan.

Some adjectives may be used with either verb, but will have different meanings according to the verb that is used:

SER (CHARACTERISTICS)	ESTAR (CONDITIONS)
Él no es aburrido.	Él no está aburrido.
He isn't boring.	He isn't bored.
Él es bueno (malo).	La comida está buena (mala).
He is good (bad).	The meal is good (bad).
Soy listo.	Estoy listo.
I'm clever (smart).	I'm ready.
Es pálida.	Está pálida.
She has a pale complexion.	She is pale.
Es seguro.	Está seguro.
It is safe (reliable).	He is sure.
Ella es viva.	Ella está viva.
She is quick (sharp).	She is alive.
Ud. es joven (viejo).	Ud. está joven (viejo).
You are young (old).	You look young (old).

ADVERBS

An adverb is often a word that describes how the subject performs an action. In English, many adverbs end in *-ly*. The Spanish equivalent ending is *-mente*. Because adverbs modify verbs, you don't need to worry about the agreement of adverbs.

Forming Adverbs

Adverbs are formed by adding *-mente* (mehn-teh) to the feminine singular form of the adjective as shown here.

MASCULINE ADJECTIVE	FEMININE ADJECTIVE	ADVERB	MEANING
claro	clara	claramente	clearly
completo	completa	completamente	completely
diligente	diligente	diligentemente	diligently
especial	especial	especialmente	especially
fácil	fácil	fácilmente	easily
final	final	finalmente	finally
frecuente	frecuente	frecuentemente	frequently
lento	lenta	lentamente	slowly
rápido	rápida	rápidamente	quickly

Adverbial Phrases

The preposition *con* (with) + noun may be used to form an adverbial phrase. You can modify a verb by saying *with* + a noun: *con claridad* (with clarity), or by using the corresponding adverb: *claramente* (clearly).

Él habla con claridad.	He speaks (with clarity) clearly.
Él habla claramente.	He speaks clearly.

CON + NOUN	ADVERB	MEANING
con claridad	claramente	clearly
con cuidado	cuidadosamente	carefully
con habilidad	hábilmente	skillfully
con paciencia	pacientemente	patiently

ADJECTIVES VERSUS ADVERBS

Pay attention to the Spanish words that have distinct forms for adjectives and adverbs:

ADJECTIVE	EXAMPLE	MEANING
bueno (good)	buenos días	good day(s)
malo (bad)	malos sueños	bad dreams
bien (well)	Baila bien.	He dances well.
mal (badly)	Canta mal.	She sings poorly.

Some Spanish words may be used as adjectives or adverbs:

	ADJECTIVE	ADVERB
más	Tengo más joyas.	Corro más rápidamente.
more	I have more jewels.	I run more rapidly.
menos	Tengo menos joyas.	Corro menos rápidamente.
less, fewer	I have fewer jewels.	I run less quickly.
poco	Tengo pocas joyas.	Corro poco.
few, little	I have few jewels.	I run little.
mucho	Tengo muchas joyas.	Corro mucho.
much, many	I have many jewels.	I run a lot.
mejor	Tengo mejores joyas.	Corro mejor.
better	I have better jewels.	I run better.
peor	Tengo peores joyas.	Corro peor.
worse	I have worse jewels.	I run worse.
demasiado	Tengo demasiadas joyas.	Corro demasiado.
too much, many	I have too many jewels.	I run too much.

When used as adjectives, *mucho*, *poco*, and *demasiado* agree in number and gender with the nouns they modify; *mejor* and *peor* only agree in number, forming the plural by adding *-es*; *más* and *menos* do not change. As adverbs, all of these words remain invariable.

Some adverbs and adverbial expressions are not formed from adjectives and, therefore, do not end in *-mente*. Here are the most common adverbs in this category.

ADVERB	PRONUNCIATION	MEANING
ahora	ah-oh-rah	now
al fin	ahl feen	finally
allá	ah-yah	there
a menudo	ah meh-noo-doh	often
aquí	ah-kee	here
bastante	bahs-tahn-teh	quite, rather
casi	kah-see	almost
cerca	sehr-kah	near
demasiado	deh-mah-see-yah-doh	too
de nuevo	deh noo-weh-boh	again
de repente	deh rreh-pehn-teh	suddenly
después	dehs-poo-wehs	afterward
lejos	leh-hohs	far
más	mahs	more
menos	meh-nohs	less
mejor	meh-hohr	better
mientras	mee-yehn-trahs	meanwhile
muy	moo-wee	very
peor	peh-yohr	worse
poco	poh-koh	little
por supuesto	pohr soo-poo-wehs-toh	of course
pronto	prohn-toh	soon
pues	poo-wehs	then
siempre	see-yehm-preh	always
tal vez	tahl behs	perhaps
también	tahm-bee-yehn	also, too
tan	tahn	so
tarde	tahr-deh	late
temprano	tehm-prah-noh	soon, early

| todavía | toh-dah-bee-yah | still, yet |
| ya | yah | already |

POSITION OF ADVERBS

In simple tenses (no helping verb), adverbs are generally placed directly after the verb they modify. Sometimes, however, the position of the adverb is variable and can be placed where you would logically put an English adverb:

| Generalmente, habla fluidamente. | Generally, he speaks fluently. |
| Frecuentemente escuché atentamente. | I frequently listened attentively. |

Bien and *mal* may precede the past participle:

| Está mal escrito. | It's poorly written. |
| Hemos bien trabajado. | We worked well. |

TIME'S UP!

Rewrite each sentence by putting the correct adjectival form in parentheses in its proper place. Be careful, sometimes you will simply need to make the adjective agree and sometimes you will have to change it to an adverb:

> Example: (fluida) Él habla.   Él habla fluidamente.
> (lindo) Ana es una niña.   Ana es una niña linda.

1. (profundo) Él piensa.

2. (alegre) La señora López es una mujer.

3. (bueno) Es un hombre.

4. (frecuente) Hablan.

5. (demasiado) Ella compra vestidos.

6. (más) Necesito dinero.

7. (primero) Es la vez.

8. (fácil) Ellos trabajan.

9. (ciento) Necesito dólares.

10. (rápido) Ellos escriben.

Making Acquaintances

MASTER THESE SKILLS

. . . .

- Using reflexive verbs to present yourself
- Choosing the correct reflexive verb
- Discussing your origins
- Using possessives to speak about family and friends

. . . .

In this chapter you'll learn how to carry on a basic, introductory conversation in Spanish in which you can offer greetings, discuss your health, and speak about your origins and family members, using reflexive verbs properly as needed.

GREETINGS AND GOOD-BYES

When traveling in a foreign country, if you want to converse with a person whom you don't know at all, a formal approach is mandatory. It is considered quite a mistake to address someone informally if a strong friendship or relationship has not been established. Be sure to start and end your conversations correctly by using the appropriate greetings and good-byes listed below.

Formal Greetings and Good-Byes

SPANISH	GREETING/GOOD-BYE
Buenos días.	Hello.
Buenas tardes.	Good afternoon.
Señor	Mr.
Señora	Mrs.
Señorita	Miss (Ms.)
¿Cómo se llama Ud.?	What's your name?
Me llamo . . .	My name is . . .
Mucho gusto en conocerle.	I'm happy to meet you.
Le presento a . . .	I'd like you to meet . . .
¿Cómo está Ud.?	How are you?
Muy bien.	Very well.
Bien.	All right.
Así así.	So-so.
Adiós.	Good-bye.
Buenas noches.	Good night.

Informal Greetings and Good-Byes

SPANISH	GREETING/GOOD-BYE
¡Hola!	Hi.
¿Cómo te llamas?	What's your name?
Me llamo . . .	My name is . . .
Encantado(a).	Pleased to meet you.
Te presento a . . .	I'd like you to meet . . .

Adiós.	Bye.
¿Cómo estás?	How are you?
Bien.	Fine.
¿Cómo te va?	How's it going?
¿Qué hay de nuevo?	What's new?
Nada en particular.	Nothing (much).
Hasta muy pronto.	See you very soon.
Hasta luego.	See you later.
Luego te veo.	I'll be seeing you.
Hasta mañana.	See you tomorrow.

NOTE

The greeting *encantado* is an adjective and must agree in gender with the speaker. Use *encantado* if you are a man and *encantada* if you are a woman.

As a sign of respect, older Spanish women are generally referred to and addressed as *Señora*, regardless of their marital status. When in doubt, use *Señora*. *Señorita* is reserved for younger, unmarried women.

REFLEXIVE VERBS

A reflexive verb indicates that the action is performed by the subject upon itself: He bathes himself. The reflexive verb (in this example, *to bathe*) has a reflexive pronoun as its object (in this example, *himself*). Thus, the subject (which may be omitted in Spanish but which should be kept in mind) and the pronoun object refer to the same person or thing:

El muchacho se llama Juan.	The boy's name is Juan. (The boy is called Juan.)
(Él) se llama.	His name is Juan. (He calls himself Juan.)

You can identify a reflexive verb by the addition of *se* at then end of the infinitive: for example, *llamarse* (to call oneself).

In many instances, you can use the same verb without the reflexive pronoun to perform the action *upon* or *for* someone else. The verb is then no longer reflexive.

Me llamo María.	My name is Maria. (I call myself Maria.)
Llamo a María.	I call Maria.

Some verbs that are generally not reflexive may be made reflexive by adding the reflexive pronoun:

| Yo hablo con Julio. | I speak to Julio. |
| Me hablo. | I speak to myself. |

Note the reflexive pronouns that are used with each subject and their placement immediately before the conjugated verb. All reflexive verbs must be preceded by these pronouns, which are directly tied to their subjects. The verb *sentirse* (*ie*) (to feel) will prove very useful when discussing your health. *Sentirse* is a stem-changing *e* to *ie* shoe verb, so expect to see that change in all forms except *nosotros* and *vosotros*. Below is the conjugation of the reflexive verb *sentirse*.

sentirse—to feel

(yo) **me** siento (I feel)	(nosotros) **nos** sentimos (we feel)
(tú) **te** sientes (you feel)	(vosotros) **os** sentís (you feel)
(él) **se** siente (he feels)	(ellos) **se** sienten (they feel)

To answer the question "How are you?" (*¿Cómo está Ud.?* [formal] or *¿Cómo estás?* [familiar]), respond:

Me siento bien.	I feel well.
Me siento mal.	I feel bad.
Me siento mejor.	I feel better.
Me siento peor.	I feel worse.

Some verbs are usually or always used reflexively in English and Spanish. The following list provides the most common reflexive verbs. Verbs with an asterisk (*) have spelling changes in the present tense and must be conjugated accordingly. Refer to Chapter 22:00 for the rules for these shoe verbs.

VERB	MEANING
*acostarse (ue)	to go to bed, to lay down
afeitarse	to shave
alegrarse	to be glad
bañarse	to bathe oneself
*despertarse (ie)	to wake up
*divertirse (ie)	to have fun

enojarse	to become angry
equivocarse	to be mistaken
lavarse	to wash oneself
levantarse	to get up
llamarse	to be called, named
peinarse	to comb one's hair
quedarse	to remain, to stay
*sentirse (ie)	to feel

Choosing the Correct Reflexive Verb

Some verbs in Spanish have special meanings when used reflexively, so be careful to choose the verb you want to use.

INFINITIVE	BASIC MEANING	REFLEXIVE MEANING
aburrir(se)	to bore	to become bored
acostar(se) (ue)	to put to bed	to go to bed
bañar(se)	to bathe (someone)	to bathe oneself
cansar(se)	to tire	to become tired
engañar(se)	to deceive	to be mistaken
levantar(se)	to raise (something)	to get up
poner(se)	to put (something)	to put (something on), to become, to place oneself
sentar(se) (ie)	to seat	to sit down

Some reflexive verbs are used idiomatically; that is, no logical grammatical explanation exists for the construction of these phrases. These verbs appear below.

EXPRESSION	MEANING
cepillarse (los dientes)	to brush one's (teeth)
romperse (la pierna)	to break one's (leg)
irse	to go away
hacerse amigos	to become friends
enfadarse con	to get angry with
darse cuenta de	to realize

The following verbs are always used reflexively in Spanish, but not necessarily in English. An asterisk (*) denotes a verb with a spelling or stem change.

VERB	MEANING
*acordarse (ue) (de)	to remember
empeñarse (en)	to insist (on)
fijarse (en)	to notice
irse	to go away
*negarse (ie) (de)	to refuse (to)
olvidarse (de)	to forget
parecerse (a)	to resemble
quejarse (de)	to complain
*reírse (i) (de)	to laugh at

Reflexive verbs in the plural may express reciprocal action corresponding to *each other* and *one another* in English: *Nos escribimos.* (We write to each other.)

Note the use of *uno a otro (una a otra)* or *el uno al otro (la una a la otra),* which mean "each other":

Ellos se miran.	They look at each other.
Ellos se miran uno al otro.	They look at each other.
Paco y Ana se escriben el uno al otro.	They write to each other.

Reflexive verbs in Spanish may be used to express the passive voice when the subject is a thing (not a person):

| Aquí se habla español. | Spanish is spoken here. |
| Se vende carne hoy. | Meat is being sold today. |

Reflexive Verbs in Compound Tenses

In compound tenses, the reflexive pronoun remains before the conjugated helping verb form of *haber*:

| Ella se ha lavado. | She has washed herself. |
| Ella se había lavado. | She had washed herself. |

| Ella se habrá lavado. | She will have washed herself. |
| Ella se habría lavado. | She would have washed herself. |

Reflexive Verbs with Infinitives and Gerunds

When a subject is followed by a conjugated verb and an infinitive, or with *estar* + gerund, the reflexive pronoun may be placed either before the conjugated verb or after it and attached to the infinitive to which its meaning is linked:

I'm going to feel better.	**Me** voy a sentir mejor.
	Voy a sentir**me** mejor.
I'm combing my hair.	**Me** estoy peinando.
	Estoy peinándo**me**.

When using the gerund that has one pronoun attached, a general rule of thumb is to count back three vowels and add an accent to get the correct stress. When two pronouns are attached, count back four vowels: *Está lavándosela.* (He is washing it for himself.)

ORIGINS

It is only natural when you meet someone new to inquire about that person's origins or to speak about your own. In order to speak correctly about coming *from*, living *in*, or traveling *to* a country, city, state, or province, you need to learn these prepositions:

PREPOSITION	MEANING
en	in
a	to
de	from

Vivo en Nueva York.	I live in New York.
Soy de California.	I'm from California.
Voy a San Juan.	I'm going to San Juan.

To formally ask a person where he or she is from, say: *¿De dónde es Ud.?* (Where are you from?) To be informal, ask: *¿De dónde eres?* (Where are you from?)

In Spanish most countries are not preceded by a definite article (*el*, *la*, *los*, or *las*), though a few are. Common everyday usage, however, tends to omit the definite article even before those countries whose names show them. The only exceptions are *El Salvador* and *La Républica Dominicana*, because *El* and *La* are part of the country's official name. There is no contraction of *a + el* when speaking about *El Salvador*.

Use the definite article with geographical names that are modified:

América es grande.

But:

La América del Sur es grande.

Voy a Guatemala.

Voy a El Salvador.

Refer to the following lists for the names of countries and continents.

Countries
. . . .

Argentina	la Argentina
Brazil	el Brasil
Canada	el Canadá
China	la China
Dominican Republic	la República Dominicana
Ecuador	el Ecuador
El Salvador	El Salvador
England	Inglaterra
France	Francia
Germany	Alemania
Greece	Grecia
Haiti	Haïti
India	la India
Italy	Italia
Japan	el Japón
Mexico	México
Panama	Panamá
Paraguay	el Paraguay

Peru	el Perú
Portugal	Portugal
Russia	Rusia
Spain	España
Sweden	Suecia
Switzerland	Suiza
United States	los Estados Unidos
Uruguay	el Uruguay

Continents

. . . .

Africa	África
Antarctica	Antártica
Asia	Asia
Australia	Australia
Europe	Europa
North America	Norte América, América del Norte
South America	Sud América, América del Sur

Now you can answer these questions:

¿De dónde es Ud.?	Soy de (los) Estados Unidos.
(Where are you from?)	(I'm from the United States.)
¿Adónde va Ud.?	Voy a España.
(Where are you going?)	(I'm going to Spain.)
¿Dónde vive Ud.?	Vivo en Grecia.
(Where do you live?)	(I live in Greece.)

NATIONALITIES

When answering a question about your origin, remember to use an adjective that agrees in number and gender with the person or persons you are describing, as explained in Chapter 19:00.

¿Cuál es su nacionalidad?	What's your nationality?
Soy alemana.	I'm German.
Somos americanos.	We are Americans.

Nationalities ending in -*és* drop the accent from the *e* in the feminine singular and all plural forms. The adjectives of nationality are:

inglés	English
escocés	Scottish
francés	French
irlandés	Irish
japonés	Japanese
portugés	Portuguese

NOTE

Unlike in English, adjectives of nationality are not capitalized in Spanish.

THE FAMILY

When meeting new people, after you've introduced yourself, it often becomes necessary to present or refer to other members of your family. The following tables give you the names of family members you may need to know.

Family Members: Males

Relative	Spanish	Relative	Spanish
boyfriend	novio	husband	esposo
brother	hermano	nephew	sobrino
brother-in-law	cuñado	son	hijo
child	niño	son-in-law	yerno
cousin	primo	stepbrother	hermanastro
father	padre	stepson	hijastro
father-in-law	suegro	uncle	tío
grandfather	abuelo		

Family Members: Females

Relative	Spanish	Relative	Spanish
aunt	tía	cousin	prima
child	niña	daughter	hija

daughter-in-law	nuera	sister	hermana
girlfriend	novia	sister-in-law	cuñada
grandmother	abuela	stepdaughter	hijastra
mother	madre	stepsister	hermanastra
mother-in-law	suegra	wife	esposa
niece	sobrina		

SHOWING POSSESSION

To show possession, you may use the preposition *de* (of) or a possessive adjective.

Using *De*

English speakers use apostrophe *s* ('s) or *s* apostrophe (s') after a noun to show possession. Because Spanish does not use apostrophes, a reverse construction is used: *el padre de Marta* (the father of Marta or Marta's father). Note that in this construction the preposition *de* (*of*) is used to express relationship and possession.

If the possessor is referred to by a common noun, such as "the boy"—for example, "She is the boy's mother"—then *de* contracts with the definite article *el* to express "of the": *Es la madre del muchacho.*

Using Possessive Adjectives

Possessive adjectives, like other Spanish adjectives, agree with the nouns they modify (the person or thing that is possessed) and not with the subject (the person possessing them) and, therefore, serve as noun markers. The first table below summarizes the use of short possessive adjectives that precede the noun, and the second table summarizes the use of longer possessive adjectives that are used less frequently and follow the noun.

Short Forms

BEFORE MASCULINE NOUNS		BEFORE FEMININE NOUNS		MEANING
Singular	Plural	Singular	Plural	
mi	mis	mi	mis	my
tu	tus	tu	tus	your
su	sus	su	sus	his, her, your, its

nuestro	nuestros	nuestra	nuestras	our
vuestro	vuestros	vuestra	vuestras	your
su	sus	su	sus	their, your

Long Forms

. . . .

AFTER MASCULINE NOUNS		AFTER FEMININE NOUNS		MEANING
Singular	Plural	Singular	Plural	
mío	míos	mía	mías	my
tuyo	tuyos	tuya	tuyas	your
suyo	suyos	suya	suyas	his, her, your, its
nuestro	nuestros	nuestra	nuestras	our
vuestro	vuestros	vuestra	vuestras	your
suyo	suyos	suya	suyas	their, your

When you use a short possessive adjective, make note of the following:

- *Su* can mean "his," "her," or "their," because the possessive adjective agrees with the noun it modifies, and not with the subject. Therefore, his mother = *su madre* because *su* agrees with the word *mother*, which is singular. *Su madre* can also mean *her mother* or *their mother*. You will know whether *su* means "his," "her," or "their" by the context of the conversation.
- Short possessive adjectives are used before *each* noun:

| su hermana y su hermano | her sister and brother |
| mi hermano y tus primos | my brother and your cousins |

- With parts of the body or clothing, the possessive adjective is usually replaced with the definite article if the possessor is clear:

| Ella se cepilla los dientes. | She brushes her teeth. |
| Él se pone el sombrero. | He puts on his hat. |

The longer adjectives are used as follows:

el hermano mío	my brother
el padre y la madre suyos	his (her, their) father and mother
unas amigas tuyas	some of your friends

To avoid ambiguity, *su* (*sus*) and *suyo* (*suya, suyos, suyas*), may be replaced by the article and *de él* (*ella*), *de Ud.* (*Uds.*), or *de ellos* (*ellas*):

el padre de ella	her father
una amiga de Uds.	one of your friends

You can now introduce someone using possessive adjectives:

Le (te) presento a mi hijo y a su esposa.	I'd like you to meet my son and his wife.
Le (te) presento a un hijo mío y a su esposa.	

Using Possessive Pronouns

A possessive pronoun replaces a possessive adjective + noun. The following pronouns agree in number and gender with the nouns they replace.

SINGULAR		PLURAL		
Masculine	Feminine	Masculine	Feminine	English
el mío	la mía	los míos	las mías	mine
el tuyo	la tuya	los tuyos	las tuyas	yours (familiar)
el suyo	la suya	los suyos	las suyas	his/her/yours (formal)
el nuestro	la nuestra	los nuestros	las nuestras	ours
el vuestro	la vuestra	los vuestros	las vuestras	yours (familiar)
el suyo	la suya	los suyos	las suyas	theirs/yours (formal)

Este periódico es el suyo.	This newspaper is his/hers.

Because the possessive pronoun agrees with the item possessed and not the possessor, the only way to distinguish between *his* and *hers* is to follow the conversation carefully.

Aquí está mi maleta.	Here is my suitcase.
¿Dónde está la suya?	Where is yours?

Spanish expressions of relationship are:

- a friend of mine, one of my friends, *un amigo mío*
- a nephew of his, one of his nephews, *un sobrino suyo*
- neighbors (f.) of theirs, some of their neighbors, *unas vecinas suyas*

TIME'S UP!

By using the phrases presented at the beginning of this chapter with the correct possessive adjective, and by following them with the noun expressing the person being introduced, you can now have a very simple introductory conversation in Spanish. Do the following without looking back:

1. Greet someone.

2. State that you are pleased to meet them.

3. Give your name.

4. State your health.

5. Tell where you are from.

6. Tell where you live.

7. Give your nationality.

8. Name a country you are going to visit.

9. Introduce a family member.

10. Say good-bye.

Fielding Invitations and Other Questions

MASTER THESE SKILLS

- Using verbs to extend invitations
- Using prepositions to join your thoughts
- Using prepositional pronouns to extend invitations
- Accepting, refusing, and showing indifference and indecision

In this chapter you'll learn how to extend, accept, and tactfully refuse invitations to a variety of interesting and popular tourist attractions and sights.

VERBS FOR INVITATIONS

By far the easiest verb to use is *desear* (to want). It is a regular *-ar* verb and, therefore, quite easy to conjugate:

desear—to want

yo deseo (I want)	nosotros deseamos (we want)
tú deseas (you want)	vosotros deseáis (you want)
él desea (he wants)	ellos desean (they want)

You may also use the verb *querer* (to wish or to want) to extend an invitation. Remember, though, that *querer* requires an *e* to *ie* change within the shoe, while the *nosotros* and *vosotros* forms use the infinitive stem.

querer—to want

yo quiero (I want)	nosotros queremos (we want)
tú quieres (you want)	vosotros queréis (you want)
él quiere (he wants)	ellos quieren (they want)

You may also use the verb *poder* (to be able to, can) to ask whether someone is available. Keep in mind that *poder* also has a stem change within the shoe from *o* to *ue* and that the n*osotros* and *vosotros* forms follow the infinitive.

poder—to be able to, can

yo puedo (I can)	nosotros podemos (we can)
tú puedes (you can)	vosotros podéis (you can)
él puede (he can)	ellos pueden (they can)

You may use the idiomatic expression *tener ganas de* (to feel like) to ask what someone is in the mood to do. Remember that *tener* also has an irregular yo form: *tengo* and a stem change from *e* to *ie* for the *tú, él, ella, Ud., ellos, ellas,* and *Uds.* forms. The *nosotros* and *vosotros* forms follow the infinitive.

tener—to have

yo tengo (I have)	nosotros tenemos (we have)
tú tienes (you have)	vosotros tenéis (you have)
él tiene (he has)	ellos tienen (they have)

To extend an invitation, use the verbs discussed in this section, plus an infinitive, to form the invitation.

FORMAL

¿Ud. desea ir . . . ?	Do you want to go . . . ?
¿Ud. pueden salir . . . ?	Can you go out . . . ?

INFORMAL

¿Tú quieres ir . . . ?	Do you want to go . . . ?
¿Tú puedes salir . . . ?	Can you go out . . . ?

PLURAL

¿Uds. pueden ir . . . ?	Can you go . . . ?

PREPOSITIONS

You can use prepositions to show the relationship of a noun to another word in a sentence. Prepositions come in handy when extending an invitation, as well as in common everyday situations.

The prepositions listed here can not only help you to offer a suggestion for something to do, but can also help you give or receive any necessary directions.

PREPOSITION	SPANISH	PREPOSITION	SPANISH
about	acerca de	by	en
above, on top of	encima de	during	durante
according to	según	far	lejos de
after	después (de)	for	por, para
against	contra	from	de
around	alrededor de	in	en
at	a, en	in front of	delante de
at the house of	en casa de	inside, within	dentro de
before	antes (de)	instead of	en lugar de
behind	detrás de	instead of	en vez de
beneath, under	debajo de	of	de
besides	además de	on	en
between	entre	opposite	enfrente de

outside of	fuera de	toward	hacia
over, above	sobre	until	hasta
near	cerca de	with	con
to	a	without	sin

Prepositions That Require Special Attention

***En* and *A*.** The selection of the correct word for *at* when referring to a place may present some difficulty. The following explanations should help eliminate some of the confusion:

- *En* means inside, or within an enclosed or specific place. *Estamos en el aeropuerto.* (We are at [inside] the airport.)
- *A* refers to a general location where specific boundaries are not suggested or implied: *Vamos al aeropuerto.* (We are going to the airport.)

***A* and *De*.** As seen above, the prepositions *a* (to) and *de* (from) are used when referring to places. It is important to contract *a* and *de* with the definite article *el* (the) as shown below before a masculine singular noun. *A* and *de* do not contract with *la*, *los*, or *las*:

a + el = al	Van al cine.	They are going to the movies.
de + el = del	Salen del cine.	They leave the movies.

***Por* and *Para*.** Because *por* and *para* have the same meaning in English, you will need to determine which to use by their Spanish context as shown in the following examples.

Por is used in the following ways:

- To show motion:

Pasé por la tienda.	I passed by the store.
Entraron por la puerta.	They came in through the door.
Pasean por esa calle.	They stroll along that street.

- To state means or manner:

Lo necesito por escrito.	I need it in writing.
Lo envió por avión.	He sent it by plane.

- To mean "in exchange for": *Pagaré un dólar por eso.* (I'll pay a dollar for that.)

- To show the duration of an action: *Estuvo enfermo por un mes.* (He was sick for a month.)
- To indicate an indefinite period of time: *Me voy por la tarde.* (I'm leaving in the afternoon.)
- To express "for the sake of" or "on behalf of":

Lo haré por Ud.	I'll do it for your sake.
Lo haré por la familia.	I'll do it on behalf of the family.

- To give a reason or motive: *Trabajo por necesidad.* (I work out of necessity.)
- To express "per" or "by the":

Va al cine una vez por semana.	He goes to the movies once a week.
Son más baratos por docena.	They are cheaper by the dozen.

- To state an opinion or estimation, equivalent to "for" or "as":

Me toman por profesora.	They took me for a teacher.
Se le conocía por Pedro.	He was known as Pedro.

- To place the agent (doer) in a passive construction: *Fue escrito por Juan.* (It was written by Juan.)
- To mean "for" after the verbs *enviar* (to send), *ir* (to go), *mandar* (to order, send), *preguntar* (to ask), *regresar* (to return), *venir* (to come), and *volver* (to return):

Fui (Envié, Pregunté) por el médico.	I went for (sent for, asked for) the doctor.
Vine (Regresé, Volví) por mis libros.	I came (returned, came back) for my books.

Por is used in the following adverbial expressions:

EXPRESSION	MEANING
por eso	therefore, so
por lo común	generally
por lo general	generally
por lo visto	apparently
por supuesto	of course

Para is used in the following ways:

- With a destination of a place or a direction: *Salimos para México.* (We are going to Mexico.)
- With the destination of a recipient: *Este regalo es para Ud.* (This gift is for you.)
- To express a time limit in the future: *Lo necesito para mañana.* (I need it for tomorrow.)
- To state a purpose or goal: *Trabajo para vivir.* (I work [in order] to live.)
- To show the use of an object: *Es una caja para vestidos.* (It's a box for clothing.)
- To make comparisons by expressing "for" or "considering that": *Para ser americano habla bien el español.* (For being an American he speaks Spanish well.)

Note the following exceptions to these rules:

- When speaking about a means of transportation for a passenger, use *en* instead of *por* to express "by":

Voy a viajar en avión.	I'm going to travel by plane.
Envío la carta por avión.	I'm sending the letter by plane.

- When using the verbs *buscar* (to look for), *esperar* (to wait for), and *pedir* (to ask for), do not use *por* or *para*, because the word *for* is already included in the meaning of the verb.

PLACES

If you are a traveler, student, or businessperson in the Spanish-speaking world, or if you happen to meet a Spanish speaker who needs assistance in your own hometown, you will find this list of place names quite useful.

amusement park	el parque de atracciones
beach	la playa
cathedral	la catedral
church	la iglesia
circus	el circo
department store	los grandes almacenes
fair	la feria
fountain	la fuente
garden	el jardín

library	la biblioteca
mall	el centro comercial
movies	el cine
museum	el museo
nightclub	el club
park	el parque
restaurant	el restaurante
theater	el teatro
zoo	el zoológico

PREPOSTITIONAL PRONOUNS

Prepositional pronouns are so named because they are pronouns that you use after prepositions. In many cases, prepositional pronouns are useful when you need to extend an invitation. The following table shows subject pronouns with their corresponding stress pronouns.

SUBJECT	PREPOSITIONAL PRONOUN	MEANING
yo	mí	I, me
tú	ti	you (familiar)
él	él	he, him
ella	ella	she
Ud.	Ud.	you
nosotros	nosotros	we, us (polite)
vosotros	vosotros	you (familiar)
ellos	ellos	they, them
ellas	ellas	they, them
Uds.	Uds.	you (polite)

The prepositional pronoun *sí* is used reflexively both in the singular and in the plural to express "yourself," "himself," "herself," "itself," "themselves," or "yourselves": *Piensa para sí mismo.* (He thinks for himself.)

You can use prepositional pronouns in situations where you would like to extend an invitation, or in other everyday conversations as follows:

- The prepositional pronoun is used as the object of a preposition and always follows the preposition: *No es para ti; es para mí.* (It's not for you; it's for me.)
- The prepositional pronouns *mí*, *ti*, and *sí* combine with the preposition *con* as follows:

conmigo	with me
contigo	with you
consigo	with him/her/your(self), them/your(selves)

EXTENDING AN INVITATION

By combining all the elements presented so far in this chapter, you can now try to extend your own invitation.

1. Start with a verb in either its polite or familiar form:

¿Ud. quiere . . . ?	¿Tú quieres . . . ?	Do you want . . . ?
¿Ud. puede . . . ?	¿Tú puedes . . . ?	Can you . . . ?
¿Ud. desea . . . ?	¿Tú deseas . . . ?	Do you wish . . . ?
¿Ud. tiene ganas de . . . ?	¿Tú tienes ganas de . . . ?	Do you feel like . . . ?

2. Add an infinitive:

ir	to go
salir	to go out
venir	to come

3. Use the correct form of *a* + definite article followed by the name of a place:

al cine	to the movies
a la playa	to the beach
a los parques	to the parks
a las iglesias	to the churches

4. Add a preposition + a prepositional pronoun:

conmigo	with me
con nosotros	with us

Your final product should look and sound something like these examples:

¿Tú quieres ir a la playa conmigo?	Do you want to go to the beach with me?
¿Uds. quieren ir al cine con nosotros?	Do you want to go to the movies with us?

ACCEPTING AN INVITATION

Perhaps you receive an invitation that intrigues you. Saying yes is easy. Just nod your head and say, "Sí" to show your eager acceptance. You may also use any of the phrases listed here.

PHRASE	SPANISH
You bet!	¡Ya lo creo!
Gladly.	¡Con mucho gusto!
Great!	!Fantástico!
If you want to.	Si tu quieres./Si Ud. quiere.
OK./I agree.	De acuerdo.
Of course.	¡Por supuesto!/¡Claro!
Thank you.	Gracias.
Thank you.	Le (te) agradezco.
Thank you very much.	Muchas gracias.
That's a good idea.	Es una buena idea.
With pleasure.	Con placer.

NOTE

To express the phrase "You're welcome," you can use *De nada* or *No hay de qué*.

REFUSING AN INVITATION

Saying no is more difficult because you must remain tactful. An invitation can be cordially and politely refused by expressing regrets and giving a valid excuse. You may need to use the following phrases in both formal and informal situations.

PHRASE	SPANISH
Unfortunately . . .	Desgraciadamente . . .
I can't.	No puedo.
I don't feel like it.	No tengo ganas.
I don't have the money.	No tengo dinero.
I don't have time.	No tengo tiempo.
I don't want to.	No quiero.
I'm busy.	Estoy ocupado(a).
I'm sorry.	Lo siento.
I'm tired.	Estoy cansado(a).
Perhaps some other time.	Tal vez en otra ocasión.

In any of the expressions listed above that begin with *I*, you can change the subject to whatever is appropriate for the situation (*they*, *we*, etc.). Make sure, however, that when you do so, you also conjugate the verb and make the adjective agree with the new subject. (Refer to Chapter 22:00 for a refresher on the present tense of verbs.)

EXPRESSING INDECISION AND INDIFFERENCE

If you receive an invitation and are at a loss as to what to do, express your indecision or indifference by using the phrases listed here.

PHRASE	SPANISH
I don't know.	No sé.
It depends.	Depende.
It doesn't matter.	No importa.
Perhaps./Maybe.	Quizás.
Whatever you want.	Lo que prefiera(s).

NO

You will sometimes need to use the simplest of all the Spanish negatives, *no*, which expresses "not." In simple and compound sentences, *no* precedes the conjugated verb; in compound tenses, *no* precedes the helping verb:

SIMPLE	COMPOUND
No estoy libre.	No he estado libre.
I'm not free.	I wasn't free./I haven't been free.
(at a particular, specific moment in time)	
No estaba libre.	No había estado libre.
I wasn't free.	I hadn't been free.
(in general—at no specific moment)	
No estaré libre.	No habré estado libre.
I will not be free.	I will not have been free.
No estaría libre.	No habría estado libre.
I wouldn't be free.	I wouldn't have been free.

When a sentence has two verbs, remember that *no* must precede the conjugated verb:

No quiero ir al parque.	I don't want to go to the park.
No podemos salir.	We can't go out.
No van a viajar.	They aren't going to travel.

No with Reflexive Verbs

In simple and compound tenses, *no* precedes the reflexive pronoun:

SIMPLE	COMPOUND
No me divierto.	No nos hemos divertido.
I'm not having a good time.	We have not had a good time.
No te divertías.	No se había divertido.
You weren't having a good time.	You hadn't had a good time.
No se divertirá.	No se habrán divertido.
He will not have a good time.	They will not have had a good time.
No se divertiría.	No se habrían divertido.
She wouldn't have a good time.	They wouldn't have had a good time.

When an infinitive is negated, *no* precedes the infinitive:

Yo decidí no venir.	I decided not to come.
Yo he decidido no levantarme temprano.	I decided not to get up early.

TIME'S UP!

1. Extend an invitation to a new acquaintance to go to a restaurant with you.

2. Extend an invitation to a friend to go to the circus with you and your family.

3. Accept an invitation to a nightclub.

4. Accept an invitation to visit a cathedral.

5. Refuse an invitation to a fair.

6. Refuse an invitation to the mall.

7. Give an excuse why you can't go to the zoo.

8. Give an excuse why you can't go the gardens.

9. Show indifference about going to the movies.

10. Show indecision about going to see the fountains.

Making Plans

MASTER THESE SKILLS

- Using cardinal numbers
- Using ordinal numbers
- Expressing days, months, seasons, and dates
- Telling time

In this lesson you'll learn the essentials for making plans: numbers, and how they are used to express the date and tell time; and how to combine these elements to plan an outing.

CARDINAL NUMBERS

The Spanish write two numbers differently than we do. The number one has a little hook on top: 1. In order to distinguish a one from the number seven, Spanish speakers put a line through the seven when they write it: 7.

In numerals and decimals, where English speakers use commas the Spanish use periods, and vice versa:

ENGLISH	SPANISH		ENGLISH	SPANISH
3,000	3.000		$16.95	$16,95
0.75	0,75			

Carefully study the Spanish numbers presented here:

CARDINAL	SPANISH	CARDINAL	SPANISH
0	cero	21	veintiuno, veinte y uno
1	uno	25	veinte y cinco
2	dos	30	treinta
3	tres	40	cuarenta
4	cuatro	50	cincuenta
5	cinco	60	sesenta
6	seis	70	setenta
7	siete	80	ochenta
8	ocho	90	noventa
9	nueve	100	ciento (cien)
10	diez	101	ciento uno
11	once	200	doscientos
12	doce	500	quinientos
13	trece	1000	mil
14	catorce	2000	dos mil
15	quince	100.000	cien mil
16	dieciséis, diez y seis	1.000.000	un millón
17	diecisiete, diez y siete	2.000.000	dos millones
18	dieciocho, diez y ocho	1.000.000.000	mil millones
19	diecinueve, diez y nueve	2.000.000.000	dos mil millones
20	veinte		

Note the following about Spanish numbers:

- The conjunction *y* (and) is used only for numbers between 16 and 99:

52	cincuenta y dos
152	ciento cincuenta y dos

- The numbers 16–19 and 21–29 are most frequently written as one word. When this is done, the numbers 16, 22, 23, and 26 have accents on the last syllable:

16	dieciséis	23	veintitrés
22	veintidós	26	veintiséis

- In compounds of *ciento* (*doscientos, trescientos*), there must be agreement with a feminine noun:

doscientos muchachos	two hundred boys
trescientas muchachas	three hundred girls

- *Ciento* becomes *cien* before nouns and before the numbers *mil* and *millones*. Before all other numbers, *ciento* is used:

cien personas	one hundred people
cien mil habitantes	one hundred thousand inhabitants
cien millones de dólares	one billion dollars
ciento cincuenta libros	one hundred and twenty books

- *Uno* is used only when counting and becomes *un* before a masculine noun and *una* before a feminine noun:

uno, dos, tres . . .	one, two, three . . .
un niño y una niña	a boy and a girl
treinta y un hombres	thirty-one men
veintiuna casas	twenty-one houses

- *Un* is not used before *cien(to)* or *mil*, but it is used before *millón*. When *millón* is followed by a noun, put *de* between *millón* and the noun.

cien años	one hundred years
ciento veinte alumnos	one hundred twenty students

| mil años | one thousand years |
| un millón de dólares | a million dollars |

▽ **NOTE**
. . . .

To express your age, use the idiomatic expression *tengo . . . años*, given in Chapter 22:00: *Tengo veintiséis años.* (I'm twenty-six years old.)

ORDINAL NUMBERS

Understanding ordinal numbers is very important when you are in an elevated building, such as an apartment house or a department store. Note that *el sótano* is the basement, *la planta baja* is the ground or main floor, and *la primera planta* or *el primer piso* is the first floor above ground level.

Carefully study these ordinal numbers:

ORDINAL	SPANISH	ORDINAL	SPANISH
1st	primero	6th	sexto
2nd	segundo	7th	séptimo
3rd	tercero	8th	octavo
4th	cuarto	9th	noveno
5th	quinto	10th	décimo

Note the following about ordinal numbers:

- Spanish speakers use ordinal numbers only through the tenth. After that, cardinal numbers are used:

el sexto día	the sixth day
la segunda semana	the second week
Carlos Cuarto	Charles IV
la página doce	page 12
el siglo veinte	the twentieth century

- Ordinal numbers must agree in gender with the nouns they modify. Ordinal numbers are made feminine by changing the final *o* of the masculine form to *a*:

| el cuarto día | the fourth day |
| la cuarta semana | the fourth week |

- *Primero* and *tercero* drop their final *o* before a masculine singular noun:

el primer acto	the first act
el tercer baile	the third dance

    But:

el siglo tercero	the third century

- The Spanish ordinal numbers are abbreviated as follows:

primero(a): $1^{o(a)}$	tercero(a): $3^{o(a)}$
primer: 1er	tercer: 3er
segundo(a): $2^{o(a)}$	cuarto(a): $4^{o(a)}$

> **▽ NOTE**
>
> 1. A cardinal number that replaces an ordinal number is always masculine, as *número*, a masculine word, is understood: *la avenida once* (Eleventh Avenue [avenue number eleven]).
> 2. In Spanish, cardinal numbers precede ordinal numbers: *las cuatro primeras personas* (the first four people).

DAYS, MONTHS, AND SEASONS

To express the date, you will need the names of the days of the week and months of the year. It will also be helpful to know the seasons. The days, months, and seasons are listed below. In Spanish all are masculine and are not capitalized unless they are used at the beginning of a sentence.

An important fact to remember if you have a lot of appointments in a Spanish-speaking country is that Spanish calendars start with Monday as the first day of the week.

DAY	SPANISH
Monday	lunes
Tuesday	martes
Wednesday	miércoles
Thursday	jueves
Friday	viernes
Saturday	sábado
Sunday	domingo

111

MONTH	SPANISH
January	enero
February	febrero
March	marzo
April	abril
May	mayo
June	junio
July	julio
August	agosto
September	septiembre
October	octubre
November	noviembre
December	diciembre

SEASON	SPANISH
winter	el invierno
spring	la primavera
summer	el verano
autumn, fall	el otoño

To express "on a certain day", the Spanish language uses the definite article *los*: *Los domingos me levanto tarde.* (On Sundays, I wake up late.)

Use the preposition *en* to express "in" with months, and *en* + definite article for seasons: *en julio* (in July), *en el verano* (in the summer).

DATES

The following list gives you a few date-related words you will need when making plans.

WORD/EXPRESSION	SPANISH
a day	un día
a week	una semana
a month	un mes
a year	un año
in	en

ago	hace
per	por
during	durante
next	próximo(a)
last	pasado(a)
last (in a series)	último(a)
yesterday	ayer
today	hoy
tomorrow	mañana
tomorrow morning	mañana por la mañana
tomorrow afternoon	mañana por la tarde
tomorrow night	mañana por la noche
day after tomorrow	pasado mañana
from	desde
a week from today	de hoy en una semana

Dates in Spanish are expressed as follows; the definite article *el* is optional: day + (*el*) + cardinal number (except for *primero*) + *de* + month + *de* + year: *lunes (el) once de julio de dos mil* (Monday, July 11, 2000).

Note the following when expressing a date:

- The first of each month is expressed by *primero*. Cardinal numbers are used for all other days:

el primero de abril	April 1st
el dos de mayo	May 2nd

- Years are expressed in thousands and hundreds, not in hundreds as they are in English:

1999	mil novecientos noventa y nueve
	one thousand nine hundred and ninety-nine

- When writing the date in numbers, Spanish follows the sequence: day + month + year:

  el 12 de enero de 2003 = 12/1/03

  January 12, 2003 = 1/12/03

- The English word *on* is expressed by *el* in Spanish dates:

Llego *el* dos de abril.	I'm arriving *on* April 2nd.
Te veré *el* viernes.	I'll see you *on* Friday.

To get information about the date or the date of an event, you need the following questions and answers:

What day is today?	¿Qué día es hoy?
—Today is . . .	—Hoy es . . .
What's today's date?	¿Cuál es la fecha de hoy?
—Today is . . .	—Hoy es . . .
What's today's date?	¿A cuánto estamos hoy?
—It is . . .	—Estamos a . . .
What is the date of the . . . ?	¿Cuál es la fecha del (de la, de los, de las) . . .
When do (does) the . . . begin?	¿Cuándo empieza(n) . . . ?
When do (does) the . . . end?	¿Cuándo termina(n) . . . ?
What day(s) is (are) the . . . open?	¿Qué día(s) está(n) abierto(a)(s) . . . ?
What day(s) is (are) the . . . closed?	¿Qué día(s) está(n) cerrado(a)(s) . . . ?

▽ **NOTE**

The adjectives *abierto* and *cerrado* must agree in number and gender with the nouns they modify:

¿Qué día está cerrado el museo?	What day is the museum closed?
¿Qué días están abiertas las bibliotecas?	What days are the libraries open?

TELLING TIME

When making plans, you need to know at what time you will meet and when an event is going to take place. The following will help you ask and answer the appropriate questions.

QUESTION	ANSWER
¿Qué hora es?	Es (Son) . . .
What time is it?	It is . . .

¿A qué hora empieza(n) . . . ?	A . . .
At what time does . . . start?	At . . .
¿A qué hora termina(n) . . . ?	A . . .
At what times does . . . end?	At . . .
¿A qué hora nos reunimos?	A . . .
At what time shall we meet?	At . . .

TIME	SPANISH
1:00	la una
2:05	las dos y cinco
3:10	las tres y diez
4:15	las cuatro y cuarto
5:20	las cinco y veinte
6:25	las seis y veinticinco
7:30	las siete y media
7:35	las ocho menos veinticinco
8:40 (20 minutes to 9:00)	las nueve menos veinte
9:45	un cuarto para las diez
10:50 (10 minutes to 11)	las once menos diez
11:55 (5 minutes to 12)	las doce menos cinco
noon	el mediodía
midnight	la medianoche

To express time properly, remember the following:

- Use *es* for "it is" when it is one o'clock. Because they are plural, for the other numbers, use *son*:

Es la una.	It's one o'clock.
Son las dos y media.	It's half past two./It's 2:30.

- Use *a la* for one o'clock and *a las* for every other hour to express "at" (at the specific time):

Me voy a la una.	I'm leaving at one o'clock.
Va a llegar a las cinco y cuarto.	He's going to arrive at a quarter after five.

- Use *y* and the number of minutes to express the time after the hour (before half past): *Es la una y veinte.* (It's one twenty./It's 1:20.)
- To express time before the next hour (after half past), use *menos* + the number of the following hour: *Son las cinco menos veinte.* (It's twenty minutes to five./It's 4:40.)

   Time before the hour may also be expressed by *faltar* + minutes + *para* + the following hour: *Faltan veinte minutos para las cinco.* (It's twenty minutes to five./It's 4:40.)

You will commonly hear the time expressed numerically, as follows: *Son las dos y cuarenta y cinco.* (It's two forty-five./It's 2:45.)

   Because *media* (half) is used as an adjective, it agrees with *hora* (hour). *Cuarto* (quarter) is used as a noun and shows no agreement:

Es la una y media.	It's half past one.
Es la una y cuarto.	It's quarter after one.

When making plans, keep the following questions in mind. You may mix and match the elements in the list to get a correct sentence. Use the forms below when you know the person well. To be polite, use the *Ud.* form, as shown in Chapter 17:00.

¿A qué hora . . . ?	At what time . . . ?
¿Cuándo . . . ?	When . . . ?
Debes . . .	You have to . . .
Puedes . . .	You can . . .
Quieres . . .	You want . . .
¿Deseas . . . ?	Do you want . . . ?
¿Tienes ganas de . . . ?	Do you feel like . . . ?
regresar	(to) return (come back)
ir	(to) go
salir	(to) go out
volver	(to) return

¿Cuándo quieres salir?	When do you want to go out?
¿A qué hora puedes salir?	At what time can you leave?

Studying the expressions presented here will help you better understand expressions with time.

EXPRESSION	SPANISH
a second	un segundo
a minute	un minuto
an hour	una hora
in the morning (A.M.)	por la mañana
in the afternoon (P.M.)	por la tarde
in the evening (P.M.)	por la noche
at what time?	¿a qué hora?
at exactly 2:00	a las dos en punto
a quarter of an hour	un cuarto de hora
a half hour	una media hora
in an hour	en una hora
in a while	dentro de un rato
until 3:00	hasta las tres
before 4:00	antes de las cuatro
after 5:00	después de las cinco
since what time?	¿desde qué hora?
since 6:00	desde las seis
an hour ago	hace una hora
early	temprano
late	tarde
late (in arriving)	de retraso

▽ **NOTE**
....

In public announcements, such as timetables, the official 24-hour system is commonly used, with midnight as the zero hour:

0 h 40 = 12:40 A.M.   16 horas = 4:00 P.M.   21 h 45 = 9:45 P.M.

TIME'S UP!

1. Tell how old you are.

2. Ask for today's date.

3. Express your birth date.

4. Ask what days the museum is closed.

5. Express the season we are in.

6. Give today's date.

7. Ask your friend when he/she wants to go out?

8. Say what time it is.

9. Ask at what time we'll be getting together.

10. Say when the movie (*la película*) begins.

Using Spanish Around the Home

MASTER THESE SKILLS

- Using *deber*

- Getting help around the house and in a store

- Understanding and forming the present subjunctive

- Using the subjunctive

- Using the imperfect, the perfect, and the pluperfect subjunctive and offering encouragement

In this chapter you'll learn how to express school and household obligations by using the verb *deber* (to have to), the idiomatic expression *tener que*, or the subjunctive mood. You'll also learn how to encourage someone to pursue a course of action.

HOUSE AND HOME

In order to refer to the different rooms and parts of a house that might need attention, you'll need the vocabulary in the following table.

ROOM/PLACE	SPANISH	ROOM/PLACE	SPANISH
apartment building	el edificio de pisos	floor	el suelo
		floor (story)	el piso
apartment	el apartamento	garage	el garaje
attic	el entretecho	ground floor	la planta baja
backyard	el jardín	house	la casa
balcony	el balcón	kitchen	la cocina
basement	el sótano	laundry room	la lavandería
bathroom	el cuarto de baño	lawn	el césped
bedroom	el dormitorio	living room	la sala
closet	el armario	shower	la ducha
door	la puerta	stairs	la escalera
elevator	el ascensor	window	la ventana
fireplace	la chimenea		

Naturally, within each room of a home there are pieces of furniture and appliances that may also need your attention. The following list gives you the names of the necessary equipment.

FURNITURE	SPANISH	FURNITURE	SPANISH
bed	la cama	microwave oven	el microondas
chair	la silla	mirror	el espejo
clock	el reloj	oven	el horno
clothes dryer	la secadora	refrigerator	el refrigerador
computer	la computadora	sofa	el sofá
dresser	la cómoda	stereo	el estéreo
freezer	el congelador	stove	la estufa
furniture	los muebles	table	la mesa
lamp	la lámpara	television	el televisor

CHORES

Among the most common household chores are those listed below.

CHORE	SPANISH
clean the house	limpiar la casa
cook	cocinar
do the dishes	lavar los platos
do the laundry	lavar la ropa
go shopping	ir de compras
iron	planchar la ropa
make the beds	hacer (tender) las camas
mow the lawn	cortar el cesped
set the table	poner la mesa
throw out the garbage	sacar la basura
vacuum	pasar la aspiradora
wash the car	lavar el coche

STORES

Learn the names of the food stores, as well as the other establishments listed in the following table. You might like to visit them while in a Spanish-speaking country.

STORE/PRODUCT	SPANISH	PRODUCT
bakery/bread	la panadería	el pan
bookstore/books	la librería	los libros
butcher shop/meat	la carnicería	la carne
dairy store/milk	la lechería	la leche
fish store/fish	la pescadería	el pescado
florist/flowers	la florería	las flores
fruit store/fruits	la frutería	las frutas
grocery/vegetables	la abastecería (el abasto)	los vegetales
newsstand/newspapers	el puesto de periódicos	los periódicos
pharmacy/medicine	la farmacia	los medicamentos

Remember that if you want to say that you are going to a store or that you'll be at a store, you must use *a* + definite article. Note that *a* + *el* = *al*. The other possibilities are *a la*, *a los*, or *a las*: *al estanco*, *a la panadería*.

To express that you are going to a store, use the form of *ir* that agrees with the subject and *a* with the appropriate definite article and noun:

Voy a la lechería.	I'm going to the dairy.
Vamos al puesto de periódicos.	We're going to the newsstand.

Getting Help in a Store

An employee in any type of store may ask you one of these questions to find out if you need assistance:

May I help you?	¿Puedo ayudarle a Ud.?
How can I help you?	¿En que puedo servirle?
What can I offer you?	¿Qué se le ofrece?

An appropriate answer would be:

No, thanks. I'm just browsing.	No, gracias. Estoy mirando solamente.
Yes, please. I would like to see . . .	Sí, por favor. Quisiera ver . . .
Yes. I'd like to buy . . . for . . .	Sí, quisiera comprar . . . para . . .
Yes, I'm looking for (I need) . . .	Sí, estoy buscando (Necesito) . . .
Are there any sales?	¿Hay gangas?
Are your prices reduced?	¿Hay una buena rebaja de precios?

After being helped, you might hear the salesperson ask:

Anything else?	¿Qué más?
	¿Algo más?

Unless you need to continue with an order or explain other needs, you can respond: *No, gracias. Me quedo con éste (ésta).* (No, thank you. I'll take this.)

DEBER (TO HAVE TO)

The verb *deber* expresses what the subject should do:

yo debo	nosotros debemos

tú debes	vosotros debéis
él debe	ellos deben

Uses of *Deber*

Deber has some special uses when you want to persuade someone to do something and when it expresses an obligation:

• *Deber* is used primarily to express obligation:

Debo salir.	I have to leave.
	I must leave.
	I am supposed to leave.
	I should leave.

• *Deber de* + infinitive is used to express probability:

Debe de estar atrasado.	He must be late.
	He is probably late.

• *Deber* in the imperfect + *de* + infinitive may also be used to express probability in the past: *Debía de estar atrasado.* (He must have been late.)
• The imperfect subjunctive of *deber* means *ought to* or *should*, and expresses obligation (for more on the imperfect subjunctive see "The Imperfect Subjunctive," "The Perfect and Pluperfect Subjunctive," and "Offering Encouragement" later in this chapter):

Debieras ir de compras.	You should go shopping.
	You ought to go shopping.

• *Deber* means to owe when followed by a noun: *Le debo cinco dólares a Juan.* (I owe John five dollars.)

TENER QUE

Like *deber*, you can use the irregular verb *tener* + *que* + infinitive to express obligation:

Yo tengo que trabajar.	I have to work.
Tú tienes que lavar el coche.	You have to wash the car.
Él tiene que poner la mesa.	He has to set the table.

Nosotros tenemos que cocinar.	We have to cook.
Vosotros tenéis que lavar la ropa.	You have to do the laundry.
Ellos tienen que ir de compras.	They have to go shopping.

HAY QUE + INFINITVE

Hay que + infinitive is used in a general way to express what people must do:

Hay que comer para vivir.	You have to eat to live.
Hay que llegar a tiempo.	You have to arrive on time.

UNDERSTANDING AND FORMING THE PRESENT SUBJUNCTIVE

Like the conditional, the subjunctive is a mood (a form of the verb showing the subject's attitude), not a tense (a form of the verb showing time). You may use the subjunctive to persuade someone to follow a course of action because it shows, among other things, wishing and wanting, need and necessity, and feelings and emotions. The subjunctive is used much more frequently in Spanish than in English.

Because the subjunctive is not a tense, the present subjunctive can be used to refer to actions in the present or the future. The imperfect, perfect, and pluperfect subjunctive refer to a completed past action.

Es necesario que él trabaje.	It is necessary for him to work./ He has to work.
Es posible que ellas lleguen a tiempo.	It's possible that they will arrive on time.
Lamenté que Ud. haya esperado.	I was sorry that you waited.

The following conditions must be present if the subjunctive is to be used:

- The sentence usually must contain two different clauses with two different subjects.
- The clauses must be joined by *que* (that), which is followed by the subjunctive.
- Among other things, the main clause must show need, necessity, emotion, or doubt.

The Subjunctive of Regular Verbs

To form the present subjunctive of regular verbs, and many irregular verbs, drop the -o from the first person singular indicative (yo) form of the present and add the subjunctive endings:

	YO	TÚ	ÉL	NOSOTROS	VOSOTROS	ELLOS
-ar verbs	-e	-es	-e	-emos	-éis	-en
-er verbs	-a	-as	-a	-amos	-áis	-an
-ir verbs	-a	-as	-a	-amos	-áis	-an

The next table shows how this is done.

-AR VERBS	-ER VERBS	-IR VERBS
lavar (to wash)	comer (to eat)	abrir (to open)
yo lavo	yo como	yo abro .
yo lave	yo coma	yo abra
tú laves	tú comas	tú abras
él lave	él coma	él abra
nosotros lavemos	nosotros comamos	nosotros abramos
vosotros lavéis	vosotros comáis	vosotros abráis
ellos laven	ellos coman	ellos abran

Notice that the endings are the reverse of the present tense endings, which can be found in Chapter 22:00: *ar* to *e*; *er* and *ir* to *a*.

Verbs Irregular in the Yo Form

The following table shows verbs that are irregular only in the yo form of the present tense and form the present subjuntive accordingly.

VERB	YO FORM	SUBJUNCTIVE STEM AND ENDINGS
escoger (to choose)	escojo	escoj (-a, -as, -a, -amos, -áis, -an)
conocer (to know)	conozco	conozc (-a, -as, -a, -amos, -áis, -an)
destruir (to destroy)	destruyo	destruy (-a, -as, -a, -amos, -áis, -an)
hacer (to do, make)	hago	hag (-a, -as, -a, -amos, -áis, -an)
oír (to hear)	oigo	oig (-a, -as, -a, -amos, -áis, -an)
poner (to put)	pongo	pong (-a, -as, -a, -amos, -áis, -an)

salir (to leave)	salgo	salg (-a, -as, -a, -amos, -áis, -an)
traer (to bring)	traigo	traig (-a, -as, -a, -amos, -áis,-an)
valer (to be worth)	valgo	valg (-a, -as, -a, -amos, -áis, -an)
venir (to come)	vengo	veng (-a, -as, -a, -amos, áis, -an)

Spelling Changes in the Present Subjunctive

In the present subjunctive, the following spelling changes are made:

-car verbs: change c to qu

-gar verbs: change g to gu

-zar verbs: change z to c

INFINITIVE	YO FORM PRETERIT	SUBJUNCTIVE STEM AND ENDINGS
buscar	busqué	busqu (-e, -es, -e, -emos, -éis, -en)
pagar	pagué	pagu (-e, -es, -e, -emos, -éis, -en)
cruzar	crucé	cruc (-e, -es, -e, -emos, éis, -en)

Note that these verbs have the same spelling changes as they did in the *yo* form of the preterite (see Chapter 21:00).

Stem-Changing Verbs in the Present Subjunctive

Stem-changing -ar, -er, and -ir verbs may or may not have the same stem changes in the present subjunctive as they do in the present indicative. Note: Changes in the stem occur in all persons, except the first- and second-person plural (*nosotros, vosotros*).

-ar and -er Verbs

· ·

	E TO IE	YO STEM	NOSOTROS/ VOSOTROS STEM
cerrar (to close)	yo cierro	cierr-	cerr-
querer (to want)	yo quiero	quier-	quer-

	O TO UE	YO STEM	NOSOTROS/ VOSOTROS STEM
contar (to tell)	yo cuento	cuent-	cont-
volver (to return)	yo vuelvo	vuelv-	volv-

-ir Verbs

	E TO *IE*	YO STEM	NOSOTROS/ VOSOTROS STEM
sentir (to regret)	yo siento	sient-	sint-

	O TO *UE*	YO STEM	NOSTROS/ VOSOTROS STEM
dormir (to sleep)	yo duermo	duerm-	durm-

	E TO *I*	YO STEM	NOSOTROS/ VOSOTROS STEM
pedir (to ask)	yo pido	pid-	pid-

Note the accent marks in some *-iar* and *-uar* verbs in all forms except *nosotros*:

enviar (to send)	yo envío	env(-íe, -íes, -íe, -iemos, -iéis, -íen)
continuar (to continue)	yo continúo	contin(-úe, -úes, -úe, -uemos, -uéis, -úen)

Verbs Irregular in the Subjunctive

Some verbs follow no rules for the formation of the subjunctive and must be memorized. The ones that are used the most frequently are:

dar (to give): dé, des, dé, demos, deis, den

estar (to be): esté, estés, esté, estemos, estéis, estén

haber (to have): haya, hayas, haya, hayamos, hayáis, hayan

ir (to go): vaya, vayas, vaya, vayamos, vayáis, vayan

saber (to know): sepa, sepas, sepa, sepamos, sepáis, sepan

ser (to be): sea, seas, sea, seamos, seáis, sean

Expressions of Need and Necessity

The subjunctive may be used to persuade someone of the need or necessity to do something or to make requests or demands. The expressions below are typically followed by the subjunctive.

SPANISH	MEANING
Es mejor que . . .	It is better that . . .
Más vale que . . .	It is better that . . .
Es importante que . . .	It is important that . . .
Es necesario que . . .	It is necessary that . . .

Es preferible que . . .	It is preferable that . . .
Es tiempo que . . .	It is time that . . .
Es urgente que . . .	It is urgent that . . .
Es útil que . . .	It is useful that . . .

Es importante que vayas al supermercado.	It is important you go to the supermarket.
Es urgente que hable al médico por telefono.	It's urgent that he call the doctor.

Be aware that the Spanish subjunctive may have many different meanings in English and will often not allow for an exact, word-for-word translation:

Es necesario que pongas la mesa.	You have to set the table.
	It is necessary that you set the table.

In Spanish, the subjunctive is often equivalent to an infinitive in English: *Quiero que tú vayas de compras.* (I want you to go to the store.)

Verbs of Wishing and Wanting

The subjunctive is often used after the verbs listed below:

decir	to tell, say	ojalá	if only . . .
desear	to desire, wish, want	pedir	to ask for, request
esperar	to hope	permitir	to permit
hacer	to make, cause	preferir	to prefer
insistir	to insist	querer	to wish, want
mandar	to command, order		

Él pide que yo haga el trabajo.	He asks that I do the work.
Prefiero que tú vayas a la farmacia.	I prefer you to go to the pharmacy.

When using the subjunctive in English, we often omit the word *that*. In Spanish however, *que* must always be used to join the two clauses:

Es importante que él lave el coche.	It's important that he wash the car.
Quiero que tú cortes el césped.	I want you to mow the lawn.

Avoiding the Subjunctive

In all of the examples shown thus far, the verb in the dependent clause (where the subjunctive is used) and the verb in the main clause (need, necessity, wishing, or wanting) have different subjects. If the subjects in both clauses are the same, *que* is omitted and the infinitive replaces the subjunctive:

Ella quiere que yo vaya a la panadería.	She wants me to go to the bakery.
Ella quiere ir a la panadería.	She wants to go to the bakery.

The verbs *dejar* (to allow), *hacer* (to make, do), *mandar* (to order), *permitir* (to permit), and *prohibir* (to forbid) may be followed by either the subjunctive or the infinitive:

Me mandan que salga.	They order me to leave.
Me mandan salir.	

THE IMPERFECT SUBJUNCTIVE

The imperfect subjunctive is used in the dependent clause (the clause after *que*) when the verb in the main clause is in the past. For the verbs *deber* and *querer*, the imperfect subjunctive form may be used to express the conditional:

Le mandaron que saliera.	They ordered him to leave.
Debieras ir a España.	You should go to Spain.
Quisiera trabajar.	I would like to work.

The imperfect subjunctive of all verbs is formed by dropping the *-ron* ending of the third person plural (*ellos*) of the preterite tense and adding either of the endings below. Either is correct as long as they are used consistently:

SUBJECT	ENDING	OR	ENDING
yo	-ra		-se
tú	-ras		-ses
él	-ra		-se
nosotros	-´ramos		-´semos
vosotros	-rais		-seis
ellos	-ran		-sen

129

> **▽ NOTE**
>
> The *nosotros* form of the imperfect subjunctive has an accent on the
> vowel immediately before the ending, whether you use the *-ra* ending or
> the *-se* ending.

The following table shows how to form the imperfect subjunctive.

INFINITIVE	PRETERIT	IMPERFECT SUBJUNCTIVE
	Third Person Plural	
hablar	hablaron	hablara, hablaras, hablara,
		habláramos, hablarais, hablaran
		OR
		hablase, hablases, hablase,
		hablásemos, hablaseis, hablasen
vender	vendieron	vendiera, vendieras, vendiera,
		vendiéramos, vendierais, vendieran
		OR
		vendiese, vendieses, vendiese,
		vendiésemos, vendieseis, vendiesen
abrir	abrieron	abriera, abrieras, abriera,
		abriéramos, abrierais, abrieran
		OR
		abriese, abrieses, abriese,
		abriésemos, abrieseis, abriesen

THE PERFECT AND PLUPERFECT SUBJUNCTIVE

The perfect and pluperfect subjunctives are formed in the same manner
as other compound tenses. Take the present subjunctive form of the helping verb *haber* (*haya, hayas, haya, hayamos, hayáis, hayan*) to form the
perfect subjunctive, and take the imperfect subjunctive of *haber* (*hubiera/
hubiese; hubieras/hubieses; hubiera/hubiese; hubiéramos/hubiésemos;
hubierais/hubieseis; hubieran/hubiesen*) to form the pluperfect subjunctive and add the past participle:

| Es importante que Uds. lo hayan visto. | It is important that you have seen it. |
| Era importante que Uds. lo hubieran (hubiesen) visto. | It was important that you had seen it. |

The perfect and pluperfect subjunctives are compound forms expressing actions completed in the past. The perfect subjunctive expresses what the subject has done, while the imperfect subjunctive expresses what the subject had done. The verb in the main clause may be in the present tense.

OFFERING ENCOURAGEMENT

We have seen how the subjunctive can be used to convince someone to follow a course of action. The best way to persuade someone to do something, whether it be a chore or a fun activity, is to offer a bit of encouragement.

PHRASE	SPANISH
A little more effort!	¡Un poquito más de esfuerzo!
Don't hesitate!	¡No vacile!
Go for it!	¡Vaya por eso!
Keep going!	¡Continúe!/¡Siga!
You have to try!	¡Tiene que tratar!
You're almost there!	¡Casi está allí!
You're getting there!	¡Ya está llegando!

All of the phrases of encouragement can be changed to familiar commands by changing to the *tú* command form, which you will learn in the next chapter.

| You're almost there! | ¡Ya casi llegas! |
| Continue! | ¡Continúa! |

TIME'S UP!

Express the following things to someone:

1. You are just browsing (in a store).

2. You'd like to buy a car for your family.

3. He/she has to listen.

4. He/she is supposed to go to the bakery.

5. He/she ought to make the beds.

6. He/she owes you five dollars.

7. It is necessary to go shopping.

8. You want him/her to throw out the garbage.

9. You want to go to the bookstore.

10. Encourage someone to wash the car.

Offering Ideas and Issuing Commands

MASTER THESE SKILLS

- Making proposals
- Giving commands
- Getting there
- Using idioms

In this lesson you'll learn how to be persuasive when you make suggestions and how to use commands to give and receive directions.

MAKING PROPOSALS

In English, to persuade someone to do something or go somewhere you ask, "How about . . . ?" or you use the contraction "Let's." Other expressions that allow you to make suggestions can also be quite idiomatic and, therefore, cannot be translated word for word from English to Spanish. There are several ways to get around this problem.

- To express *"Why don't we . . . ?"* use *¿Por qué no* + the present tense *nosotros* form of the verb: *¿Por qué no vamos a España?* (Why don't we go to Spain?)
- Use *tener ganas de* + an infinitive to ask what a person feels like doing: *¿Tiene(s) ganas de ir a España?* (Do you feel like going to Spain?)
- Use *querer* + an infinitive of a verb to ask if a person wants to do something: *¿Quiere(s) ir a España?* (Do you want to go to Spain?)
- Use *vamos a* + an infinitive to make a suggestion similar to the English contraction "Let's": *Vamos a ir a España.* (Let's go to Spain.)
- Use the *nosotros* form of the present subjunctive of the verb to also express "Let's": *Vayamos a España.* (Let's go to Spain.)

COMMANDS

Commands are very useful for directing people to locations. The subject of a command is understood to be *you*, because you are being told where to go or what to do.

Remember, there are four ways to say *you* in Spanish and you must always use the polite forms (*Ud., Uds.*) when you don't know the other party:

	SINGULAR	PLURAL
Familiar	tú	vosotros
Polite	Ud.	Uds.

Polite Commands

To form polite commands with regular verbs:

1. Take the *yo* form of the present tense and drop the final -*o*.
2. For infinitives ending in -*ar*, add -*e* for the singular and -*en* for the plural command.
3. For infinitives ending in -*er* or -*ir*, add -*a* for the singular and -*an* for the plural.

INFINITIVE	YO IN PRESENT	UD. COMMAND	UDS. COMMAND	MEANING
hablar	hable	hable	hablen	speak
comer	come	coma	coman	eat
escribir	escribe	escriba	escriban	write

Verbs with irregular *yo* forms follow the same rules for forming commands as regular verbs:

tener:	tenge	tenga	tengan	have
decir:	dige	diga	digan	tell

The following verbs are irregular:

dar:	doy	dé	den	give
ir:	voy	vaya	vayan	go
ser:	soy	sea	sean	be

The subject pronoun may or may not be used with commands in Spanish:

Vuelva (Ud.).   Return.

Vengan (Uds.).   Come.

To make a command negative, simply put *no* in front of the verb: *No hable (Ud.).* (Don't speak.)

Familiar Commands

Affirmative and negative familiar commands are formed in different ways:

- The singular affirmative *tú* command is formed by dropping the final *s* from the present tense, *tú* form of the verb.

    Hablas.   Habla.

- The plural affirmative *vosotros* command is formed by dropping the final *r* from the infinitive and adding *d*.

    Hablar.   Hablad.

- The negative *tú* and *vosotros* command forms are identical to the corresponding present subjunctive forms (see Chapter 15:00).

    No hables.   No habléis.

The table below illustrates the formation of the familiar commands.

INFINITIVE	AFFIRMATIVE	NEGATIVE
hablar	habla (tú)	no hables (tú)
	hablad (vosotros)	no habléis (vosotros)
comer	come (tú)	no comas (tú)
	comed (vosotros)	no comáis (vosotros)
escribir	escribe (tú)	no escribas (tú)
	escribid (vosotros)	no escribáis (vosotros)

Irregular Commands

Irregular commands occur only in the affirmative singular *tú* form. All other command forms are regular as shown here.

INFINITIVE	AFFIRMATIVE	NEGATIVE
	Tú/Vosotros	Tú/Vosotros
decir (to tell)	di/decid	no digas/digáis
hacer (to do)	haz/haced	no hagas/hagáis
ir (to go)	ve/id	no vayas/vayáis
poner (to put)	pon/poned	no pongas/pongáis
salir (to leave)	sal/salid	no salgas/salgáis
ser (to be)	sé/sed	no seas/seáis
tener (to have)	ten/tened	no tengas/tengáis
valer (to be worth)	val/valed	no valgas/valgáis
venir (to come)	ven/venid	no vengas/vengáis

Refer to the following for the high-frequency verbs you will need in order to give and receive directions.

DIRECTION	TÚ/VOSOTROS	UD./UDS.
Continue	Continúa/Continuad	Continúe/Continúen
Do not continue	No continúes/continuéis	No continúe/continúen
Cross	Cruza/Cruzad	Cruce/Crucen
Do not cross	No cruces/crucéis	No cruce/crucen

Get off	Baja/Bajad	Baje/Bajen
Do not get off	No bajes/bajéis	No baje/bajen
Go down	Baja/Bajad	Baje/Bajen
Do not go down	No bajes/bajéis	No baje/bajen
Go up	Sube/Subid	Suba/Suban
Do not go up	No subas/subáis	No suba/suban
Go	Ve/Id	Vaya/Vayan
Do not go	No vayas/vayáis	No vaya/vayan
Pass	Pasa/Pasad	Pase/Pasen
Do not pass	No pases/paséis	No pase/pasen
Take	Toma/Tomad	Tome/Tomen
Do not take	No tomes/toméis	No tome/tomen
Turn	Dobla/Doblad	Doble/Doblen
Do not turn	No dobles/dobléis	No doble/doblen
Walk	Camina/Caminad	Camine/Caminen
Do not walk	No camines/caminéis	No camine/caminen

To give proper directions, you will need the names of the means of transportation. When explaining the means of transportation a person will take, use a definite article (*el*, *la*, *los*, *las*) and say: *Toma el autobús.* (Take the bus.) When saying that someone travels by a certain means of transportation, be careful to use to the correct preposition:

TRANSPORTATION	SPANISH
airplane	en avión (m.)
bicycle	en bicicleta
bus	en autobús (m.)
car	en coche (m.), en carro
on foot	a pie (m.)
subway	en metro
taxi	en taxi
train	en tren

Also use *a* + definite article (*al, a la, a los, a las*) to express where to get the transportation you need. Study the following:

I am going . . .   Voy . . .

PLACE	SPANISH
to the airport	al aeropuerto
to the bus stop	a la parada de autobús
to the dock	al muelle
to the gate	a la puerta
to the platform	al andén
to the station	a la estación
to the taxi stand	a la parada de taxis
to the terminal	a la terminal
to the track	a la vía

Use the numbers given in Chapter 16:00 to obtain or give gate, platform, or track numbers: *Tú vas al aeropuerto y tomas el avión a la puerta número seis.* (You go to the airport and you take the plane at gate number six.)

To give or receive adequate directions, you also need the prepositions and prepositional idioms showing location and direction:

PREPOSITION	MEANING
a	at, to
arriba	above, on top of
cerca	nearby
en	in, into, within, on
hacia	toward
por	by, through
sobre	over, above

PHRASE	MEANING
a la derecha	to the right
a la izquierda	to the left
al centro	downtown
al centro (de)	in the middle (of)

al otro lado (de)	on the other side (of)
alrededor de	around
debajo de	beneath
enfrente de	opposite, facing, across from
junto a	alongside
por aquí (allá)	this way, that way, nearby
todo derecho	straight ahead

In English, when we give directions, we often refer to the number of blocks a person has to walk. In Spanish, use the word *una cuadra* (a block): *Vivo a dos cuadras de aqui.* (I live two blocks from here.)

Commands with Reflexive Verbs

With reflexive verbs, the subject pronoun is usually dropped but the reflexive pronoun must be used. In negative commands, the reflexive pronoun precedes the verb:

Don't get up early!	¡No se levante (Ud.) temprano!
	¡No se levantan (Uds.) temprano!
	¡No te levantas (tú) temprano!
	¡No os levantéis (vosotros) temprano!

In affirmative commands, the reflexive pronoun follows the verb and is attached to it. Note that the final *d* is dropped from the *vosotros* form before adding the reflexive pronoun. An accent mark is placed on the stressed vowel of the *tú*, *Ud.*, and *Uds.* forms. To find the stressed vowel in most instances, simply count back three vowels and add the accent:

Get up!	¡Levántese (Ud.)!
	¡Levántense (Uds)!
	¡Levántate (tú)!
	¡Levántaos (vosotros)!

GETTING THERE

Being able to understand and knowing how to give directions is an important survival skill for those traveling abroad. Should you get lost and find yourself in need of instructions, the following sentences will prove useful. The blanks can be filled in with proper names or a tourist attraction, store, sporting event, etc.

I'm lost.	Estoy perdido(a).
Can you tell me how to get to . . . ?	¿Puede decirme cómo se va a . . .
Where is (are) . . . ?	¿Dónde está(n) . . .

Being able to follow directions that are given to you will be of utmost importance, whether you are lost or simply looking for a place that you can't seem to locate:

It's (Is it) far away.(?)	(¿)Está lejos.(?)
It's (Is it) nearby.(?)	(¿)Está cerca.(?)
It's (Is it) this way.(?)	(¿)Está por aquí.(?)
It's (Is it) that way.(?)	(¿) Está por allá.(?)
It's (Is it) straight ahead.(?)	(¿) Es derecho.(?)
Turn right (left) at the light.	Doble a la derecha (a la izquierda) en el semáforo.
Stop!	¡Alto!
Follow me.	Sígame.
There it (they) is (are).	Allá está(n).

It would be better to take (definite article + means of transportation) . . .

Sería mejor tomar (el/la + means of transportation) . . .

And if you are far from your destination:

Is it to the north?	¿Está al norte?
Is it to the south?	¿Está al sur?
Is it to the east?	¿Está al este?
Is it to the west?	¿Está al oeste?

USING IDIOMS

In English, we use idioms and idiomatic expressions all the time without even realizing that we are doing so. An example will help you understand exactly how an idiom works. The phrase "She fell head over heels for him" does not mean in a literal sense that she fell head first and tripped over her feet. To someone who doesn't speak English well, this sentence could be extremely confusing. But a native speaker immediately understands the underlying meaning of this phrase—that she really liked him a lot.

Idioms occur in every language, are generally indigenous to that specific language, and do not translate well from one language to the next. If a Spanish speaker were to say, "*Este coche cuesta un ojo de la cara,*" she would mean that the car costs a small fortune, even though the literal translation of the sentence is, "This car costs an eye from your face."

An idiom, then, is a word or expression whose meaning cannot be easily understood by analyzing or translating every word in the sentence.

Use the idioms in the following table to express your opinions and accentuate the positive.

IDIOM	SPANISH
as for me	a pesar de todo
in my opinion	en mi opinión
of course	por supuesto
OK	de acuerdo
on the contrary	al contrario
to tell the truth	a decir verdad
without a doubt	sin duda

POSITIVE REINFORCEMENT

If you would like to persuade someone to do something, positive reinforcement might work. Reinforcing your opinions by using the words and expressions presented below should help you convince even the most stubborn among you.

PHRASE	SPANISH	PHRASE	SPANISH
It's a good idea!	¡Es una buena idea!	It's magnificent!	¡Es magnífico(a)!
It's great!	¡Es excelente!	It's sensational!	¡Es sensacional!
It's important!	¡Es importante!	It's super!	¡Es estupendo(a)!
It's interesting!	¡Es interesante!	It's superb!	¡Es fenomenal!

Combine expressions from the previous two tables to be persuasive:

A decir verdad, es fenomenal!	To tell the truth, it's superb!
A pesar de todo, es magnífico.	All the same, it's magnificent.

COMPLAINTS

If you have persuaded someone to go along with you and they are not satisfied, you can expect to hear one of the following phrases:

COMPLAINT	SPANISH
It's annoying!	¡Es fastidioso(a)!
It's boring!	¡Es aburrido(a)!
It's disgusting!	¡Es asqueroso(a)!
It's frightful!	¡Es terrible!
It's horrible!	¡Es horrible!
It's ridiculous!	¡Es ridículo(a)!

 TIME'S UP!

Without looking back, do the following:

1. Use *¿Por qué no . . .* to suggest going to a restaurant.

2. Propose going to the movies by using *tener ganas de.*

3. Ask a friend if he/she wants to go shopping.

4. Suggest to a friend: "Let's go to the Prado museum."

5. Using an affirmative command, tell someone to continue walking three blocks.

6. Using a negative command, tell someone not to go straight ahead.

7. Tell a friend to wake up early.

8. Give a positive reason for going to visit El Morro castle in Puerto Rico.

9. Say that in your opinion, it's great.

10. Give a negative reaction toward going to the theater.

Asking Questions

MASTER THESE SKILLS

- Asking yes/no questions
- Asking for information
- Getting around
- Questioning new acquaintances

In this lesson you'll learn how to ask questions in a variety of different ways. No matter what the situation, no matter what your needs, you'll be able to get the information you seek.

ASKING YES/NO QUESTIONS

The easiest questions, by far, are those that demand a simple yes or no answer. There are four ways to obtain this information. You can use:

- Intonation
- The tag *¿No es verdad?* (Isn't that so?)
- The tag *¿Está bien?*
- Inversion

Using Intonation

Questions are often asked by changing your intonation and raising your voice at the end of a statement. In conversation, just put an imaginary question mark at the end of your thought and speak with a rising inflection. When writing a question, make sure to put an inverted question mark (¿) at the beginning of the sentence and a regular one at the end of the sentence: *¿Tienes ganas de ir al cine?* (Do you feel like going to the movies?)

When you speak with a rising inflection, your voice starts out lower and gradually keeps rising until the end of the sentence. In a sentence that states a fact, your voice rises and then lowers by the end of the sentence.

To form a negative question, simply put *no* before the conjugated verb in simple and compound tenses and whenever there are two verbs:

¿No tienes ganas de ir al cine?	Don't you feel like going to the movies?
¿No has escrito la carta?	Didn't you write the letter?

Using *¿No Es Verdad?* and *¿Está Bien?*

¿No es verdad? and *¿Está bien?* are tags that can have a variety of meanings: isn't that so?; right?; isn't (doesn't) he/she?; aren't (don't) they?; aren't (don't) we?; aren't (don't) you?; and so on. *¿No es verdad?* and *¿Está bien?* may be placed at the end of a statement, especially when the expected answer is yes:

Tienes ganas de ir al cine. ¿No es verdad?	You feel like going to the movies, don't you?
Vamos al cine. ¿Está bien?	We're going to the movies. OK?

Using Inversion

Inversion refers to reversing the word order of the subject noun or pronoun and verb form. Remember to raise your voice at the end of the phrase to show that you are asking a question:

Ud. va al cine.	¿Va Ud. al cine?

Juan es de España.	¿Es Juan de España?
Ud. se levanta tarde.	¿Se levanta Ud. tarde?

When there are two verbs or a compound tense, put the subject noun or pronoun after the phrase containing the second verb:

Ella quiere salir.	¿Quiere salir ella?
María quería trabajar allí.	¿Quería trabajar allí María?
Ana está estudiando arte.	¿Está estudiando arte Ana?
Él ha escrito esta carta.	¿Ha escrito esta carta él?

To make a question with inversion negative, put *no* before the inverted verb and pronoun. For reflexive verbs, remember to keep the reflexive pronouns before the conjugated verb, from which it may not be separated.

¿No es español el niño?	Isn't the boy Spanish?
¿No querías salir?	Didn't you want to go out?
¿No se levantó temprano Marta?	Didn't Martha wake up early?
¿No han lavado el coche ellas?	Didn't they wash the car?

INFORMATION QUESTIONS

No matter what your reason for studying Spanish, many occasions will arise when a simple yes/no response is inadequate. For this reason, it is important to know how to ask for information. Interrogative adjectives, adverbs, and pronouns will allow you to accomplish this task.

Interrogative Adjectives

The interrogative adjectives *qué* (which, what), *cuánto(-a)* (how much), and *cuántos(-as)* (how many) are used before nouns. *Cuánto* must agree in number and gender with the noun it modifies as shown here:

	MASCULINE	FEMININE
Singular	¿cuánto?	¿cuánta?
Plural	¿cuántos?	¿cuántas?

An interrogative adjective may be placed at the beginning of the sentence or after the verb, but it must always precede its noun and any modifiers of that noun. In spoken Spanish you may hear the second form, shown below, but only for emphasis.

¿Qué revista lees?	What magazine are you reading?
¿Lees qué revista?	
¿Cuánto tiempo necesitas?	How much time do you need?
¿Necesitas cuánto tiempo?	
¿Cuánta comida van a comer?	How much food are they going to eat?
¿Van a comer cuánta comida?	
¿Cuántos miembros hay?	How many members are there?
¿Hay cuántos miembros?	
¿Cuántas personas vienen?	How many people are coming?
¿Vienen cuántas personas?	

Interrogative adjectives may be preceded by a preposition:

¿A qué hora llegó?	At what time did he arrive?
¿De cuántas personas hablaba?	About how many people was he speaking to?
¿Con cuánto dinero vas a viajar?	How much money will you travel with?

Interrogative Adverbs

Adverbs asking for information help you find out what you need to know. Use the interrogative adverbs listed in the table below with inversion to form questions.

ADVERB	SPANISH
how?	¿cómo?
when?	¿cuándo?
where (to)?	¿dónde?
why? (for what reason)	¿por qué?
why? (for what purpose)	¿para qué?

Interrogative adverbs are followed by inversion:

¿Cómo se llama (Ud.)?	What's your name?
¿Por qué está (él) atrasado?	Why is he late?

Some interrogative adverbs can also be preceded by prepositions:

¿Para cuándo necesita (Ud.) los papeles?	When do you need the papers by?
¿De dónde son (ellas)?	Where are they from?

¿Para Qué? and ¿Por Qué? *¿Para qué?* asks about a purpose:

¿Para qué usas este libro?	Why (For what purpose) do you use this book?
—Uso este libro para aprender el español.	—I use this book to learn Spanish.

¿Por qué? asks about a reason:

¿Por qué vas a la biblioteca?	Why (For what reason) do you go to the library?
—Voy a la biblioteca porque necesito un libro.	—I go to the library because I need a book.

> **▽ NOTE**
>
> Questions with *¿por qué?* call for an answer with *porque* (because),
> while questions with *¿para qué?* call for an answer with *para* (for, to).

Interrogative Pronouns

If you were in a store trying to make a decision about which of two or more items to choose, you might want to ask the salesperson which one would be the right choice, or what the price is. The interrogative pronouns listed below will help you ask your questions properly.

PRONOUN	SPANISH
Who?	¿quién(es)?
What?	¿qué?
What? Which one(s)	¿cuál(es)?
How much?	¿cuánto?
How many?	¿cuántos(as)?

The interrogative pronouns *¿quién(es)?* and *¿cuál(es)?* agree in number with the nouns they replace, while *¿cuánto?* agrees in both number and gender with the noun being replaced:

¿Quién trabaja?	Who is working?

(The answer requires the name of one person.)

¿Quiénes trabajan?	Who is working?

(The answer requires at least two names.)

¿Cuál de estas películas prefieres?	Which (one) of these films do you prefer?

(The answer requires the name of one film.)

¿Cuáles de estas películas prefieres?	Which (ones) of these films do you prefer?

(The answer requires at least two names.)

¿Cuánto cuesta esta camisa?	How much does this shirt cost?
¿Cuántos están aquí?	How many are here?
¿Cuántas son?	How many (females) are there?

A preposition + *quién* refers to people. A preposition + *que* refers to things.

¿De quién hablas?	¿De qué hablas?
Whom are you speaking about?	What are you speaking about?
¿A quién se refiere?	¿A qué se refiere?
To whom are you referring?	What are you referring to?
¿Adónde vas?	¿De dónde eres?
Where are you going?	Where are you from?

¿Qué? and ¿Cuál? *¿Qué?* usually means "what" and asks about a definition, description, or an explanation. When it comes before a noun, however, *¿qué?* means "which."

¿Qué es esto?	What is this?
¿Qué está pensando?	What are you thinking?
¿Qué programa estás mirando?	Which program are you watching?

¿Cuál? means "what" or "which (one, ones)" and asks about a choice or a selection:

¿Cuál es su nombre?	What is your name?
¿Cuál de los tres quiere Ud.?	Which (one) of the three do you want?
¿Cuáles son los días de la semana?	What are the days of the week?

HAY

The verb *haber* is used impersonally to ask and answer questions. The expression *hay* can mean "there is (are)" as a statement or "is (are) there" as a question. Note the following about the uses of *hay*:

- As a question, *hay* can be used by itself using intonation: *¿Hay un restaurante por aquí?* (Is there a restaurant nearby?)
- It can be used with a preceding question word: *¿Dónde hay un restaurante por aquí?* (Where is a nearby restaurant?)
- *Hay* can also be used to ask a negative question: *¿No hay un restaurante por aquí?* (Isn't there a restaurant nearby?)
- You can use *hay* in a non-interrogative sentence to answer a question: *Hay un restaurante por aquí.* (There is a restaurant nearby.)

Expressions with *Hay*

Hay is generally used to refer to certain weather or physical conditions:

There's moonlight.	Hay luna.
It's foggy.	Hay neblina.
It's sunny.	Hay sol.

Hay que + infinitive means to be necessary to: *Hay que beber agua para vivir.* (One must drink water to live.)

ASKING FOR DIRECTIONS

You can ask for directions by using the following phrases:

Where is . . . ?	¿Dónde está . . . ?
Where are . . . ?	¿Dónde están . . . ?
Can you tell me how to get to . . . ?	¿Puede Ud. decirme cómo se va a . . . ?

Where is the Prado?	¿Dónde está el Prado?
	¿Puede Ud. decirme cómo se va al Prado?
	El Prado, por favor.
Where are the bathrooms?	¿Dónde están los baños/los servicios?
	¿Puede Ud. decirme cómo se va a los baños/los servicios?
	Los baños/los servicios, por favor.

ASKING FOR A PRICE

Being able to ask for prices in a foreign country is always a valuable tool. Use the following phrases when you need to know how much something costs:

¿Cuánto cuesta (un/una) . . . ?	What's the price of (a) . . . ?
¿Cuánto cuesta este (esta)/ ese (esa) . . . ?	How much does this/that . . . cost?
¿Cuánto cuestan estos (estas)/ esos (esas) . . . ?	How much do these/those . . . cost?
¿Cuánto cuesta un periódico?	How much does a newspaper cost?
¿Cuánto cuesta(n) este (estos) periódico(s)?	How much does this (do these) newspaper(s) cost?
¿Cuánto cuesta(n) esta (estas) revista(s)?	How much does this (do these) magazine(s) cost?

When asking for a price, make sure that all the singular and plural, masculine and feminine elements of the sentence agree:

¿Cuánto cuestan estas cartas?	How much do these cards cost?
¿Cuánto cuesta el pantalón blanco?	How much do the white pants cost?

QUESTIONING NEW ACQUAINTANCES

When you meet someone for the first time, there are many questions you would like to ask to get to know that person better. Here are some of the most common questions that could be used to get information by using the polite or familiar verb forms:

What's your name?	¿Cómo se llama (Ud.)?
	¿Cómo te llamas?
What is your wife's (child's) name?	¿Cómo se llama su (tu) esposa (niño, niña)?
Where are you from?	¿De dónde es (eres)?
What is your nationality?	¿Cuál es su (tu) nacionalidad?
What is your profession?	¿Cuál es su (tu) profesión?
How old are you?	¿Cuántos años tiene(s)?
How many people are in your family?	¿Cuántas personas hay en su (tu) familia?
Where are you staying?	¿Dónde se (te) aloja(s)?
Where do you live?	¿Dónde vive(s)?
What is your address?	¿Cuál es su (tu) dirección?
What is your phone number?	¿Cuál es su (tu) número de teléfono?

LACK OF COMMUNICATION

When you've asked a question and don't understand the answer or need more information, use the following expressions to help you get the information you need.

PHRASE	SPANISH
Excuse me.	Perdón.
Excuse me.	Perdóneme. (polite)
Excuse me.	Perdóname. (familiar)
Excuse me.	Con permiso.
I don't understand.	No comprendo.
I don't understand.	No entiendo.
I didn't hear you.	No le (te) oí.
I didn't understand you.	No le (te) entendí.
What?	¿Cómo?
Please repeat it.	Repita, por favor. (polite)
Please repeat it.	Repite, por favor. (familiar)

Speak more slowly.	Hable más despacio. (polite)
Speak more slowly.	Habla más despacio. (familiar)
What did you say?	¿Qué dijo (dijiste)?
One more time.	Otra vez.
I'm sorry.	Lo siento.

▽ **NOTE**

You can use *perdón* and *perdóneme* if you have disturbed or bumped into someone, whereas you should use *con permiso* when leaving, asking permission to pass through a group or crowd, or when walking in front of a person.

 TIME'S UP!

Without looking back in the chapter, try to complete the following:

1. Ask a person for his/her name.

2. Ask a person for his/her address.

3. Ask a person for his/her phone number.

4. Ask where a person is from.

5. Ask a person's age.

6. Ask if there is a restaurant nearby.

7. Ask which one of the films he/she prefers.

8. Ask a person his/her profession.

9. Ask for the price of a newspaper.

10. Say that you are sorry and that you don't understand.

Answering Questions

MASTER THESE SKILLS

- Answering yes and no questions
- Using negative expressions
- Answering questions with *¿qué?* and *¿cuál?*
- Answering questions with interrogative adverbs
- Talking on the phone
- Facing phone problems

In this lesson you'll learn how to correctly answer the questions people ask you by giving affirmative or negative responses or by providing necessary information. You'll also learn how to conduct a phone conversation.

ANSWERING YES

Use *sí* to answer a question affirmatively:

¿Quieres ir al cine?	Do you want to go to the movies?
—Sí, es una buena idea.	—Yes, that's a good idea.
Esta película es fantástica.	This film is great.
— Creo que sí.	—I think so.

ANSWERING NO

In Chapter 17:00 you learned how to use *no* to respond negatively. Other common negatives are listed below. Negative answers may begin with *no*.

NEGATIVE	SPANISH
neither . . . nor	ni . . . ni
neither, not either	tampoco
never, (not) ever	jamás, nunca
no one, nobody	nadie
no, none, (not) any	ninguno(-a)
no, not	no
nothing	nada

To answer negatively, do the following:

- In simple and compound tenses, always put *no* before the conjugated verb. *No* may be repeated for emphasis:

¿Bailas bien?	No bailo bien.	No, no bailo bien.
Do you dance well?	I don't dance well.	No, I don't dance well.
¿Quiere comer?	No quiero comer.	No, no quiero comer.
Do you want to eat?	I don't want to eat.	No, I don't want to eat.
¿Ha terminado?	No ha terminado.	No, no ha terminado.
Did he finish?	He didn't finish.	No, he didn't finish.

- Direct and indirect object pronouns, discussed in greater detail in Chapter 10:00, also remain before the conjugated verb when a negative construction is used:

¿Vio el hombre?	No lo vi.	No, no lo vi.
Did you see the man?	I didn't see him.	No, I didn't see him.

- Spanish sentences may have more than one negative. When *no* is one of the negatives, it precedes the conjugated verb. If *no* is omitted, another negative precedes the verb:

No canto nunca.	Nunca canto.	I never sing.
No habla nadie.	Nadie habla.	No one is speaking.
No le creo a nadie nunca.	Nunca le creo a nadie.	I never believe anyone.
No lo vi tampoco.	Tampoco lo vi.	I didn't see it either.
No prefiero ni rojo ni verde.	Ni rojo ni verde prefiero.	I don't prefer either red or green.

- Each part of the *ni . . . ni* construction precedes the word or words stressed:

No como ni frutas ni legumbres.	I eat neither fruits nor vegetables.
La comida no estaba ni buena ni mala.	The meal was neither good nor bad.
No le gusta ni bailar ni cantar.	He doesn't like to dance or to sing.

- An infinitive may be negated as follows: *Es mejor no decir nada.* (It's better not to say anything.)
- The negatives *nadie*, *nada*, *nunca*, and *jamás* are used after comparisons and in phrases beginning with *sin* (without) or *antes* (*de* or *que*) (before):

Juega mejor que nadie.	He plays better than anyone.
Lo comprendo más que nunca.	I understand it better than ever.
Lo aprecia más que nada.	She treasures it more than anything.
Llegó sin traer nada.	He arrived without bringing anything.
Hablé antes que nadie.	I spoke before anyone else.
Antes de hacer nada, ella tiene que hacer su tarea.	Before doing anything, she has to do her homework.

- Negatives may be used alone (without *no*):

¿Qué estás haciendo?	What are you doing?
—Nada.	—Nothing.
¿Ha estado en España?	Have you been to Spain?
—Jamás.	—Never.

- Negatives may be used with two verbs by placing *no* before the conjugated verb and another negative word after the second verb:

No quiero hacer nada.	I don't want to do anything.
No he visto a nadie.	I didn't see anyone.

- *Ninguno* (not any) drops the final *-o* and adds an accent to the *u* = *ningún* before a masculine singular noun. The feminine singular form is *ninguna*. There are no plural forms. When used as an adjective, *ninguno* may be replaced by *alguno* (a more emphatic negative), which follows the noun:

No tengo ninguno.	I don't have any.
No tengo ningún problema.	I have no problem.
No tengo problema alguno.	I don't have a problem.

- A negative expression that begins with a preposition retains that preposition when placed before the verb: *En nada pienso.* (I'm not thinking about anything.)

The words in the first column below, when used in questions, produce the corresponding negative response listed in the second column:

alguien (someone)	nadie (no one)
siempre (sometimes)	jamás/nunca (never)
algo (something)	nada (nothing)
también (also)	tampoco (neither)
alguno(a) (some, any)	ninguno(a) (none, not any)
¿Buscas algo?	No busco nada.
Are you looking for something?	I'm not looking for anything.

NEGATIVE EXPRESSIONS

The following common negative expressions will prove useful in any number of everyday situations:

- *No importa.* (It doesn't matter.):

Él estará atrasado.	He's going to be late.
—No importa.	—It doesn't matter.

- *De nada.* (You're welcome.) or *No hay de qué.* (You're welcome.):

Muchas gracias por todo.	Thank you for everything.
—De nada. (No hay de qué.)	—You're welcome.

- *¡De ninguna manera!* (Certainly not!/Not at all!):

¿Te molesta?	Does that bother you?
—¡De ninguna manera!	—Not at all!

- *Todavía no.* (Not yet.):

Quieres salir?	Do you want to leave?
—Todavía no.	—Not yet.

- *Ahora no.* (Not now.):

¿Quiere comer?	Do you want to eat?
—Ahora no.	—Not now.

- *Ya no.* (No longer.): *Ya no estudio el español.* (I'm no longer studying Spanish.)
- *Ni yo tampoco.* (Neither do I.):

Ella no quiere bailar.	She doesn't want to dance.
—Ni yo tampoco.	—Neither do I.

- *No hay remedio.* (It can't be helped.):

Tienes que esperar.	You have to wait.
—No hay remedio.	—It can't be helped.

- *No obstante* (Nevertheless/However/In spite of): *Está nevando. No obstante él va a trabajar.* (It's snowing. Nevertheless he's going to work.)

- *No cabe duda.* (There's no doubt.): *No cabe duda que ella va a tener éxito.* (There's no doubt that she's going to succeed.)

PERO VERSUS *SINO*

Pero and *sino* both express "but." *Pero* is used in a more general sense and may also mean "however":

> No puedo telefonearle ahora, pero voy a telefonearle más tarde.
>
> I can't call him now, but I'll call him later.
>
> No tiene mucho dinero, pero está contento.
>
> He doesn't have much money, but (however) he is happy.

Sino is only used after a negative statement to express a contrast (on the contrary):

> No canta música popular sino romántica.
>
> He doesn't sing popular music, but he sings romantic music.
>
> No compra el grande sino el pequeño.
>
> He doesn't buy the big one but (rather) the little one.

ANSWERING INFORMATION QUESTIONS

Certain key words and phrases will help you answer just about any question that might arise. Note carefully how to present the correct information for which you are being asked.

Answering Questions with ¿Qué? and ¿Cuál?

Answering questions with the interrogative adjective *¿qué?* and with the interrogative pronoun *¿cuál(es)?* requires that you keep in mind the number and gender of the nouns to which they refer. Simply use a definite article + an appropriate adjective that agrees in number and gender with the noun referred to and you have a quick, easy answer.

To express "the . . . one(s)" you must use an adjective as a noun. The adjective must agree in number and gender with the noun it is describing. This is usually done with adjectives showing color (*el blanco*—the white one), size (*las grandes*—the big ones), and nationality (*la española*—the Spanish one).

¿Cuáles camisas prefieres?	Which (ones of the) shirts do you prefer?
¿Qué camisas prefieres?	What shirts do you prefer?

Las azules.	The blue ones.
Las pequeñas.	The small ones.
Las españolas.	The Spanish ones.
¿Cuál de los carros quiere?	Which one of the cars do you want?
¿Qué carro quiere?	What car do you want?
El blanco.	The white one.
El grande.	The big one.
El español.	The Spanish one.

Some answers to the most commonly asked questions should be at your fingertips:

¿Cómo se (te) llama(s)?	What's your name?
—Me llamo . . .	—My name is . . .
¿Cuál es su (tu) dirección?	What's your address?
—Mi dirección es . . .	—My address is . . .
¿Cuál es su (tu) profesión?	What's your profession?
—Soy . . .	—I am . . .
¿Cuál es su (tu) número de teléfono?	What's your phone number?
—Mi número de teléfono es . . .	—My phone number is . . .
¿Cuántos años tiene(s)?	How old are you?
—Tengo . . . años.	—I am . . . years old.

Remember that when *a* or *de* (or any of their forms) is in the question, *a* or *de* (or any of their forms) must appear in the answer:

¿De qué libro hablas?	Which book are you talking about?
—De Don Quijote.	—Don Quijote.

¿A quiénes de sus amigas le ha escrito?	To which of your friends have you written?
—A María y a Juanita.	—To Maria and Juanita.

Answering Questions with Interrogative Adverbs

Use the following guidelines to answer questions containing interrogative adverbs:

- *¿Cómo?* (how) may be answered with a preposition (*por*, *en*, or *a*) followed by a noun or an explanation:

¿Cómo vas a Madrid?	How are you going to Spain?
—En tren.	—By train.
¿Cómo te llamas?	What's your name?
—Me llamo . . .	—My name is . . .
¿Cómo estás?	How are you?
—Muy bien.	—Very good.

- *¿Cuánto(a)(s)* (How much, many) must be answered with a number or a quantity:

¿Cuánto cuesta este CD?	How much does this CD cost?
—Cien pesos.	—A hundred pesos.
¿Cuánta carne quieres?	How much meat do you want?
—Quinientos gramos.	—Five hundred grams.

- A question with *¿Cuándo?* (when) is answered by giving a time or an expression of time (see Chapter 16:00):

When do you want to leave?	¿Cuándo quieres salir?
In fifteen minutes.	En quince minutos.
At eight o'clock.	A las ocho.
Immediately.	Inmediatamente.

- Answer a question with *¿dónde?* by naming a place, using the preposition *en*:

¿Dónde vives?	Where do you live?
—Vivo en . . .	—I live in . . .

- Answer a question with *¿adónde?* by using the preposition *a* (*al, a los, a las*):

¿Adónde vas?	Where are you going?
—Voy al banco.	—I'm going to the bank.

- Answer *¿de dónde?* by using the preposition *de* (*del, de la, de los*) + place:

¿De dónde eres?	Where are you from?
—Soy de . . .	—I'm from . . .

- Answer a question that asks *¿por qué?* (why) with *porque* (because) and a reason:

¿Por qué está atrasado?	Why are you late?
—Porque perdí mi tren.	—Because I missed my train.

- Answer a question with *¿quién?* (who, whom), whether it is used as a subject, direct object, or after a preposition, by naming a person:

¿Quién habla?	Who is speaking?
—Juan.	—John.
¿A quién busca?	Whom are you looking for?
—A un vendedor.	—A salesperson.
¿Con quién quiere hablar?	Whom do you want to speak with?
—Con la Señora López.	—With Mrs. Lopez.

- Answer *¿qué?* with the name of a thing:

¿Qué se cayó?	What fell?
—Mis gafas.	—My glasses.
¿Qué busca Ud.?	What are you looking for?
—Una pluma.	—A pen.

¿Con qué escribe Ud.?	What are you writing with?
—Con un lápiz.	—With a pencil.

When a preposition is used in a question, the same preposition must also be used in the answer:

¿Para quién trabajó?	For whom did he work?
—Para su padre.	—For his father.

ON THE PHONE

Having a phone conversation with a person speaking another language is difficult at best. Without the help of body language, communication can be a chore. Use the phrases presented below to provide and obtain information on the phone.

Calling

SPANISH	MEANING
A ver. (Colombia)	hello
Hola. (Argentina)	hello
Bueno. (Mexico)	hello
Diga. (Spain)	hello
Oigo. (Cuba)	hello
Aló.	hello
¿Está . . . ?	Is . . . in (there)?
Es . . .	It's . . .
¿Está en casa . . . ?	Is . . . in (there)?
Habla . . .	This is . . .
Quisiera hablar con . . .	I would like to speak to . . .
¿Cuándo regresa?	When will he (she) be back?
Llamo más tarde.	I'll call back later.
No importa.	It's (not) important.
Tengo que colgar.	I have to hang up.

Answering

SPANISH	MEANING
A ver. (Colombia)	hello
Hola. (Argentina)	hello
Bueno. (Mexico)	hello
Diga. (Spain)	hello
Oigo. (Cuba)	hello
Aló.	hello
¿Quién habla?	Who's calling?
No cuelgue.	Hold on./Don't hang up.
Un momentito.	Just a moment.
No está.	He/She is not in.
¿Desea Ud. dejar algún recado?	Do you want to leave a message?
Lo siento. No puedo entenderle.	I'm sorry, I can't understand you.
Un poco más alto, por favor.	A little louder, please.
Siga . . . Escucho.	Go on . . . I'm listening.

Phone Problems

If you've made a mistake or if you're having trouble getting connected, or if there's trouble on the line, here are the phrases you will need to explain the problem:

It's a mistake.	Es un error.
I have the wrong number.	Tengo el número equivocado.
There's no answer.	No contesta.
We got cut off (disconnected).	Se nos cortó la línea.
The line is busy.	La línea está ocupada.
Please redial the number.	Marque (Ud.) de nuevo el número, por favor.
The telephone is out of order.	El teléfono está fuera de servicio (dañado, descompuesto).

There's no dial tone.	No hay tono (señal).
There's a lot of static on the line.	Hay mucha estática.
We have a bad connection.	Tenemos una comunicación mala.
I'm sorry to have bothered you.	Disculpe la molestia.

If you want to speak to an operator, say: *El (la) operador(a), por favor.*

TIME'S UP!

Without looking in the lesson, see if you can answer these questions:

1. ¿No quiere ir al cine esta noche? (say yes)
2. ¿Tiene ganas de comer en un restaurante? (say no)
3. ¿Ud. fuma? (say no)
4. ¿Cómo se llama Ud.?
5. ¿Dónde vive Ud.?
6. ¿Cuál es su número de teléfono?
7. ¿Cuántos años tiene Ud.?
8. ¿Cuánto cuesta un viaje a España?
9. ¿Cuáles películas populares prefiere Ud?
10. ¿Qué hay en su escritorio (desk)?

11:00

Seeking Help

MASTER THESE SKILLS

- Getting help anywhere
- At the post office
- At the hair salon
- At the dry cleaner's
- At the optician's
- At the camera store
- At the jeweler's
- Getting special services for special needs

In this lesson you'll learn how to get all the personal services you might need while traveling in a Spanish-speaking country.

GETTING HELP ANYWHERE

Whether you are seeking certain services or are trying to have something repaired, use the phrases below at the post office, the hair salon, the dry cleaner, the shoemaker, the optometrist, the jeweler, or the camera store:

Can you help me, please?	¿Puede Ud. ayudarme, por favor?
I need . . .	Necesito . . .
I'm looking for . . .	Busco . . .
Where is the nearest . . . ?	¿Dónde está la . . . más cercana?

PLACE	SPANISH
post office	oficina de correos
hair salon	peluquería
dry cleaner's	tintorería
optician's	óptica
jeweler's	joyería
camera store	tienda de fotografía

Do you have . . . ?	¿Tiene Ud. . . . ?
Do you sell . . . ?	¿Vende Ud. . . . ?
What time do you open?	¿A qué hora abre Ud.?
What time do you close?	¿A qué hora cierra Ud.?
What days are you open (closed)?	¿Qué días abre (cierra) Ud.?
Can you fix . . . for me?	¿Puede Ud. arreglarme . . . ?
Can you fix it (them) today?	¿Puede Ud. arreglármelo/la (los/las) hoy?
May I have a receipt?	¿Puede darme un recibo?
Can you fix it (them) temporarily (while I wait)?	¿Puede Ud. arreglármelo/la (los/las) temporalmente (mientras espero)?
How much does it cost?	¿Cuánto cuesta?

AT THE POST OFFICE

If you travel to a foreign country, you will quite likely have to make a stop or two at a post office to purchase stamps or to send packages. Use the following table for the postal phrases you will need.

TERM	SPANISH
address	la dirección
envelope	el sobre
letter	la carta
to mail (send)	mandar por correo
mailbox	el buzón
package	el paquete
postage	el franqueo
postal worker	el cartero
rate	la tarifa de franqueo
stamp	el sello

Special forms, paperwork, and postal rates apply to different types of letters and packages. If you need to send something C.O.D., you will be sending it *contra reembolso*. Use the phrases below to get the type of service you require: *¿Cuál es la tarifa de franqueo de . . . a los Estados Unidos?* (What is the postal rate of . . . to the United States?)

an airmail letter	una carta por correo aéreo
a registered letter	una carta certificada
a special delivery letter	una carta urgente

Use the preposition *por* (as opposed to *para*) to explain how you would like to send a letter or package: *Quisiera mandar esta carta por correo . . .* (I would like to send this letter by . . . mail.)

regular	regular
air	aéreo
special delivery	urgente
How much do these stamps cost?	¿Cuánto cuestan estos sellos?

AT THE HAIR SALON

Men and women alike have to look for a sign that says *peluquero(a)* for a hairdresser. *Un salón de belleza* indicates a beauty parlor. To express what you need, say: *Quisiera . . . por favor.* (I would like . . . please.) followed by these words:

SERVICE	SPANISH	SERVICE	SPANISH
a coloring	un tinte (vegetal)	a pedicure	una pedicura
a haircut	un corte de pelo	a permanent	una permanente
a manicure	una manicura	a shampoo	un champú

To say how you would like your hair, use the phrase *Quisiera tener el cabello . . .* (I would like to have my hair . . .) with the words listed here:

long	largo	straight	lacio (liso)
medium	mediano	auburn	rojizo
short	corto	black	negro
wavy	ondulado	blond	rubio
curly	rizado	brunette	castaño

If you would like to be a redhead, you would say: *Quisiera ser pelirrojo(a).*

AT THE DRY CLEANER'S

Should you have a problem with your clothing, explain what services you need: *¿Puede Ud. . . . (este/esta/estos/estas) . . . por favor?* (Can you . . . [this, these . . .] please?)

dry clean	lavar en seco	remove	quitar
mend	remendarme	sew	coser
press	plancharme	starch	almidonarme

Make sure to tell the dry cleaner if there's a problem: *Hay . . .* (There is [are] . . .)

a hole	un hoyo
a button missing	un botón que falta
a loose button	un botón flojo
a spot, stain	una mancha
a tear	un desgarrón

REPAIRS AND MORE REPAIRS

Use the verb *remendar* when referring to clothing or shoe repairs: *¿Por favor, puede Ud. remendarme esta camisa (estos zapatos)?* (Can you please repair this shirt [these shoes] for me?)

Use the verb *reparar* when referring to equipment: *¿Por favor, puede Ud. repararme este reloj?* (Can you please repair this watch for me?)

AT THE OPTICIAN'S

For those who depend upon glasses or contact lenses, a ripped lens or a broken pair of glasses can ruin a vacation if proper measures aren't taken immediately. Optical centers are available in all countries, but it helps to know the proper vocabulary words, terms, questions, and expressions so that you can have your problem solved as quickly as possible. One day the following phrases may come in handy:

I have a problem with my . . .	Tengo un problema con mis . . .
glasses	lentes/gafas
contact lenses	lentes de contacto
bifocals	gafas bifocales
progressive lenses	mis lentes progresivos
The lens (frame) is broken.	El lente (el armazón) está roto.
My lens (contact) is torn.	Mi lente de contacto está rasgado.
Can you replace it?	¿Puede Ud. darme otra?

AT THE CAMERA SHOP

The words and expressions listed below will be useful should you have to make a trip to a camera store.

camera	una cámara
video camera	una videocámara
roll of film	una película, un rollo
36 exposures	de treinta y seis exposiciones
black and white	en blanco y negro
color	a color

Being Impulsive

Perhaps you just can't wait to get home to see if your pictures turned out all right. Or maybe you met someone on your trip and want to give that person a copy of a picture to be treasured forever as a souvenir of this wonderful vacation. Off you go to the nearest camera or drug store, roll of film in hand. If you want to have your film developed, say: *Quisiera que me revele este carrete (rollo) (inmediatamente)*. (I would like to have this film developed [immediately].)

AT THE JEWELER'S

It's always best to leave your expensive jewelry home, but if you take something along and need a repair, or if you simply want to treat your-self to something new, use the words in the table below to refer to the specific items you are wearing, that you want repaired, or that you want to buy.

JEWELRY	SPANISH
bracelet	la pulsera
earrings	los aretes
necklace	el collar
ring	el anillo
engagement ring	el anillo de compromiso
watch	el reloj

To find out the price you would ask:

¿Cuánto cuesta?	How much is it?
¿Cuánto vale?	How much is it worth?

Sometimes an item of jewelry needs further description by naming the stones it contains. The names of different jewels that might interest you are listed here:

JEWEL	SPANISH	JEWEL	SPANISH
diamond	un diamante	ruby	un rubí
emerald	una esmeralda	sapphire	un zafiro
pearls	las perlas		

If you are unsure about a stone or want its weight, you would ask:

¿Qué es esa piedra?	What is that stone?
¿De cuántos quilates es?	How many carats is it?

SPECIAL SERVICES AND NEEDS

When there's a problem, people can have special needs, whether it's obtaining help in finding a lost item or dealing with physical challenges. Refer to these sentences when you need help:

Ayúdeme por favor. — Please help me.

Necesito un intérprete. — I need an interpreter.

¿Dónde está la comisaría de policía? — Where is the police station?

¿Dónde está la Embajada Americana? — Where is the American Embassy?

He perdido . . . — I've lost . . .

ITEM	SPANISH
my checkbook	mi chequera
my documents	mis documentos
my money	mi dinero
my passport	mi pasaporte
my traveler's checks	mis cheques de viajero
my wallet	mi cartera/mi billetera

For those who are physically challenged, the words below may prove invaluable, along with the phrase: *¿Dónde puedo conseguir . . . ?* (Where can I get . . . ?)

NEED	SPANISH
cane	un bastón
closed-captioned TV	una sistema de subtitulación
hearing aid	un aparato para sordos
wheelchair	una silla de ruedas

These items can be purchased, rented from, or located by organizations dedicated to the needs of the physically challenged. There are also many pharmacies (*farmacias*) that specialize in the rental of medical appliances—*el alquiler de aparatos médicos*.

TIME'S UP!

Ask the following without looking back at the lessons:

1. For help in general

2. What time a store opens

3. For a receipt

4. For the price of an airmail stamp

5. For a haircut

6. To have a suit dry-cleaned

7. If you can have your contact lens replaced

8. For a roll of 36-exposure film

9. To have your watch fixed

10. For the nearest police station

10:00

Expressing Positive Opinions

MASTER THESE SKILLS

- Making suggestions
- Going to the movies and watching television
- Using demonstrative pronouns
- Using direct object nouns and pronouns
- Using indirect object pronouns
- Using *gustar* and other similar verbs
- Positioning object pronouns
- Using the subjunctive to express emotions and feelings

In this lesson you'll learn how to invite someone to participate in leisure activities using direct and indirect object pronouns. You'll also see how to express positive opinions, feelings, and emotions with and without the subjunctive.

MAKING SUGGESTIONS

Certain key phrases are readily available to you if you'd like to suggest an outing or an activity to someone. These phrases include indirect object pronouns, which will be explained in greater depth later in this chapter. For the phrases that follow, you only need to pay attention to using the correct indirect object form for *you*. Note that the singular polite forms are presented and the familiar forms are enclosed in brackets. When you become more familiar with indirect object pronouns, you may substitute the plural forms for *you* in any of these sentences. In each case, the conjugated verb must be followed by an infinitive. For now, concentrate on committing these phrases to memory, because they are so useful in a wide variety of situations.

Do(n't) you want to . . . ?	¿(No) le (te) parece . . . ?
Are(n't) you interested in . . . ?	¿(No) le (te) interesa . . . ?
Would(n't) it please you to . . . ?	¿(No) le (te) gustaría . . . ?
Do(n't) you want to go to the country?	¿(No) Le (Te) parece bien ir al campo?
—Yes, I would.	—Sí, me parece bien ir al campo.
Are(n't) you interested in going to the movies?	¿(No) le (te) interesa ir al cine?
—No, I'm not interested.	—No, no me interesa.
Would(n't) it please you to go out?	¿(No) le (te) gustaría salir?
—Yes, it would.	—Sí me gustaría salir.

LEISURE ACTIVITIES

Leisure activities play an important role in travel and tourism. The list below gives a variety of popular attractions, events, and pastimes.

ACTIVITY	SPANISH	ACTIVITY	SPANISH
ballet	el ballet	hike	la caminata
beach	la playa	movies	el cine
cards	los naipes	opera	la ópera
concert	el concierto	party	la fiesta
exhibit	la exposición	television	la televisión

The Spanish language designates certain verbs to accompany certain activities. Use the verb *mirar* to say that you watch *la televisión*. Use *jugar(ue) a* + a definite article to say that you play games. Use *dar* with *una caminata* to describe a hike. And use *ir* + *a* + a definite article with other places listed.

Yo miro la televisión.	I watch television.
Yo juego a los naipes.	I play cards.
Yo doy una caminata.	I go for a hike.
Yo voy al ballet.	I go to the ballet.

To invite someone to go on a picnic say: *¿Quiere(s) hacer una gira al campo?* (Would you like to go on a picnic?)

Going to the Movies and Watching Television

The same types of themes (horror, adventure, mystery, comedy, drama, romance) appear in films and on television. Use the words listed here when you want to see or ask about a movie or program.

PROGRAM	SPANISH
adventure film	una película de aventura
cartoon	los dibujos animados
comedy	una comedia
drama	un drama
game show	un programa de concursos
horror movie	una película de horror
love story	una película de amor
news	las noticias
police story	una película policíaca
science-fiction	una película de ciencia ficción
soap opera	una telenovela
spy movie	una película de espía
talk show	un programa de entrevistas
weather	el pronóstico del tiempo meteorológico

What's on TV?	¿Qué hay en la televisión?
What film is showing?	¿Qué película están pasando?
What program is playing?	Qué programa están pasando?
What kind of film is it?	¿Qué tipo de película es esa?

DEMONSTRATIVE PRONOUNS

Demonstrative pronouns (*this [one], that [one], these, those*) replace a noun referring to a person, place, thing, or idea and may be used alone. These pronouns must agree in number and gender with the nouns to which they refer. Demonstrative pronouns are distinguished from demonstrative adjectives by an accent mark.

Demonstrative Pronouns

MASCULINE	FEMININE	NEUTER	MEANING
éste	ésta	esto	this (one)
éstos	éstas		these
ése	ésa	eso	that (one) [near]
ésos	ésas		those
aquél	aquélla	aquello	that (one) [far]
aquéllos	aquéllas		those

Note the following about how to use demonstrative pronouns:

- Demonstrative pronouns can be distinguished from demonstrative adjectives by their accented letter: *este libro y ése* (this book and that one).
- Demonstrative pronouns agree in number and gender with the nouns to which they refer:

I prefer this coat and those.	Prefiero este abrigo y ésos.
I'll take this skirt and that one.	Me llevo esta falda y aquélla.

- Demonstrative pronouns can be followed by the words *aquí, ahí* (which indicates proximity to the the person spoken to), and *allá* (which recognizes distance from the speaker and the person spoken to):

these ones	estos ahí
that one	aquél allá
Which (pair of) pants do you prefer?	¿Cuáles pantalones prefieres?
These or those?	¿Éstos aquí o esos allá?

- The neuter forms, *esto*, *eso*, and *aquello*, are invariable because they do not refer to specific nouns but to statements, ideas, and understood nouns. These forms contain no accent as they have no corresponding demonstrative adjectives.

He is late and that makes me angry.	Él está atrasado y eso me enoja.
What is this (that)?	¿Qué es esto (eso, aquello)?

In a question asking about something unknown, such as the preceding question, the neuter form of the pronoun is used until the noun is identified, after which the pronoun must correspond in number and gender with the noun to which it refers.

Phrases using the definite articles *el* (*la, los, las*) + *de*, meaning "that of" or "the one of" and *el* (*la, los, las*) + *que*, meaning "the one that," are used as demonstrative pronouns.

El (La, Los, Las) de Marta es (son) importante(s).

The one(s) of Martha are important.

El (La, Los, Las) que está(n) aquí me interesa(n).

The one(s) that is (are) here interest(s) me.

El coche de Juan es distinto del de Julio, pero es muy parecido al que tiene Roberto.

Juan's car is different from Julio's, but it is very similar to the one Robert has.

The Former and the Latter

To express "the latter" (the latest, the most recently mentioned), use *éste* (*ésta, éstos, éstas*) and to express "the former" (the most remotely mentioned), use *aquél* (*aquélla, aquéllos, aquéllas*).

In English, we usually speak about "the former and the latter." In Spanish, the word order is reversed, and they refer to "the latter and the former," which is often less confusing:

¿Qué piensas de estas gafas de sol grandes y de éstas pequeñas?

What do you think of these large and small sunglasses?

Pienso que éstas (las pequeñas) son más bonitas que aquéllas (las grandes).

I think that these (the latter—the small ones) are prettier than those (the former—the big ones).

OBJECT PRONOUNS

Object pronouns are used so that an object noun doesn't have to be continuously repeated. This allows for a more free-flowing conversational tone. Object pronouns are classified as either direct or indirect. The following table lists the object pronouns.

DIRECT OBJECT PRONOUNS		INDIRECT OBJECT PRONOUNS	
Pronoun	English	Pronoun	English
me	me	me	(to) me
te	you (familiar)	te	(to) you (familiar)
le	him	le	(to) him, her, you, it
lo	him, it, you		
la	her, it, you		
se	himself, herself, itself	se	(to) himself, herself, itself
nos	us	nos	(to) us
os	you (polite)	os	(to) you
los	them, you	les	(to) them, you
las	them, you		
se	themselves	se	(to) themselves

▽ **NOTE**
. . . .

1. The forms *me*, *te*, *se*, *nos*, and *os* are direct and indirect object pronouns. They are also reflexive pronouns (see Chapter 18:00).
2. The direct object pronoun *lo* is preferred to *le* to express *him* or *you* in Latin America.

Yo invito a Carlos.	I invite Carlos.
Yo le invito.	I invite him. (In Spain)
Yo lo invito.	I invite him. (In Latin America)

Direct Object Pronouns

Direct objects (which can be nouns or pronouns) answer the question *whom* or *what* the subject is acting upon and may refer to people, places, things, or ideas. A direct object pronoun replaces a direct object noun.

Tú compras el libro.	You buy the book.
Tú lo compras.	You buy it.
Yo miro las películas.	I watch the movies.
Yo las miro.	I watch them.
Yo te quiero.	I love you.
Tú me quieres.	You love me.
Ud. nos ve.	You see us.
Nosotros le vemos.	We see you.

When using object pronouns, make sure that your conjugated verb agrees with the subject and not the object pronoun.

The Personal *A*

The personal *a* has no meaning and merely indicates that the direct object is a person. The personal *a* is only used before a direct object noun (not before a pronoun) when the direct object is:

- A person or persons: *Visito a mis amigos.* (I visit my friends.)
- A pet: *Cuido a su perro.* (I watch her dog.)
- A pronoun referring to an indefinite person: *¿Ves a alguien?* (Do you see anyone?)

The personal *a* is not used with the verb *tener*: *Tengo muchos amigos.* (I have many friends.)

Indirect Object Pronouns

Indirect objects (which can be nouns or pronouns) answer the question *to* or *for whom* the subject is doing something. Indirect objects only refer to people. An indirect object pronoun replaces an indirect object noun but is used in Spanish when the noun is mentioned. A key to the correct usage of an indirect object pronoun is the preposition *a* (*al, a la, a los,* or *a las*), which means "to" or "for" (unlike the personal *a*, which has no meaning) followed by the name or reference to a person. Use *a él, a ella,* or *a Ud.* to clearly differentiate to whom you are referring.

Ella le escribe a Juan.	She writes to John.
Ella le escribe (a él).	She writes to him.
Él le habla a la muchacha.	He speaks to the girl.
Él le habla (a ella).	He speaks to her.
Ud. me compra un regalo.	You buy a gift for me.
Yo le compro un regalo.	I buy a gift for you.

Some Spanish constructions with direct and indirect object pronouns differ from the English:

- Verbs that take an indirect object in English do not necessarily take an indirect object in Spanish. The following verbs take a direct object in Spanish:

VERB	MEANING	VERB	MEANING
esperar	to wait for	llamar	to call, name
buscar	to look for	pagar	to pay for (something)
escuchar	to listen to	mirar	to look at
esperar	to hope for (to)		

- Verbs that take a direct object in English do not necessarily take a direct object in Spanish. These verbs take an indirect object in Spanish because *to* or *for* is implied or because the verb is followed by *a*:

VERB	MEANING	VERB	MEANING
contestar	to answer	pagar	to pay ([to] someone)
dar	to give	pedir	to ask
decir	to tell	preguntar	to ask
escribir	to write	regalar	to give a gift
explicar	to explain	telefonear	to call (on the phone)
mandar	to send		

Gustar and Other Similar Verbs. Although *gustar* (to please, to like) is perhaps the most common of the verbs using indirect objects, there are many others, which are listed here:

VERB	MEANING	VERB	MEANING
agradar	to please, to be pleased with	importar	to matter, care
bastar	to be enough	interesar	to interest
doler (ue)	to be painful	parecer	to seem
encantar	to adore	quedar	to remain, have left
faltar	to lack, need	tocar	to be one's turn

Verbs requiring an indirect object follow these rules:

- The Spanish indirect object is the subject of the English sentence, so using these verbs requires that you think backwards a bit:

Me gustan los libros.	I like the books. (The books are pleasing to me.)
Nos falta una pluma.	We need a pen. (A pen is lacking to us.)

- Always use the third person singular form of *gustar* with an action or actions:

Le gusta bailar y cantar.	He likes to dance and sing. (Dancing and singing are pleasing to him.)

- The indirect object pronoun may be preceded by the preposition *a* + the corresponding prepositional pronoun *mí, ti, él, ella, Ud., nosotros, vosotros, ellos, ellas, Uds.* for stress or clarification:

A mí me parece imposible.	It seems impossible to me.
A ellos les toca jugar.	It is their turn to play.

- The indirect object noun generally precedes the indirect object pronoun:

A Paco no le queda nada.	Paco has nothing left.
A las niñas les gusta ir al centro.	The girls like to go downtown.

The Prepositions *to*, *for*, and *from*

The prepositions *to*, *for*, and *from* are not expressed in Spanish before indirect object pronouns, and they may or may not be expressed in English. Note that if one of these prepositions could be used, then an indirect pronoun is called for.

Me mostró su batería.	He showed his drums to me.
	(He showed me his drums.)
Le compré este libro.	I bought this book for him.
	(I bought him this book.)
Nos cobraron el dinero.	They collected the money from us.

Position of Object Pronouns

Study the following rules for the placement of pronouns:

- Object pronouns, direct or indirect, including reflexive pronouns, in simple and compound tenses, are placed before the verb:

Yo lo tomo.	I take it.
Él no la ha visto.	He hasn't seen her.
Nosotros nos levantamos temprano.	We get up early.

- With an affirmative command, the object pronoun follows the verb and is attached to it. An accent mark is normally required on the stressed vowel (count back three vowels and add the accent):

| Affirmative: Cómpralo. | Buy it. |

But:

| Negative: No lo compres. | Don't buy it. |

- With an infinitive or a gerund, the object pronoun may precede the conjugated verb, or follow the infinitive or gerund and be attached to it. When attached to the gerund, add the required accent on the stressed vowel:

Lo quiero comprar.	I want to buy it.
Quiero comprarlo.	
Lo estoy haciendo.	I'm doing it.
Estoy haciéndolo.	

Double Object Pronouns

More than one pronoun may be used in a sentence at a time. In Spanish, unlike in English, the indirect object pronoun (usually a person) precedes the direct object pronoun (usually a thing):

Él me lo describe.	He describes it to me.
Ella te la da.	She gives it to you.

Note the following:

- The indirect object pronouns *le* and *les* change to *se* before the direct object pronouns *lo, la, los, las*: *Yo se los leo.* (I read them to you [him, her].)
- The phrases *a Ud./Uds., a él/ellos* and *a ella/ellas* may be used to clarify the meaning of *se*: *Yo se la doy a ella (a Uds.).* (I give it to her [you].)
- The same rules for the position of single object pronouns apply for double object pronouns:

Infinitive:	Me lo quiere dar.	He wants to give it to me.
	Quiere dármelo.	
Gerund:	Me lo está dando.	He's giving it to me.
	Está dándomelo.	
Affirmative command:	Démelo.	Give it to me.
Negative command:	No me lo dé.	Don't give it to me.

USING ACCENTS

When attaching two pronouns to an infinitive, the general rule of thumb is to count back three vowels and then add an accent: *Él va a comprármelo.* (He is going to buy it for me.) When the pronouns are placed before the conjugated verb, no accent is added: *Él me lo va a comprar.* (He is going to buy it for me.)

When the affirmative command has more than one syllable, count back four vowels and then add the accent: *Dígamelo.* (Tell it to me.) No accent is added for the negative command: *No me lo diga.* (Don't tell it to me.)

When the pronouns are attached to a present participle, count back four vowels and add the accent: *Élla está leyéndoselo.* (She is reading it to him [her].)

POSITIVE FEELINGS

An invitation can be extended using a direct object pronoun: *¿Ud. quiere (Tú quieres) acompañarme (nos) . . . ?* (Would you like to acompany me [us]?) To accept, use *sí* and one of the following phrases:

EXPRESSION	SPANISH
Why not!	¡Cómo no!
Gladly!	¡Con mucho gusto!
Great!	¡Magnífico!
I adore . . .	Me encanta(n) . . .
I like . . .	Me gusta(n) . . .
Of course.	Claro.
Of course.	Por supuesto.
OK.	De acuerdo.
That would please me.	Me gustaría.
What a good idea.	¡Qué buena idea!
Why not?	¿Por qué no?
With pleasure.	Con placer.

USING THE SUBJUNCTIVE TO EXPRESS EMOTIONS AND FEELINGS

The subjunctive is used after verbs and expressions of feeling and emotion, such as fear, joy, sorrow, and surprise. To express your feelings to someone else, use this formula: subject pronoun + *estar* (conjugated) + adjective + *(de) que* + . . .The adjectives below will help you.

ADJECTIVE	SPANISH	ADJECTIVE	SPANISH
afraid	asustado(a)	furious	furioso(a)
angry	enojado(a)	happy	alegre, feliz
delighted	encantado(a)	proud	orgulloso(a)
displeased	enfadado(a)	sad	triste
embarrassed	avergonzado(a)	unhappy	infeliz

Ella está alegre de que Uds. acepten su invitación.	She is happy that you will accept her invitation.
Estoy triste que ellos no vengan.	I'm sad that they aren't coming.

Conjugate *tener* with the following nouns when you want to express feelings and emotions:

miedo de   fear (of)

vergüenza de   shame (of)

Tengo miedo de que él no diga la verdad.	I'm afraid that he won't tell the truth.

The following reflexive verbs may be conjugated and used with the subjunctive:

VERB	MEANING
enojarse	to become angry
enfadarse	to become angry
alegrarse (de)	to rejoice, be happy

Me alegro de que hagas el viaje a Francia.	I am happy that you are taking a trip to France.

 TIME'S UP!

1. Ask a friend if he wants to go to the beach.

2. Ask what's on television.

3. Ask what kind of film is playing.

4. Say you'd like to see a comedy.

5. Invite someone to have a picnic in the country.

6. Say: "I love you."

7. Say that the gifts please you.

8. Say: "I need a pen."

9. Say: "Show it to me, please."

10. Express a positive feeling about a play you saw.

Planning Outdoor Activities

MASTER THESE SKILLS

. . . .

- Engaging in sports
- Playing the game
- Describing the weather
- Expressing negative opinions and indifference
- Using the subjunctive with expressions of doubt and after impersonal expressions

. . . .

In this lesson you'll learn how to talk about sports and the weather. You'll also learn how to express your dissatisfaction or indifference toward various activities by using the subjunctive and relative pronouns.

SPORTS

Because sports are popular around the world, the sports listed below might be of interest to you.

The verbs *hacer* and *jugar* + *a* + definite article are commonly used to describe participation in a sport. In the list of sports, a 1 indicates that you should use the verb *hacer*, while a 2 indicates that you use *jugar*. All other verbs in the chart are listed beneath the name of the sport.

SPORT	SPANISH
aerobics	los ejercicios aeróbicos[1]
baseball	el béisbol[2]
basketball	el baloncesto[2]/el básquetbol[2]
bicycling	montar a bicicleta
cycling	el ciclismo[1]
fishing	ir de pesca
football	el fútbol americano[2]
golf	el golf[2]
ice skating	patinar
roller skating	patinar
skiing	esquiar
soccer	el fútbol[2]
swimming	la natación[1]/nadar
tennis	el tenis[2]

Engaging in Sports

When speaking about sports, one might say:

Let's play a game of . . .	Let's have a . . . match.
Vamos a jugar a . . .	Hagamos un partido de . . .
Vamos a jugar al fútbol.	Hagamos un partido de tenis.

Once you've determined the sport in which you want to engage, refer to the words below to select the appropriate playing field.

FIELD	SPANISH
beach	la playa
course (golf)	el campo (de golf)
court	la cancha
field	el campo
gymnasium	el gimnasio
ocean	el océano
park	el parque
pool	la piscina
stadium	el estadio
track	la pista

Let's go to the gym.   Vamos al gimnasio.

It's also important to make sure you have the appropriate and necessary equipment as listed below. Use these phrases to get you started.

I need . . .	I need . . .	Could you lend (rent) me . . .
Me falta(n) . . .	Necesito . . .	Podrías prestarme (alquilarme) . . .

EQUIPMENT	SPANISH
ball	la pelota
ball (basketball)	el balón
bat	el bate
bathing suit	el traje de baño
bicycle	la bicicleta
boat	el barco
fishing rod	la caña de pesca
golf clubs	los palos de golf
helmet	el casco
jogging shoes	los tenis
skates	los patines
ski bindings	las ataduras
skis	los esquís

THE WEATHER

In order to participate in any sport or outdoor activity, favorable weather conditions should prevail. The expressions in the table below will help you determine whether *el pronóstico* (the forecast) is encouraging: *¿Qué tiempo hace?* (What's the weather?)

The third person singular of the verb *hacer*—*hace*—is used to express many weather conditions. *Hay* is used to express visible conditions.

WEATHER	SPANISH
It's beautiful.	Hace bien tiempo.
It's cloudy.	Está nublado.
It's cold.	Hace frío.
It's foggy.	Hay niebla.
It's hot.	Hace calor.
It's humid.	Hay humedad.
It's overcast.	Está cubierto.
It's pouring.	Hay lluvias torrenciales.
It's raining.	Llueve.
It's snowing.	Está nevando.
It's sunny.	Hay sol.

What's the Temperature?

If you want to know the temperature, keep in mind that in Europe and Latin America the Centigrade (Celsius) thermometer is used.

To convert Fahrenheit to Centigrade, subtract thirty-two from the Fahrenheit temperature and multiply the remaining number by $\frac{5}{9}$. This will give you the temperature in degrees Centigrade.

To convert Centigrade to Fahrenheit, multiply the Centigrade temperature by $\frac{9}{5}$, then add thirty-two. This will give you the temperature in degrees Fahrenheit.

Some questions and answers you will need in order to express the temperature are:

What's the temperature?	¿Cuál es la temperatura?
It's ten below.	Hay una temperatura de diez grados bajo cero.
It's zero.	Hay una temperatura de cero grados.
It's seventy degrees.	Hay una temperatura de setenta grados.

> ▽ **NOTE**
>
> Use *hacer* to express weather conditions: *Hace calor.* (It's hot weather.)
> Use *tener* to express physical conditions of a person: *Tiene calor.*
> (He is hot.)

EXPRESSING NEGATIVE OPINIONS

An invitation, whether made in the affirmative or negative, might elicit a negative response. Use the phrases listed here to decline an invitation:

Don't you want to come with me (us)?	¿No quiere(s) ir conmigo (con nosotros)?

EXPRESSION	SPANISH
I hate . . .	Odio . . .
I don't like . . .	No me gusta . . .
I'm not a fan of . . .	No soy aficionado(a) a . . .
I'm sorry but . . .	Lo siento pero . . .
It's too difficult.	Es demasiado difícil.
That doesn't interest me.	No me interesa.
Why?	¿Por qué?
You've got to be kidding!	¡Qué va!

EXPRESSING INDIFFERENCE

If you've been invited out and are indifferent or indecisive about whether to go or not, use one of the expressions below.

EXPRESSION	SPANISH
I don't care.	No me importa.
I doubt it.	Lo dudo.
I really don't know.	No sé.
It depends.	Depende.
It doesn't matter.	Me da igual.
It's the same to me.	Me da lo mismo.
Perhaps./Maybe.	Quizás./Tal vez.
Whatever you want.	Como quiera(s).

USING THE SUBJUNCTIVE WITH EXPRESSIONS OF DOUBT

The subjunctive is used after verbs and expressions of doubt, denial, disbelief, and probability. The indicative (simple and compound tenses) is used after verbs and expressions of certainty. When certain verbs and expressions are used in the negative or the interrogative, they imply uncertainty or doubt and the subjunctive is required. When doubt is negated, certainty or probability exists and the indicative is used.

No pienso que ella pueda venir.	I don't think she can come.
No dudo que él nos acompañará.	I don't doubt that he will accompany us.
Él sabe que tú irás al partido.	He knows you will go to the game.

Note that all of the following expressions are followed by *que* and another clause.

INDICATIVE (CERTAINTY)		SUBJUNCTIVE (UNCERTAINTY)	
Spanish	**English**	**Spanish**	**English**
yo creo	I believe	yo no creo	I don't believe
		¿Cree Ud. . . . ?	Do you believe . . . ?
yo estoy seguro(a)	I'm sure	yo no estoy seguro(a)	I'm not sure
yo no dudo	I don't doubt	yo dudo	I doubt
yo no niego	I don't deny	yo niego	I deny
yo opino	I'm of the opinion	yo no opino	I'm not of the opinion
yo pienso	I think	yo no pienso	I don't think
		¿Piensa Ud . . . ?	Do you think . . .?
yo sé	I know	yo no sé	I don't know

USING THE SUBJUNCTIVE AFTER IMPERSONAL EXPRESSIONS

The subjunctive is also used after the impersonal expressions that show doubt, emotion, or opinion. The following expressions can be used to state either positive or negative feelings and can also be used to persuade someone to follow a course of action.

EXPRESSION	SPANISH
it's a pity	es una lástima
it could be	puede ser
it's curious	es curioso
it's doubtful	es dudoso
it's enough	es suficiente
it's fair	es justo
it's good	es bueno
it's impossible	es imposible
it's incredible	es increíble
it's interesting	es interesante
it's nice	es bueno
it's normal	es normal
it's possible	es posible
it's strange	es extraño
it's surprising	es sorprendente
it's unfair	es injusto
it seems	parece

Note that these expressions take the subjunctive even when preceded by *no*:

It is not surprising that you will accompany us.	No es sorprendente que Ud. nos acompañe.
It is not probable that he wants to go out.	No es probable que él quiera salir.

The following impersonal expressions show certainty and, therefore, require the indicative:

SPANISH	MEANING	SPANISH	MEANING
es cierto	it is certain, sure	es exacto	it is exact
es claro	it is clear	es seguro	it is sure
es evidente	it is evident	es verdad	it is true

Es claro que ella vendrá.   It's clear that she will come.

But:

No es claro que ella venga.   It's not clear that she will come.

CONTRARY-TO-FACT CONDITIONS

A contrary-to-fact condition expresses what would have happened had circumstances been different from what they currently are. In other words, you are talking about a hypothetical situation. The conditional mood expresses what would happen and the *si* clause, using a verb in the imperfect subjunctive, expresses if something else occurred: *Yo estaría contenta si tú aceptaras la invitación.* (I would be happy if you accepted the invitation.) (See Chapter 20:00 for more on *si* clauses.)

SEQUENCE OF TENSES OF THE SUBJUNCTIVE

The tense (time frame) of the subjunctive in a dependent clause depends on the tense of the verb used in the main clause. Always keep in mind the time to which you are referring when choosing the tenses to use. For example, look at the chart below. If the main clause is in the present, you may use either the present or perfect subjunctive in the dependent clause, depending on the meaning you wish to convey. If, however, the verb in the main clause is in the preterite, you may only use either the imperfect or pluperfect subjunctive. Use the following chart to help pick the correct tense of the subjunctive.

MAIN CLAUSE	DEPENDENT CLAUSE
present	present subjunctive
present perfect	OR
future	perfect subjunctive
command	
que	
imperfect	imperfect subjunctive
preterite	OR
conditional	pluperfect subjunctive
pluperfect	

194

TIME'S UP!

1. Invite someone to go swimming.

2. Ask someone if he/she plays golf.

3. Suggest that someone play tennis with you.

4. Say you need skates.

5. Ask someone if they could lend you a bicycle.

6. Ask someone for today's weather.

7. Give a simplified version of today's weather forecast in Spanish. Make sure to include the temperature.

8. Say that you don't like to play tennis because it's too difficult.

9. Say that you doubt that your friend will play basketball.

10. Say that you are sure that the weather will be nice.

Making Comparisons

MASTER THESE SKILLS

. . . .

- Making comparisons of inequality
- Comparing adjectives
- Comparing adverbs
- Comparing nouns
- Making comparisons of equality

. . . .

In this lesson you'll learn how to make comparisons of inequality using adjectives, adverbs, and nouns. You'll also learn how to use these words to make statements showing equality.

ANIMALS

Animals are compared all the time for their prowess, their size, their speed, their intelligence, and their good and bad traits. The list below gives the names of animals commonly used in comparisons:

ANIMAL	SPANISH	ANIMAL	SPANISH
bird	el ave, el pájaro	giraffe	la jirafa
bull	el toro	horse	el caballo
cat	el gato	leopard	el leopardo
cheetah	el guepardo	lion	el león
chicken, hen	la gallina	monkey	el mono
cow	la vaca	pig	el cochino
dog	el perro	rabbit	el conejo
elephant	el elefante	tiger	el tigre
fish	el pez	whale	la ballena
fox	el zorro		

IN THE CLASSROOM

In a classroom setting, students are constantly comparing grades, teachers, classes, class requirements, and homework assignments. Teachers also have a habit of comparing their students. The following list will give you the vocabulary you need to make classroom comparisons.

ITEM	SPANISH	ITEM	SPANISH
backpack	la mochila	homework	la tarea
board	la pizarra	principal	el director
book	el libro	pupil	el (la) estudiante
chalk	la tiza	school	la escuela
classroom	la sala de clase	teacher	el profesor
desk	el escritorio	test	el examen, la prueba
grade	la nota	textbook	el libro de texto
grammar	la gramática	university	la universidad

> ▽ **NOTE**
> ....
>
> In Spanish there is a distinction between the terms for *course* and *subject. El curso* has more of a connotation of an individual lesson, while *la materia* refers to the discipline of the subject itself:
>
> | | |
> |---|---|
> | Da un curso de español. | He gives Spanish lessons. |
> | El español es una materia fácil. | Spanish is an easy subject. |

By the end of this chapter you will be able to compare the subjects listed here:

SUBJECT	SPANISH	SUBJECT	SPANISH
art	el arte	geography	la geografía
biology	la biología	history	la historia
chemistry	la química	mathematics	las matemáticas
English	el inglés	music	la música
French	el francés	science	la ciencia

COMPARISONS OF INEQUALITY

Comparisons of inequality show that two things are not equal. These comparisons have three forms:

• The positive states the fact:

Adjective:	Spanish is easy.
Adverb:	A tiger runs quickly.
Noun:	I make mistakes.

• The comparative states *more* or *less*:

Adjective:	Spanish is easier than math. Math is harder than history.
Adverb:	A tiger runs more quickly than a turtle. A tiger runs less quickly than a cheetah.
Noun:	I make more mistakes than Robert. I make fewer mistakes than Maria.

• The superlative states *the most* or *the least*:

Adjective:	Spanish is the easiest. Math is the hardest.
Adverb:	A turtle runs the slowest of all animals. A cheetah runs the fastest of all animals.

Noun: Maria makes the most mistakes of anyone. Robert makes the fewest mistakes of anyone.

Most comparatives in English end in -*er* or use the word *less* or *more*. Most superlatives in English end in -*est* or use the word *least* or *most*.

El tigre es grande.	The tiger is big.
El caballo es más grande.	The horse is bigger.
El elefante es el más grande.	The elephant is the biggest.

Comparison of Adjectives

Adjectives are compared as follows:

- Positive: *interesante* (interesting): *El español es interesante.* (Spanish is interesting.)
- Comparative: *menos interesante* (less interesting), *más interesante* (more interesting):

Las matemáticas son menos interesantes que la historia.	Math is less interesting than history.
El español es más interesante que la historia.	Spanish is more interesting than history.

- Superlative: *el (la/los/las) menos interesante(s)* (the least interesting), *el (la/los/las) más interesante(s)* (the most interesting):

Las matemáticas son las menos interesantes.	Math is the least interesting.
El español es el más interesante.	Spanish is the most interesting.

A few adjectives have irregular comparatives and superlatives:

POSITIVE	COMPARATIVE	SUPERLATIVE
bueno(a)(s)	mejor(es)	el/la (los/las) mejor(es)
good	better	(the) best
malo(a)(s)	peor(es)	el/la (los/las) peores
bad	worse	(the) worst
pequeño(a)(s)	más pequeño(a)(s)	el/la (los/las) más pequeño(a)(s)
small	smaller (size)	the smallest (size)

pequeño(a)(s)	menor(es)	el/la (los/las) menor(es)
small	lesser, younger	the least, the youngest
grande(s)	más grande(s)	el/la (los/las) más grande(s)
big	bigger	biggest
grande(s)	mayor(es)	el/la (los/las) mayor(es)
great	greater, older	the greatest, the oldest

El perro es el mejor amigo del hombre.	A dog is man's best friend.
Sus notas son peores que las mías.	His grades are worse than mine.
Él es más pequeño que su hermano.	He is smaller than his brother.
Es el hermano menor.	He is the youngest brother.
Es la casa más grande.	It's the biggest house.
Es el mayor de la familia.	He is the oldest in the family.

In order to form the comparative and superlative of adjectives correctly, take note of the following rules:

- In the comparative, use adjectives to compare two or more things in one sentence and introduce the second element with *que* (than):

El español es más interesante que la historia.	Spanish is more interesting than history.
El tigre es menos grande que el elefante.	The tiger is shorter (less big) than the elephant.

- The second element of the comparison may be a noun, a subject pronoun, a possessive pronoun, an adjective, an adverb, or a clause:

Noun: *La biología es más fácil que la física.*
(Biology is easier than physics.)

Subject Pronoun: *Ella es más baja que yo.*
(She is shorter than I.)

Possessive Pronoun: *Su perro es más grande que el mío.*
(His dog is bigger than mine.)

Adjective: *Ellos son más dotados que inteligentes.*
(They are more gifted than intelligent.)

Adverb: *Estudió más que antes.*
(He studied more than before.)

Clause: *Ellas son más importantes de lo que yo pensaba.*
(They are more important than I thought.)

- Comparative and superlative adjectives agree in number and gender with the nouns they modify:

Una vaca es menos feroz que un tigre.	A cow is less ferocious than a tiger.
Los profesores son más inteligentes que los alumnos.	Teachers are more intelligent than students.

- To express "in" or "of" in a superlative sentence, use the preposition *de* + definite article: *La jirafa es el animal más alta del mundo.* (The giraffe is the tallest animal in the world.)
- In a superlative sentence, you may place the noun between the article (*el/la/los/las*) and the adjective: *Es el perro más precioso de todos.* (It's the most beautiful dog of all.)
- *Mejor* and *peor* generally precede the noun, whereas *mayor* and *menor* generally follow the noun (when comparing differences in age):

mi mejor amigo	my best friend
las peores películas	the worst films
mi hermana mayor	my older sister
su hermano menor	his younger brother

But:

de mayor importancia	of more importance

The antonyms (opposites) in the following chart should help you when making comparisons using adjectives.

ADJECTIVE		ANTONYM	
Spanish	English	Spanish	English
ancho	wide	estrecho	narrow
antiguo	old	moderno	modern
bajo	low	alto	high

caliente	hot	frío	cold
contento	happy	triste	unhappy
corto	short	largo	long
fácil	easy	difícil	hard
fuerte	strong	débil	weak
grande	big	pequeño	little
guapo	handsome	feo	ugly
limpio	clean	sucio	dirty
pobre	poor	rico	rich
viejo	old	nuevo	new

Comparison of Adverbs

Adverbs are compared as follows:

- Positive: *rápidamente* (quickly): *Los perros corren rápidamente.* (Dogs run quickly.)
- Comparative: *menos rápidamente* (less quickly), *más rápidamente* (more quickly):

  Los perros corren menos rápidamente que los caballos.

  Dogs run slower (less quickly) than horses.

  Los guepardos corren más rápidamente que los caballos.

  Cheetahs run faster than horses.

- Superlative: *menos rápidamente* (the least quickly), *más rápidamente* (the most quickly):

  Los guepardos son los que corren más rápidamente.

  Cheetahs are the ones that run the fastest.

  Los perros son los que corren menos rápidamente.

  Dogs are the ones that run the slowest.

Because there is no distinction between the comparative and superlative forms of adverbs, use *que* to express "than" in the comparative:

Los guepardos corren más rápidamente que los perros.

Cheetahs run faster than dogs.

Los perros corren menos rápidamente que los guepardos.

Dogs run slower than cheetahs.

In order to form the comparative and superlative of adverbs correctly, take note of the following rules:

* In the comparative, use adverbs to compare two or more things in one sentence and introduce the second element with *que* (than):

    Los perros corren menos rápidamente que los caballos.

    Dogs run slower than horses.

    Los tigres corren más rápidamente que los gatos.

    Tigers run faster than cats.

* In an affirmative sentence, *de* (than) replaces *que* before a number:

    Gané más (menos) de cien dólares.

    I earned more (less) than a hundred dollars.

But:

    No gané más que cien dólares.

    I didn't earn more than a hundred dollars.

* The second element of the comparison may be a noun, a subject pronoun, a possessive pronoun, an adverb, or a clause:

    Noun: *Los gatos juegan más silenciosamente que los leones.*
    (Cats play more quietly than lions.)

    Subject Pronoun: *Ella habla más rápidamente que yo.*
    (She speaks more quickly than I.)

    Possessive Pronoun: *Su perro corre más rápidamente que el mío.*
    (Her dog runs faster than mine.)

    Adverb: *Él trabaja más rápidamente que bien.*
    (He is working more quickly than well.)

    Clause: *Los guepardos corren más rápidamente de lo que yo pensaba.*
    (Cheetahs run faster than I thought.)

- If the second clause in a comparison has a different verb, use *de* together with a form of the article (*el, la, los, las*) when necessary: *Yo compré más libros de los que Ud. me recomendó.* (I bought more books than you recommended.)
- To express "in" or "of" in a superlative sentence, use the preposition *de* + definite article: *Los guepardos son los animales que corren más rápidamente de todos los animales.* (Cheetahs are the animals that run the fastest of all animals.)

Comparison of Nouns

Nouns are compared in the same way as adjectives and adverbs:

- Comparative: *menos que* (fewer [than]), *más que* (more [than]):

  Tengo menos materias que Ud.

  I have fewer subjects than you.

  Un perro come más carne que legumbres.

  A dog eats more meat than vegetables.

- Superlative: *lo menos* (the least), *lo más* (the most):

  Hace lo menos posible de la clase.

  She does the least possible in the class.

  Haces lo más errores posibles de todos los alumnos

  You make the most possible mistakes of all the students.

To form the comparative and superlative of nouns correctly, take note of the following rules:

- In the comparative, use nouns to compare two or more things in one sentence and introduce the second element with *que* (than):

  Tengo menos tareas que tú.   I have less homework than you.

  Tienes más trabajo que yo.   You have more work than I (do).

- The second element of the comparison may be a noun, a subject pronoun, a possessive pronoun, or a clause:

  Noun: *Tengo mejores notas que esos alumnos.*
  (I have better grades than those students.)

  Subject Pronoun: *Tiene más libros que yo.*
  (He has more books than I.)

Possessive Pronoun: *Mi clase tiene más alumnos que la tuya.*
(My class has more students than yours.)

Clause: *Una jirafa come más hierba de lo que yo pensaba.*
(A giraffe eats more grass than I thought.)

- To express "in" or "of" in a superlative sentence, use the preposition *de* + definite article: *Hace lo más trabajo posible de todos los profesores.* (He does the most possible work of all the teachers.)

Comparison of Verbs

When comparing infinitives of verbs, use *que* + an infinitive in the second part of the comparison:

Prefiero ir al cine que ir al teatro.

I prefer going to the theater rather than to the movies.

Me gustaría más comer pescado que comer carne.

I'd rather eat fish than meat.

COMPARISONS OF EQUALITY

Comparisons of equality show that two things are the same. Follow these simple formulas:

- *Tan* + adjective or adverb + *como* (as . . . as):

    Ella es tan inteligente como su hermano.

    She is as intelligent as her brother.

    Hablo español tan elocuentemente como tú.

    I speak Spanish as eloquently as you.

- *Tanto(-a, -os, -as)* [used as an adjective] + noun + *como* (as much/many . . . as). *Tanto* remains invariable when used as an adverb.

    Él tiene tantos amigos como tú.

    He has as many friends as you.

    No tengo tanta paciencia como mi esposo.

    I don't have as much patience as my husband.

Ella lee tanto como su hermano y yo.

She reads as much as her brother and I (do).

THE ABSOLUTE SUPERLATIVE

Use the absolute superlative when no comparison is involved. Simply add
-ísimo, *-ísima*, *ísimos*, *ísimas* to the adjective according to the gender
(masculine or feminine) and number (singular or plural) of the noun
being described. The meaning is the same as *muy* + adjective:

La blusa es muy cara.	The blouse is very expensive.
La blusa es carísima.	

Los perros son muy lindos.	The dogs are very sweet.
Los perros son lindísimos.	

Note the following exceptions to the rule:

• To express "very much" use *muchísimo*:

Lo quiero mucho.	I love him a lot.
Lo quiero muchísimo.	

• Drop the final vowel of an adjective before adding *-ísimo*:

La casa es muy grande.	The house is very big.
La casa es grandísima.	

• Adjectives ending in *-co* (*-ca* for feminine adjectives), *-go* (*-ga* for
feminine adjectives), or *-z* change *c* to *qu*, *g* to *gu*, and *z* to *c* before
adding *-ísimo*:

La limonada es muy fresca.	The lemonade is very fresh.
La limonada es fresquísima.	

Las avenidas son muy largas.	The streets are very long.
Las avenidas son larguísimas.	

El tigre es muy feroz.	The tiger is very fierce.
El tigre es ferocísimo.	

An adverb may be formed by adding *-mente* to the feminine form (*-ísima*) of the adjective:

Ella canta muy lentamente.   She sings very slowly.

Ella canta lentísimamente.

COMPARATIVE AND SUPERLATIVE EXPRESSIONS

The following comparative and superlative expressions will help you speak more colloquially:

* *hacer lo mejor que puede* (to do one's best): *Hacemos lo mejor que podemos.* (We do our best.)
* *hacer lo más (menos) posible* (as much [little] as possible): *Este muchacho hace lo más posible.* (This boy does as much as possible.)
* *lo más (menos) . . . posible* (as . . . as possible): *Ella trabaja lo menos rápidamente posible.* (She works as slowly as possible.)
* *cuanto más . . . más* (the more . . . the more): *Cuanto más come, más quiere.* (The more you eat, the more you want.)
* *cuanto menos . . . menos* (the less . . . the less): *Cuanto menos estudia, menos aprende.* (The less you study, the less you learn.)
* *cuanto más . . . menos* (the more . . . the less): *Cuanto más come, menos tiene hambre.* (The more you eat, the less hungry you are.)
* *cada vez más* (more and more): *Aprendes cada vez más rápidamente.* (You learn more and more quickly.)
* *cada vez menos* (less and less): *Los alumnos descansan cada vez menos.* (The students rest less and less.)

THE SUBJUNCTIVE AFTER SUPERLATIVE EXPRESSIONS

Use the subjunctive after superlative expressions to show an opinion, a feeling, or an emotion:

El español es la mejor lengua (indicative) que Ud. pueda estudiar (subjunctive).

Spanish is the best language you can study.

Sé que este mapa es el peor (indicative) que se venda (subjunctive).

I know that this map is the worst that they sell.

Use the indicative after a superlative to state a fact when no opinion on the part of the speaker is involved. The indicative is also used after the superlative of an adverb:

Es su mejor amiga que llamó.   It's his best friend who called.

Corre lo más rápidamente que puede.   He is running as fast as he can.

TIME'S UP!

1. Compare two animals.

2. Compare two classroom subjects.

3. Compare two people using adjectives.

4. Use the superlative to describe a person you know.

5. Compare the way in which two people do things using adverbs.

6. Use the superlative to say what someone does best.

7. Say that you have more work than I.

8. Make a comparison of equality between you and a family member.

9. Say that you have as much patience as your friend.

10. Use the subjunctive to say that you think this is the best book you can buy.

Meeting Your Needs on the Road and Elsewhere

MASTER THESE SKILLS

- Acquiring hotel accommodations
- Using the subjunctive
- Using relative pronouns

In this lesson you'll learn much about selecting the proper accommodations and getting the facilities and services you require. You'll also learn more about the subjunctive, and how to make exclamations and use relative pronouns.

HOTEL ACCOMMODATIONS AND AMENITIES

The following is a list of the amenities you may desire when staying in a hotel. Start with the question: *¿Hay . . . ?* (Is [Are] there . . . ?)

AMENITY	SPANISH
air conditioning	el aire acondicionado
a doorman	un portero
an elevator	un ascensor
a laundry service	una lavandería
a maid service	el servicio de limpieza
rooms for the disabled	habitaciones equipadas para los minusválidos
a swimming pool	una piscina
television	la televisión
tennis courts	canchas de tenis
valet parking	la atendencia del garaje

If you are traveling with a pet, you may be surprised to learn that animals are accepted as family members in most hotel and restaurant establishments. You may want to ask: *¿Acepta Ud. perros en el establecimiento?* (Do you accept dogs?)

Room Needs

When booking a room, if you have a preference as to view or location, you can make your wishes known by saying the following: *Quisiera una habitación . . .* (I would like to have a room . . .):

with a balcony	con balcón
with a garden	con jardín
with a terrace	con una terraza
on the courtyard	que dé al patio
on the garden	que dé al jardín
on the sea	con vista al mar

If you've found that you are missing something you need, use the words and expressions that follow to get what you desire:

I would like . . .	Quisiera . . .
I need . . .	Me falta(n) . . .
I need . . .	Necesito . . .
a bar of soap	una barra de jabón
a blanket	una manta
a hair dryer	un secador de cabello
hangers	unas perchas
a pillow	una almohada
a towel	una toalla
toilet paper	un rollo de papel higiénico

NOTE

Not all hotel rooms in Spanish-speaking countries have private bathroom facilities. If that is what you want, ask the following: ¿*Tienen las habitaciones baño privado?* (Do the rooms have private toilet facilities?)

EXCLAMATIONS

Exclamations can be used to give your positive or negative opinion about something. Make sure to use an inverted exclamation point (¡) before the exclamation and a regular one (!) after it. Use the adjectives below to express your pleasure or displeasure by saying *What a . . . !* or *How much/many . . . !*

¡Qué . . . !	What (a) . . . ! How . . . !
¡Cuánto(a) . . . !	How much . . . !
¡Cuántos(as) . . . !	How many . . . !
¡Qué hotel!	What a hotel!
¡Qué grande es!	How large it is!
¡Cuántas ventanas tiene!	How many windows it has!

To make an exclamation more emphatic, use *más* or *tan* before the adjective: ¡*Qué habitación tan (más) lujosa!* (What a luxurious room!)

THE SUBJUNCTIVE IN THIRD PERSON COMMANDS

Use the subjunctive in third person singular or plural commands:

Que entre él (ella).	Let (Have) him (her) come in.
Que hablen ellos (ellas).	Let (Have) them speak.
Que sean felices.	May they be happy.
¡Viva el rey!	Long live the king!

THE SUBJUNCTIVE AFTER CONJUNCTIONS

Use the subjunctive after certain conjunctions when uncertainty, doubt, purpose, or anticipation is implied.

Conjunctions are words that connect and relate vocabulary words and pronouns, as well as two clauses in a sentence. You use them repeatedly in speaking and writing. Conjunctions do not change their form to indicate meaning.

You may use the subjunctive with the following conjunctions. Those with an asterisk (*) always take the subjunctive, because doubt, uncertainty, or purpose is implied:

- Conjunctions that express time:

CONJUNCTION	MEANING
hasta que	until
*antes (de) que	before

Yo esperaré hasta que venga el portero.

I'll wait until the porter comes.

(Expresses doubt: he may not come.)

Yo esperé hasta que vino.

I waited until he came.

(Expresses certainty: he showed up.)

- Conjunctions that express purpose:

CONJUNCTION	MEANING
a fin de que	in order that
*para que	in order that
de modo que	so that
de manera que	so that

Yo saldré a fin de que la criada pueda limpiar la casa.

I'll leave so that the maid can clean the room.

(Expresses purpose: so that she may clean.)

- Conjunctions that express condition:

CONJUNCTION	MEANING
*con tal (de) que	provided that
*a menos que	unless
*en caso de que	in case (that)
*a condición (de) que	on condition of

Me quedaré en este hotel con tal de que tengan una piscina.

I'll stay in this hotel provided that they have a pool.

(Expresses doubt: maybe there is a pool and maybe there isn't.)

- Conjunction that expresses concession:

CONJUNCTION	MEANING
aunque	although

Aceptaré esta habitación aunque sea pequeña.

I'll take this room although it may be small.

(Expresses doubt: maybe the room is small and maybe it isn't.)

Aceptaré esta habitación aunque es pequeña.

I'll take this room although it is small.

(Expresses certainty: the room is small.)

- Conjunction that expresses negation:

CONJUNCTION	MEANING
*sin que	without

El portero se fue sin que yo lo supiera.

The porter left without my knowing it.

(Expresses purpose: in such a way that I didn't notice.)

- Conjunction that expresses fear:

CONJUNCTION	MEANING
por miedo (de) que	for fear that

Telefoneo por miedo de que la criada no venga.

I'm calling for fear that the maid isn't coming.

(Expresses emotion: shows fear)

The following conjunctions use the indicative to refer to past or present actions or events, and the subjunctive to refer to future events that are considered uncertain:

CONJUNCTION	MEANING
así que	as soon as
cuando	when
después (de) que	after
en cuanto	as soon as
hasta que	until
luego que	as soon as
mientras que	while
tan pronto como	as soon as

Ella limpió su habitación mientras comían.

She cleaned their room while they ate.

But:

Ella limpiará su habitación mientras coman.

She will clean their room while they are (will be) eating.

Use the infinitive after these conjunctions when the subject does not change:

CONJUNCTION	MEANING
para	in order to
porque	because
sin	without
antes de	before

Llamó para reservar una habitación.	He called to reserve a room.
Salío sin decir nada.	He left without saying anything.
Te telefonearé antes de salir.	I'll call you before leaving.

THE SUBJUNCTIVE IN RELATIVE CLAUSES

Use the subjunctive in a relative clause if the antecedent (the person or thing mentioned in the main clause) is indefinite, desired but not yet found, or nonexistent (or whose existence is in doubt):

Busco un hotel que sea cómodo.

I'm looking for a comfortable hotel.

¿Conoce Ud. a alguien que pueda ayudarme?

Do you know anyone who can help me?

No puedo encontrar a nadie que sepa ese número de teléfono.

I can't find anyone who knows that phone number.

But:

Conozco a alguien que puede ayudarle.

I know someone who can help you.

RELATIVE PRONOUNS

A relative pronoun (who, which, that) joins a main clause to a dependent clause. This pronoun introduces the dependent clause that describes someone or something mentioned in the main clause. The person or thing the pronoun refers to is called the antecedent. A relative clause may serve as a subject, a direct object, or an object of a preposition. The following list shows the relative pronouns in Spanish:

	ANTECEDENT		ANTECEDENT
	Person	Thing	Clause/Idea
Subject	que	que	lo que/lo cual
Direct object	que	que	lo que/lo cual
Object of all prepositions	a	a	
	de quien(es)	de que	
	en	en	
	con	con	

Que

Que (who, whom, which, that), the most frequently used relative pronoun, is the subject or object of a relative clause and may refer to people or things.

Es *el hombre* que ganó un premio.

He's the man who won a prize.

(antecedent = person = subject of relative clause)

Es *el hotel* que ganó un premio.

It's the hotel that won a prize.

(antecedent = thing = subject of relative clause)

Es *un hombre* que yo admiro.

He's a man I admire.

(antecedent = person = object of relative clause)

Es *una pintura* que yo admiro.

It's a painting I admire.

(antecedent = thing = object of relative clause)

Although frequently omitted in English, the relative pronoun is always expressed in Spanish: *Es un país que yo visito frecuentemente.* (It's a country [that] I visit often.)

Que and Quien (Objects of a Preposition)

Que (which, whom) is used as the object of a preposition referring primarily to things: *Es el hotel de que yo hablo.* (That's the hotel about which I am speaking.) *Quien* (whom) is used as the object of a preposition referring to people: *Miguel es el muchacho con quien yo viajo.* (Michael is the boy with whom I am traveling.) Note that in both cases the preposition precedes the relative pronoun *quien* or *que*.

Quien may be used in the following circumstances:

- Instead of *que* to introduce a clause not necessary to the meaning of the sentence: *Arturo, quien me ha escrito, quiere hablarme.* (Arturo, who wrote to me, wants to speak to me.)
- As a direct object. The personal *a* is required in *a quien* (whom), which may replace *que* as the direct object in more formal style: *Son los hombres a quienes (que) yo vi esta mañana.* (Those are the men I saw this morning.)

- As a subject to express "he (she, those, the one, the ones) who": *Quien trabaja mucho, gana mucho.* (The one who works a lot, earns a lot.)

> **▽ NOTE**
>
> *El (la, los, las) que* may be used in place of *quien* as a subject:
> *El que trabaja mucho, gana mucho.* (He who works a lot, earns a lot.)

El Cual and *El Que*

The longer forms of the relative pronouns, *el cual (la cual, los cuales, las cuales)* and *el que (la que, los que, las que)*, are used as follows:

- For clarity and emphasis when there are two antecedents:

El (la, los, las) que or *el (la, los, las) cual(es)* may be used to refer to the latter (the one that is mentioned last):

La madre de Julio, el que (el cual) esta enfermo, le prepara sopa.

The mother of Julio, who is sick, prepares soup for him.

(Julio is sick.)

El (la, los, las) que or *el (la, los, las) cual(es)* can also be used to refer to the former (the one that is mentioned first), especially when the two antecedents are of the same gender:

La madre de Julio, la que (la cual) esta enferma, esta en cama.

Julio's mother, who is sick, is in bed.

(The mother is sick.)

El padre de Julio, el que (el cual) esta enfermo, esta en cama.

Julio's father, who is sick, is in bed.

(The father is sick.)

- After prepositions other than *a*, *con*, *de*, and *en* to refer to things: *Es la compañía para la cual (la que) él trabaja.* (It's the company for which he works.)

Note that *de + el = del* before *que* and *cual*: *Es el edificio delante del que (del cual) él se cayó.* (That's the building in front of which he fell.)

Lo Que and Lo Cual

The relative pronoun *lo que* (*lo cual*) is the neuter form of *el que* and is used when there is no antecedent noun as follows:

- *Lo que* means "what (that which)" and is the subject of a verb:
  Me pregunto lo que pasó. (I wonder what happened.)
- *Lo que* means "what (that which)" and is the object of a verb:
  Yo sé lo que quiere decir eso. (I know what that means.)
- *Lo que* is used after the pronoun *todo* to express "everything that" or "all that":

Me gusta todo lo que es español.	I like everything that is Spanish.
No escuché todo lo que Ud. dijo.	I didn't hear everything you said.

Cuyo

Cuyo(*-a,-os,-as*) (whose) is a relative adjective that must agree in gender and number with the people or things possessed, not with the possessor:
La casa, cuyas puertas son rojas, es la mía. (The house, whose doors are red, is mine.)

TIME'S UP!

1. Ask if your hotel has a garage.

2. Say you want a room with an ocean view.

3. Say you need another pillow.

4. Use an exclamation to say: "What a great room!"

5. Use the subjunctive to say: "Let them come in!"

6. Say that you will stay at the hotel provided there are tennis courts.

7. Say that you're searching for a luxurious hotel.

8. Ask if there's a person who speaks English.

9. Say: "That's the room I want."

10. Say that you have everything that you need.

Speaking of Food

MASTER THESE SKILLS

- Using adverbs and nouns of quantity
- Selecting an eating establishment and getting started
- Selecting meats, poultry, and fish
- Selecting vegetables and fruits
- Cooking to perfection
- Using or avoiding herbs, condiments, and spices
- Selecting a drink and a dessert
- Using proper restaurant etiquette

In this chapter you'll learn how to buy the quantity of food you want and how to order in a restaurant.

QUANTITIES

Should you decide to purchase food in a store in a Spanish-speaking area, you'll want to be able to express the correct quantity. In the Spanish-speaking world, the metric system is used for measuring quantities of food: Liquids are measured in liters, and solids are measured in kilograms. If you are accustomed to dealing with ounces, pounds, pints, quarts, and gallons, the list below gives you a quick conversion chart:

APPROXIMATE DRY MEASURES	APPROXIMATE LIQUID MEASURES
1 ounce = 28 grams	1 ounce = 30 milliliters
¼ pound = 125 grams	16 ounces (1 pint) = 475 milliliters
½ pound = 250 grams	32 ounces (1 quart) = 950 milliliters (approximately 1 liter)
¾ pound = 375 grams	1 gallon = 3.75 liters
1.1 pounds = 500 grams	
2.2 pounds = 1000 grams (1 kilogram)	

Adverbs and adjectives of quantity can help you to generalize or be more specific about the amounts you need. They are used to give an unspecified amount:

as much, many	tanto(-a,-os,-as)
enough	bastante, suficiente
how much, many	cuanto(-a,-os,-as)
less, fewer	menos
a little, few	poco(-a,-os,-as)
more	más
much, many	mucho(-a,-os,-as)
so much, many	tanto(-a,-os,-as)
too much, many	demasiado

Adverbs of quantity do not require the use of the preposition *de* (of): *No tengo bastante carne.* (I don't have enough meat.)

NOUNS OF QUANTITY

Nouns of quantity allow for a measurement based on weight or the type of container as shown here:

MEASUREMENT	SPANISH
2 pounds of	un kilo de
a bag of	un saco de
a bar of	una tableta de, una barra de
a bottle of	una botella de
a box of	una caja de
a can of	una lata de
a dozen	una docena de
a package of	un paquete de
a slice of	un trozo de

Nouns of quantity are followed by *de* to express *of*. No definite article is used: *Deme quinientos gramos de carne, por favor.* (Give me a pound of meat, please.)

To ask for or to refer to an unspecified quantity (to say that you want part of a whole [*some* or *any*]) simply use the noun:

Deme jamón, por favor.	Please give me some ham.
No tenemos carne.	We don't have any meat.

Use the definite article (*el*, *la*, *los*, *las*) with nouns in a general sense:

Me gusta el chocolate.	I like chocolate.

But:

Deme chocolate.	Give me some chocolate.

Use *un* or *una* when speaking about one portion or serving.

Un café, por favor.	A coffee, please.
Una lata de café, por favor.	A can of coffee, please.

EATING ESTABLISHMENTS

The Spanish-speaking world offers a wide variety of eating establishments to suit your hunger and your pocketbook, whether you are eating breakfast (*el desayuno*), lunch (*el almuerzo*), dinner (*la cena*), or a midmorning or late afternoon snack (*la merienda*):

- *Un bar, una tasca,* or *una taberna*: A pub or bar in Spain in which drinks and small snacks known as *tapas* or *pinchos* are served.
- *Un café*: A small neighborhood restaurant.
- *Una cafetería*: A small, informal café where snacks and drinks are served.
- *Una cantina*: A Spanish-American men's bar where women are excluded.
- *Una cervecería*: A pub specializing in barreled German beer and wine.
- *Una fonda, hostería, venta,* or *posada*: An inn specializing in regional dishes.
- *Una hacienda*: A Spanish-American ranch-style restaurant.
- *Un merendero* or *chiringuito*: An outdoor stand, generally located at the beach, that sells seafood, drinks, and ice cream.

FOODS

Whether you are dining in or out, knowing the names of Spanish foods will help you get exactly what you like to eat. The tables and lists that follow will help you with your choices from soup to nuts and will serve as useful tools in deciphering a Spanish menu.

Appetizers (*Los Aperitivos*)

Chances are that you will not be ordering a cocktail in the restaurant before your dinner. This is because in the Spanish-speaking world, it is customary to stop off before dinner at a bar, and in Spain, a tapas bar. Some tapas bars offer a wide variety of appetizers, while others serve only one or two kinds. Tell your waiter: *Para empezar, me gustaría (yo deseo, yo quiero)* . . . (To begin, I'll have . . .) Then choose from the appetizers listed below.

artichokes	alcachofas
eggs	huevos
mushrooms	champiñones
snails	caracoles
spicy sausage	chorizo
tortilla chips	tostadas

Soups (*Las Sopas*)

You can expect to find the following soups on a Spanish menu:

cazuela	spicy fish, vegetable, or meat soup
gazpacho	cold puréed uncooked vegetables
potaje madrileño	thick, puréed cod, spinach, and chickpea soup
pozole	pork and hominy soup
sopa de ajo	garlic soup
sopa de verduras	green vegetable soup

Main Meals (*Los Platos Principales*)

Whether you go to the butcher (*a la carnicería*), to the delicatessen (*a la charcutería*), or to dine out, the names of the meats, fowl, and fish will come in handy. To select the meal you want, say: *Quisiera* . . . (I would like . . .)

Meat (*Las Carnes*)

bacon	el tocino
beef	la carne de res
chop	la chuleta
ham	el jamón
lamb	el cordero, el borrego
oxtails	el rabo de buey
pork	el cerdo
roast beef	el rosbif
sausage	la salchicha
sirloin	el solomillo
steak	el bistec
veal	la ternera

Fowl and Game (*La Carne Ave y de Caza*)

chicken	el pollo
duck	el pato
goose	el ganso

turkey	el pavo
venison	el venado

Fish and Seafood (*Los Pescados y los Mariscos*)

anchovy	la anchoa
bass	la merluza
clam	la almeja
codfish	el bacalao
crab	el cangrejo
lobster	la langosta
mussel	el mejillón
octopus	el pulpo
oyster	la ostra
shrimp	los camarones, las gambas
squid	el calamar
tuna	el atún

NOTE

Rice (*el arroz*) is a very important staple in Spain and is used as the base for the ever-popular *paella*. This dish varies from region to region but always contains saffron-flavored rice. The most popular is *paella valenciana*, with chicken, seafood, peas, and tomatoes.

Salad (*La Ensalada*)

Refer to the following lists for the names of vegetables, fruits, and nuts that you might like in your salad.

Vegetables (*Las Legumbres*)

beans (green)	las judías
broccoli	el brécol
cabbage	la col
carrots	las zanahorías
corn	el maíz

cucumber	el pepino
lettuce	la lechuga
onion	la cebolla
peas	los guisantes
peppers	las pimientas
potato	la patata
spinach	la espinaca
squash	el calabacín
tomato	el tomate

Fruits (*Las Frutas*)

apple	la manzana
avocado	el aguacate
banana	la banana
grape	la uva
lemon	la lima
lime	el limón
olive	la aceituna
orange	la naranja
pear	la pera
pineapple	la piña
raisin	la pasita
strawberry	la fresa

Nuts (*Las Nueces*)

almond	la almendra
chestnut	la castaña
hazelnut	la avellana
walnut	la nuez

Eggs (*Huevos*)

Eggs (*huevos*) are quite popular in the Spanish-speaking world, but not for breakfast. Refer to the following list to ask for eggs prepared the way you like them:

fried with spicy tomato sauce	fritos rancheros
hard-boiled	duros
omelette	una tortilla
poached	escalfados
scrambled	revueltos

Cooking It to Perfection

To ensure that your main course is cooked to your liking, specify how you want it by saying: *Lo (La, Los, Las) quiero . . .* (I want it . . .)

baked	horneado
boiled	hervido
fried	frito
grilled	asado a la parrilla
roasted	rostizado
rare	poco asado
medium	a término medio
well-done	bien cocido

Herbs, Condiments, and Spices
(*Las Hierbas, los Condimentos y las Especias*)

Use the following words to specify what seasonings you would like in your meal:

butter	la mantequilla
garlic	el ajo
jam, jelly	la mermelada
mayonnaise	la mayonesa
mustard	la mostaza
oil	el aceite

parsley	el perejil
pepper (black)	la pimienta
pepper (red)	el pimiento
saffron	el azafrán
salt	la sal
sugar	el azúcar

Drinks (*Las Bebidas*)

If you would like to order a beverage, *una bebida*, look for something listed here:

beer	la cerveza
champagne	el champán
cocoa	el chocolate
coffee	el café
black	solo
with milk	con leche
decaffeinated	descafeinado
juice	el jugo
mineral water	el agua mineral
milk	la leche
tea	el té
wine	el vino

If you want to be specific about a type of juice, use *de* + the name of the fruit: *el jugo de naranja* (orange juice).

The Spanish usually drink wine with dinner. The wines you might order include the following:

red wine	el vino tinto
white wine	el vino blanco
dry wine	el vino seco
champagne	el champán

Desserts (*Los Postres*)

Desserts are always a sweet ending to a delicious meal. Consider ordering one of the following:

caramel custard	el flan
cookies	las galletitas
ice cream	el helado
marzipan	el marzapán
pie	el pastel
rice pudding	el arroz con leche
sponge cake	el bizcocho
yogurt	el yogur

TABLE SETTINGS

If something is missing from your place setting or if you need something additional at the table, use the following terms to ask your server as follows:

I need . . .	Necesito . . .
I'm missing . . .	Me falta(n) . . .
bowl	un tazón
cup	una taza
dinner plate	un plato
fork	un tenedor
glass	un vaso
knife	un cuchillo
menu	un menú
napkin	una servilleta
saucer	un platillo
teaspoon	una cucharita
tablespoon	una cuchara
wine glass	una copa

A waiter is called *el camarero* and a waitress is called *la camarera*.

RESTAURANT ETIQUETTE

When reserving a table, you can use the following information:

I would like to reserve a table . . .	Quisiera reservar una mesa . . .
for this evening.	para esta noche.
for tomorrow evening.	para mañana por la noche.
for Saturday evening.	para el sábado por la noche.
for six people at 8:00 P.M.	para seis personas a las ocho de la noche.
on the terrace.	en la terraza.

To find out about the menu, you would ask:

What is today's specialty?	¿Cuál es el plato del día?
What do you recommend?	¿Qué recomienda Ud.?
What is the house specialty?	¿Cuál es la especialidad de la casa?

Good manners dictate that when your meal arrives, you wish your fellow diners *buen provecho*, a hearty appetite.

DIETARY RESTRICTIONS

Whether because of personal preference, or in order to follow the advice of a doctor, it is very important to be able to express any dietary restrictions you might have:

I am on a diet.	Estoy a régimen (dieta).
I'm a vegetarian.	Soy vegetariano(a).
I can't have anything made with . . .	No puedo comer nada con . . .
I can't have . . .	No puedo tomar . . .
dairy products	productos lácteos.
alcohol	alcohol.
saturated fats	grasas saturadas.
shellfish	mariscos.
I'm looking for a dish (that is) . . .	Estoy buscando un plato . . .

high in fiber.	con mucha fibra.
kosher.	comida permitida por la religión judía.
low in cholesterol.	con poco colesterol.
low in fat.	con poca grasa.
low in sodium.	con poca sal.
non-dairy.	no lácteos.
salt-free.	sin sal.
sugar-free.	sin azúcar.
with . . .	con . . .
without . . .	sin . . .
without artificial coloring	sin colorantes artificiales
without preservatives	sin preservativos

PROBLEMS

If your meal isn't up to par, explain the problem using the phrases in this list.

It . . .	El (La) . . .
is cold	está frío(a)
is too rare	está demasiado crudo(a)
is overcooked	está sobrecocido(a)
is burned	está quemado(a)
is too salty	está muy salado(a)

At the end of the meal, to ask for the check, you would say: *La cuenta, por favor.* (The check, please.)

TIME'S UP!

1. Ask the butcher for 500 grams of meat.

2. Say that you will begin your meal with snails.

3. Name a vegetable you like.

4. Say you want your dish cooked medium.

5. Order a dessert.

6. Say you need another wine glass because yours is dirty.

7. Reserve a table for this evening for four people at 9:30 P.M. on the terrace.

8. Ask for today's specialty.

9. Explain that you can't have any dairy products.

10. Ask for the check.

Medical Needs

MASTER THESE SKILLS

- Going to the pharmacy

- Using prepositional modifiers

- Expressing medical problems

- Going to the doctor

- Asking and answering "how long?"

In this chapter you'll learn how to get the drugstore items and medical attention you need. You'll also learn how to use body language to convey your feelings and to say how long you've been suffering.

AT THE PHARMACY

If you've accidentally left a toiletry article at home, run out of something you need, or are just feeling under the weather, you'll probably want to take a fast trip to a local pharmacy.

Una farmacia, easily identifiable by a green cross above the door, sells prescription drugs, over-the-counter medications, and items intended for personal hygiene. When the pharmacy is closed, there may be a sign on the door indicating where a nearby all-night pharmacy, *una farmacia de guardia* (*de turno*) is located.

To ask for an over-the-counter cure, you would say: *¿Tiene Ud. algo para . . . ?* (Do you have a cure for . . . ?)

To fill a prescription, tell the druggist:

Necesito esta medicina.	I need this medication.
¿Podría Ud. preparar esta receta (en seguida)?	Could you please fill this prescription (immediately)?

If you're looking for a product you can purchase off the shelf, begin by telling a clerk what you're looking for and then use the words listed below to express your needs:

Busco . . .	I'm looking for . . .
Necesito . . .	I need . . .
¿Tiene Ud . . . ?	Do you carry . . . ?

ITEM	SPANISH
aspirin	la aspirina
bandages	las vendas
brush	un cepillo
condoms	los condones
cough syrup	el jarabe para la tos
deodorant	el desodorante
makeup	el maquillaje
mouthwash	el elixir bucal
razor	la maquinilla de afeitar
sanitary napkins	las toallas higiénicas
scissors	las tijeras
shampoo	el champú

shaving cream	la crema de afeitar
sleeping pills	las pastillas para dormir
soap (bar)	una barra de jabon
tampons	los tampones
thermometer	un termómetro
tissues	los pañuelos de papel
toothbrush	el cepillo de dientes
toothpaste	la pasta dentífrica

If you're traveling with a baby, you might need the following:

bottle	un biberón
diapers (disposable)	los pañales (desechables)
pacifier	un chupón

PREPOSITIONAL MODIFIERS

Prepositions relate two elements of a sentence. Some of the examples below use the preposition in the Spanish version but not in the English one.

- Noun to noun: *Me corté el dedo del pie.* (I cut my toe.)
- Verb to verb: *Empieza a llorar.* (He begins to cry.)
- Verb to noun: *Ella trabaja con sus manos.* (She works with her hands.)
- Verb to pronoun: *Ella habla bien de él.* (She speaks well about him.)
- A preposition + a noun modifying another noun is equivalent to an adjective:

el jarabe para la tos	cough medicine
las gotas para los ojos	eye drops
las hojas de afeitar	razor blades
los pañuelos de papel	paper handkerchiefs (tissues)

- A preposition + a noun modifying a verb is equivalent to an adverb: *El doctor trabaja con cuidado.* (The doctor works carefully.)

Note the following about the use of prepositions:

- The preposition *para* or *de* + noun is used to express the use, the function, or the characteristic of an object:

el jarabe para la tos	cough syrup
una bolsa de hielo	ice pack
un dedo del pie	toe

- The preposition *para* or *de* + verb may be used to describe the purpose of a noun:

la loción para broncearse	suntan lotion
la maquinilla de afeitar	electric razor

- The preposition *de* + noun is used to express the source, the goal, or the content of an object:

la almohadilla de calefacción	heating pad
los pañuelos de papel	tissues

PARTS OF THE BODY

If illness strikes while you are traveling, it is best to know the parts of the body so that you can describe exactly what ails you.

BODY PART	SPANISH	BODY PART	SPANISH
ankle	el tobillo	lip	el labio
arm	el brazo	lung	el pulmón
back	la espalda	mouth	la boca
chest	el pecho	nail	la uña
ear	la oreja	neck	el cuello
elbow	el codo	nose	la nariz
eye	el ojo	shoulder	el hombro
face	la cara	skin	la piel
finger	el dedo	stomach	el estómago
foot	el pie	throat	la garganta
hand	la mano	toe	el dedo del pie
head	la cabeza	tongue	la lengua
heart	el corazón	tooth	el diente
knee	la rodilla	wrist	la muñeca
leg	la pierna		

MEDICAL PROBLEMS

When someone is concerned about your health, you would expect to hear:

¿Qué le (te) pasa?	What's the matter with you?
¿Cómo está(s)?	How are you?

To say that you or someone else has an ache or hurt, you could answer in one of two ways:

1. Use the verb *tener* (to have) to express what you have and where. Remember to conjugate *tener* and use the correct form of *de*: *Tengo dolor de* . . . (I have a . . . ache.): *Tiene dolor de cabeza.* (She has a headache.)

   Although Spanish speakers use *tener* to express what's bothering them, English may not include the word *have*: *Tengo dolor de oídos.* (My ears hurt.)

2. Use the verb *doler* (to hurt) plus an indirect object to express that something hurts. Pay special attention to the following:

- Use the appropriate indirect object pronoun to refer to those who might be in pain. Literally, you are explaining the body part is hurting (*to* + person). The indirect object pronouns are:

me	to me	nos	to us
te	to you	os	to you
le	to him, her	les	to them

- Use the correct form of the definite article (*el*, *la*, *los*, *las*) that agrees with the body part in question. (See the list on page 238 for the names of the body parts with their corresponding definite article.) Because the indirect object pronoun is used, it would be redundant to use the possessive adjective.
- *Doler* must agree in number (singular or plural) with the part that is hurting:

  singular: duele

  plural: duelen

Me duelen los oídos.	My ears hurt me.
Le duele la espalda.	His back hurts.

Should you need to explain your symptoms to the doctor, use the words in the following list. Preface your explanation with: *Tengo* . . . (I have (*a/an*) . . .)

SYMPTOM	SPANISH	SYMPTOM	SPANISH
broken bone	un hueso roto	indigestion	la indigestión
cough	una tos	infection	una infección
cramp	un calambre	migraine	una jaqueca
cut	una cortadura	pain	un dolor
diarrhea	la diarrea	sprain	una torcedura
fever	una fiebre		

Other expressions for health symptoms you may need to know include:

I'm coughing a lot.	Estoy tosiendo mucho.
I'm sneezing.	Estoy estornudando.
I'm bleeding.	Estoy sangrando.
I'm nauseous.	Tengo náuseas.
I'm constipated.	Estoy estreñido(a).
I feel bad.	Me siento mal.
I have trouble sleeping.	No puedo dormir.
I'm exhausted.	Estoy agotado(a).
I hurt everywhere.	Me duele todo el cuerpo.

Use the following phrase when you need a dentist: *Tengo un dolor de muelas.* (I've got a toothache.)

AT THE DOCTOR'S

A visit to the doctor will require that you answer these questions based on your medical history. Some common medical problems are listed here:

Have you had . . . ?	¿Ha sufrido . . . ?
Do you suffer from . . . ?	¿Sufre Ud. de . . . ?

PROBLEM	SPANISH
allergic reaction	una reacción alérgica
asthma	el asma
cancer	el cáncer
cold	un resfriado, un catarro

dizziness	el vértigo
flu	la gripe
heart attack	un ataque al corazón
stroke	un ataque de apoplejía

To answer questions about your medical history say:

| I've had . . . | He sufrido . . . |
| I suffer from . . . | Sufro de . . . |

You may also use the reflexive verb, *sentirse* (*ie*), to express how you feel:

I feel well.	Me siento bien.
Do you feel very well?	¿Te sientes muy bien?
He (She, You) feel(s) better.	Se siente mejor.
We feel poorly.	Nos sentimos mal.
Do you feel very poorly?	¿Os sentís muy mal?
They (You) feel worse.	Se sienten peor.

Asking and Answering "How Long?"

The phrases below suggest the different ways you may hear the question that asks how long you've had your symptoms or complaints, and the ways in which to answer correctly. The phrases vary in difficulty but all mean the same thing:

QUESTION	ANSWER
¿Desde cuándo . . . ?	(Present tense) Desde hace . . .
Since when + present tense . . . ?	(Present tense) Since + time . . .
¿Desde cuándo sufre Ud.?	(Sufro) Desde hace una semana.
Since when have you been suffering?	(I've suffered) Since last week.
¿Cuánto tiempo hace que . . . ?	Hace + time + que +present tense.
How long has (have) . . . been . . . ?	(Present tense) For + time
¿Cuánto tiempo hace que Ud. sufre?	Hace dos días (que sufro).
(How long have you been suffering?)	(I've been suffering) For two days.

To express these questions in the past, use the imperfect:

QUESTION	ANSWER
¿Desde cuándo . . . Ud.?	(Sufría) desde hacía . . .
How long had . . . been . . . ?	(Imperfect) For + time.
¿Desde cuándo sufría Ud.?	(Sufría) Desde hacía un día.
How long had you been suffering?	(I had suffered) For one day.
¿Cuánto tiempo hacía que . . .	Hacía + time (+ que + imperfect).
How long had . . . been . . . ?	It had been + time.
¿Cuánto tiempo hacía que Ud. sufría.	Hacía una semana (que sufría).
How long had you been suffering?	It had been a week.

If you need to pay a visit to the doctor or dentist, you might ask the concierge, *el conserje*, at your hotel: *¿Dónde está el consultorio del doctor (del dentista) más cercano?* (Where is the nearest doctor's [dentist's] office?)

The doctor's office is referred to as *el consultorio*, the waiting room is *la sala de espera*, and the nurse is *el (la) enfermero(a)*.

Before paying the doctor's bill, *la nota* or *la factura*, remember to ask: *¿Podría darme un recibo para mi seguro médico?* (Could you please give me a receipt for my medical insurance?)

TIME'S UP!

1. Ask to have a prescription filled immediately.

2. Say that you're looking for aspirin.

3. Ask where they have tissues.

4. Say you have a headache.

5. Ask someone what's the matter.

6. Say that your feet hurt.

7. Say that you have a toothache.

8. You have the flu. Give your symptoms.

9. Say you suffer from dizziness.

10. Tell how long you've been suffering.

Clothing Needs

MASTER THESE SKILLS

- Selecting clothing

- Selecting sizes and getting alterations

- Expressing a problem

- Selecting colors

- Making a purchase

In this chapter you'll learn how to describe and buy clothing in just the right size. You'll also learn how to give your opinion about items you see, and how to use demonstrative pronouns.

CLOTHING

While traveling you'll undoubtedly want to do some shopping, or at least some window shopping. Articles of clothing (*la ropa*) that you may want to purchase are listed here:

CLOTHING/ACCESSORY	SPANISH
bathing suit	el traje de baño
belt	el cinturón
blouse	la blusa
boots	las botas
bra	el sostén
briefs	los calzoncillos
coat	el abrigo
dress	el vestido
gloves	los guantes
handkerchief	el pañuelo
hat	el sombrero
jacket	la chaqueta
jacket (men's)	el saco
jeans	los vaqueros
lingerie	la ropa interior femenina
pajamas	las pijámas
panties	los pantaloncillos de mujer, pantaletas
pants	los pantalones
panty hose, tights	las pantimedias
pocketbook	la bolsa
raincoat	el impermeable
robe	la bata
scarf	la bufanda
shirt	la camisa
shoes	los zapatos
shorts	los pantalones cortos

skirt	la falda
sneakers	los tenis
socks	los calcetines
sports coat	la chaqueta deportiva
stockings	las medias
suit	el traje
sweater	el suéter
tie	la corbata
T-shirt	la camiseta, la playera
underwear	la ropa interior
wallet	la cartera

If you are looking for a particular department in a store, ask for *el departamento de*: *¿Dónde está el departamento de ropa para hombres (mujeres)?* (Where is the department for men's [women's] clothing?)

To tell the salesperson what you are looking for, say:

I'm looking for . . .	Busco . . .
I need . . .	Necesito . . .
I would like . . .	Quisiera . . .

SIZES

Europe and Latin America use the metric system; consequently, their clothing sizes are different from ours. The conversion chart on page 246 will help determine the sizes you wear. You will be asked your size as follows:

| ¿Qué talla es Ud.? | What is your size (clothing)? |
| ¿Qué número calza Ud.? | What is your size (shoes)? |

To give an appropriate answer for clothing, say:

Soy una talla . . .	I wear . . .
Mi talla es . . .	My size is . . .
pequeña	small
mediana	medium
grande	large

Or give the number of your size: *Mi talla es treinta y ocho.* (I wear size 38.) For shoes, you would say: *Mi número es* . . . (I wear shoe size . . .)

Women's Shoes

American	5–5½	6–6½	7–7½	8–8½	9–9½	10–10½
Continental	36	37	38	39	40	41

Women's Dresses and Suits

American	0	2	4	6	8	10	12	14	16	18
Continental	28	30	32	34	36	38	40	42	44	46

Men's Shoes

American	7	7½	8	8½	9–9½	10–10½	11–11½
Continental	39	40	41	42	43	44	45

Men's Shirts

American	14	14½	15	15½	16	16½	17	17½
Continental	36	37	38	39	40	41	42	43

Men's Suits

American	34	36	38	40	42	44	46	48
Continental	44	46	48	50	52	54	56	58

If the item you select is too small or too large, you can ask for the appropriate size as follows:

Quisiera una talla más grande.	I would like the next larger size.
Quisiera una talla más pequeña.	I would like the next smaller size.

ALTERATIONS

There might be times when you buy something and need to have it altered, or need to repair the clothing you have. You will have to find a tailor, *un sastre* (oon sahs-treh), or a shoemaker, *un zapatero* (oon sah-pah-teh-roh), who can help you. The words listed below will help you describe the problem or the parts of the garment in need of servicing. An appropriate way to begin your conversation is: *¿Podría Ud. remendar este (esta, estos, estas)* . . . *por favor?* (Could you please alter [repair] this . . . ?)

PART	SPANISH
button	el botón
cuff (shirt)	el puño
cuff (pants)	la vuelta
heel	el tacón
hem	el bajo, el ruedo
lining	el forro
pleat	el pliegue, la pinza
pocket	el bolsillo
sleeve	la manga
waist	la cintura
zipper	el cierre

If you need a dressing room to change your clothes, ask: *¿Dónde está el vestuario?*

PROBLEMS

To explain a problem to a salesperson or a tailor, you would say:

No me gusta(n).	I don't like it (them).
No me queda(n) bien.	It doesn't (They don't) suit (fit) me.

And then give your reasons:

El (La) es demasiado . . .	It is too . . .
Los (Las) son demasiados . . .	They are too . . .

Remember to add an *s* to the adjective when using the plural:

La camisa es demasiada holgada.	The shirt is too baggy.
Los pantalones son demasiados holgados.	The pants are too baggy.

ADJECTIVE	SPANISH
baggy	holgado(a)
long	largo(a)
loose	holgado(a), suelto(a)

low-cut	escotado(a)
narrow	estrecho(a)
short	corto(a)
small	pequeño(a)
tight	apretado(a)
wide	ancho(a)

If you're still not satisfied, ask or say:

Do you have anything . . . ?	¿Tiene Ud. algo . . . ?
Show me something . . .	Muéstreme algo . . .

more inexpensive	más barato
more expensive	más caro
smaller	más pequeño
larger	más grande
shorter	más corto
longer	más largo
else	más

When your clothing has been adjusted to your liking, you might respond:

I like it (them).	Me gusta(n).
It fits me perfectly.	Me queda perfectamente.
It suits (fits) me.	Me queda bien.
It's elegant.	Es elegante.
It's nice.	Es agradable.
It's practical.	Es práctico.

COLORS

To describe your color preferences, use the colors in this list:

COLOR	SPANISH	COLOR	SPANISH
beige	beige	blue	azul
black	negro(a)	brown	café

gray	gris	purple	morado(a)
green	verde	red	rojo(a)
navy	azul marino	white	blanco(a)
orange	anaranjado(a)	yellow	amarillo(a)
pink	rosa		

To clarify a color as light, add the word *claro*. To clarify a color as dark, add the word *oscuro*.

| light green | verde claro |
| dark blue | azul oscuro |

To express your color preference, use the definite article (*el*, *la*, *los*, or *las*) that agrees with the noun and say:

| What color do you prefer? | I prefer red. |
| ¿Qué color prefiere? | Prefiero el rojo. |

To express what color you would like to have a garment, use the preposition *en* before the name of the color:

| What color shirt do you want? | ¿En qué color prefiere Ud. la camisa? |
| I want it in blue. | La prefiero en azúl. |

The definite article can be used to express "the one" as follows:

- *el* (*la*, *los*, *las*) + adjective : *la corbata azul* (the blue tie), *la azul* (the blue one).
- *el* (*la*, *los*, *las*) + *de*: *el suéter de lana* (the wool sweater), *el de lana* (the wool one).
- *el* (*la*, *los*, *las*) + *que*: *las camisas que compré* (the shirts I bought), *las que compré* (the ones I bought).

Remember to put the Spanish adjective in its proper place. Refer to Chapter 19:00 for a refresher course.

a white sweater	un suéter blanco
a red skirt	una falda roja
white sweaters	suéteres blancos
white skirts	faldas blancas

FABRICS

Tell your salesperson if you are interested in a certain fabric. The following list gives the materials (*las telas*) that are popular.

MATERIAL	SPANISH
cotton	el algodón
leather	el cuero, la piel
linen	el hilo
nylon	el nilón
silk	la seda
suede	la gamuza
wool	la lana

Use the preposition *de* to express that an item of clothing is made out of a certain material: *Quisiera un vestido de seda.* (I'd like a silk dress.)

THE NEUTER *LO*

The neuter *lo* can be used with an adjective, with *que*, or with a past participle to express *what* (in the sense of *that which*) when discussing things you can buy, or in common, general situations:

- *lo* + adjective: *Compro sólo lo necesario.* (I only buy what is necessary.)
- *lo* + *que*: *Muéstreme lo que compró.* (Show me what you bought.)

PATTERNS

When selecting a garment, the pattern can make a difference in how you look. Use the phrase below with the patterns listed to select what will be best for you:

I need something . . .   Necesito algo . . .

PATTERN	SPANISH
checked	de cuadros
in a solid color	de color liso
in plaid	de tartán
striped	con rayas

SALES

If you're interested in purchasing something on sale, you would ask:

Are there . . . ?	¿Hay . . . ?
discounts	ganga, rebajas
sales	saldos, ventas

MAKING A PURCHASE

Don't forget to ask for the price:

¿Cuánto cuesta . . . ?	How much is . . .
¿Cuánto cuestan . . . ?	How much are . . .

If you want to have an item of clothing custom-made, use the verb *hacer* followed by an infinitive, meaning "to make (have) someone do something," "to have something done," "to cause to do," or "to be done." The construction *mandar* + *hacer* may also be used:

Ella hace tejer un suéter.	She is having a sweater knit.
Él manda hacer un traje.	He is having a suit made.

Hacer and the infinitive form a unit. All nouns follow this unit and all pronouns precede it.

Me hizo comprar este abrigo.	He made me buy this coat.
Me lo hizo comprar.	He made me buy it.

GETTING MEASURED

If you need your measurements taken, speak to the tailor, *el sastre*, or the dressmaker, *el (la) modisto(a)*, and ask: *¿Podría tomarme las medidas?* (Could you please take my measurements?)

TIME'S UP!

1. Tell what size pants you wear.

2. Give your shoe size.

3. Tell someone his suit is in style.

4. Ask for the children's department.

5. Describe what you are wearing today.

6. Ask for the dressing room.

7. Ask to have your pants altered.

8. Ask the salesperson if you can see something else.

9. Ask the salesperson to show you a red and white checked shirt.

10. Ask if there are any sales today.

Taking Care of Travel Needs

MASTER THESE SKILLS

- Navigating the airport
- Getting to the train station
- Traveling by car
- Dealing with problems on the road
- Dealing with an accident

In this chapter you'll learn how to get around the airport and then around the country by train and by car. You'll also learn how to use the passive voice.

AT THE AIRPORT

Although there are plenty of signs pointing you in various directions in an airport, it's a good idea to become acquainted with the words that may be unfamiliar to you. The terms you need in order to get around an airport quickly and efficiently are listed below. To get your bearings, start with this expression: *¿Dónde está(n)* . . . *?* (Where is [are] . . . ?)

TERM	SPANISH
airline	la aerolínea
airport	el aeropuerto
arrival	la llegada
baggage claim area	el reclamo de equipaje
bathrooms	los baños, los servicios
(to) cancel	cancelar
carry-on luggage	el equipaje de mano
customs	la aduana
departure	la salida
destination	el destino
exit	la salida
flight	el vuelo
domestic	nacional
international	internacional
gate	la puerta
information	la información
landing	el aterrizaje
currency exchange	el cambio de dinero
passport control	el control de pasaportes
suitcase	la maleta
take-off	el despegue
terminal	la terminal aerea
ticket	el boleto
trip	el viaje

> ▽ **NOTE**
> ....
> To express that you are flying standby, say: *Tengo un billete (un boleto)*
> *en lista de espera.* (I have a stand-by ticket.)

Some key questions you may want to ask include:

Is the flight late in arriving (departing)?	¿El vuelo llega (sale) con retraso?
Is there a delay?	¿Hay una demora?
Where does this flight originate?	¿En dónde se origina este vuelo?
Is the flight canceled?	¿Está anulado este vuelo?
At what time is take-off?	¿A qué hora sale el avión?
Are there empty seats?	¿Hay asientos libres?
Is the flight full?	¿El vuelo está completo (lleno)?
Are there any stopovers? Where?	¿Hace escalas? ¿Dónde?
What cities does this airline serve?	¿A cuáles ciudades presta servicio esta línea?

You should also familiarize yourself with the words and phrases describing the inside of the plane. You can never tell when these terms will come in handy:

TERM	SPANISH
airplane	el avión
aisle	el pasillo
baggage compartment	el compartimento de equipaje
blanket	la manta
crew	la tripulación
life vest	el chaleco salvavidas
passenger	el pasajero
seat	el asiento
seatbelt	el cinturón de seguridad
tray	la bandeja

AT THE TRAIN STATION

The following list gives you the words you need to know for train travel.

WORD	SPANISH
compartment	el departamento
smoking	fumadores
nonsmoking	no fumadores
platform	el andén
schedule	el horario
station	la estación
ticket	el billete
first class	de primera clase
second class	de segunda clase
one-way	de ida
round-trip	de ida y vuelta

TRAVEL BY CAR

Many tourists opt to see the countryside and discover out-of-the-way places by renting a car at a local car agency (*un alquiler de carros*). Use the phrases below if this is your plan:

I would like to rent a . . .

Quisiera alquilar una . . . (make of car).

I prefer automatic transmission.

Prefiero el cambio automático.

How much does it cost per day (per week) (per kilometer)?

¿Cuánto cuesta por día (por semana) (por kilómetro)?

How much is the insurance?

¿Cuánto cuesta el seguro?

Is the mileage included?

¿Está incluida el kilometraje?

Do you accept credit cards? Which ones?

¿Acepta Ud. tarjetas de crédito? ¿Cuáles?

The Car's Exterior and Interior

Familiarize yourself with the words listed below in case you have to describe a problem with the car's exterior.

EXTERIOR PARTS	SPANISH
battery	la batería
gas tank	el tanque de gasolina
headlight	el faro delantero
hood	la capota
hubcap	el tapacubos
license plate	la placa de matrícula
motor	el motor
muffler	el silenciador
rearview mirror	el retrovisor
tail light	el faro trasero
tire	la goma, la llanta
transmission	la transmisión
trunk	la cajuela, el baúl
wheel	la rueda
windshield	el parabrisas
windshield wiper	el limpiaparabrisas

Once you've made sure that everything on the outside is in good working order, check the car's interior and refer to any problems you have by using the terms below.

INTERIOR PARTS	SPANISH
accelerator	el acelerador
air bag	la bolsa de aire
brakes	los frenos
clutch pedal	el embrague
turn signal	la direccional
gear shift	el cambio de velocidades

glove compartment	la guantera
ignition	la ignición
steering wheel	el volante

▽ NOTE

Un semáforo or *una luz de tráfico* refers to a traffic light and is often followed by *rojo* (red) or *verde* (green). The number of lights you have to pass is often used in giving directions: *Doble a la derecha en el segundo semáforo.* (Turn right at the second light.) *Una carretera de peaje (de cuota)* is a toll road.

Measuring Distances

In Europe, distance is measured in kilometers. Refer to the following list for the approximate equivalents.

MILES	KILOMETERS
0.62	1
3.1	5
6.2	10
12.4	20
31	50
62	100

Problems on the Road

Here are some phrases you will need if you have car problems:

Could you help me please?	¿Podría ayudarme por favor?
The car has broken down.	El coche se ha averiado.
Where is the nearest gas station (garage)?	¿Dónde está la gasolinería (el garaje) más cercano?
. . . doesn't (don't) work.	. . . no funciona(n).
Please check . . .	Inspeccione Ud. por favor . . .
The car is overheating.	El coche se calienta.
There's a flat tire.	Hay una llanta ponchada.
The battery is dead.	La batería está descargada.

There is a leak.	Hay un agujero.
Can you fix it (immediately)?	¿Podría repararlo (la) en seguida?
When will it be ready?	¿Cuándo estará listo?

To get your gas tank filled with the proper gas, say: *Llénelo* . . . (Fill it up . . .)

with regular	con normal
with super	con super
with unleaded	sin plomo
with diesel	con diesel

Accidents

Should you bear witness to or be involved in an accident (*un accidente*), you may need the following verbs in order to have a conversation with a police officer (*un policía*) whose English is limited. Refer to *el peatón* if a pedestrian is involved.

VERB	SPANISH	VERB	SPANISH
to collide	chocar(se)	to run over	atropellar
to drive	conducir, manejar	to signal	señalar
to hit	chocar (con)	to skid	patinar
to hurt	hacer daño a	to turn around	dar una vuelta
to knock down	atropellar a	to yield	ceder
to park	estacionar		

Should you need to refer to the parts of the road, use the words and expressions in this list.

PART	SPANISH	PART	SPANISH
crosswalk	el punto de cruce	lane	el carril
entrance	la entrada	road surface	la superficie
exit	la salida	shoulder	el saliente
intersection	el crucero	traffic circle	la glorieta

THE PASSIVE VOICE

In the active voice, the subject generally performs the action. In the passive voice, the subject is acted upon.

Active: The car knocked her down.

Passive: She was knocked down by a car.

The passive construction in Spanish resembles English: subject + form of *ser* + past participle + *por* + agent (doer) if mentioned.

The car was driven by that man.	El coche fue conducido por este hombre.
The truck has been hit.	La camioneta ha sido chocada.
The driver will be arrested.	El conductor será arrestado.

In the passive, because the past participle is used like an adjective, it agrees in number and gender with the subject: *Las mujeres fueron atropelladas.* (The women were run over.)

The reflexive construction may substitute for the passive, because the passive is used less frequently in Spanish than in English. Note that the subject usually follows the verb:

Spanish is spoken here.	Aquí se habla español.
The cars were bought.	Se compraron los coches.

 TIME'S UP!

1. Ask for help.

2. Ask when your flight departs.

3. Ask if your flight is cancelled.

4. Say you need a round-trip ticket.

5. Tell what car you'd like to rent.

6. Say that your car has broken down.

7. Ask for the nearest service station.

8. Ask to have your car filled with regular gas.

9. Say that two cars collided.

10. Say that a dog was hit by a car.

Managing
Your Money

MASTER THESE SKILLS

- Attending to your banking needs

- Playing the stock market

- Using present and perfect participles

In this chapter you'll learn all the terms necessary to conduct banking and stock market transactions.

AT THE BANK

There are any number of reasons to go to a bank, *un banco*, in a foreign country. As a tourist, you may simply want to exchange money. For those who conduct business, however, you will have deposits and withdrawals to make. And for the adventuresome few, the purchase of vacation or retirement property requires a knowledge of more sophisticated banking terms.

The following is a list of some banking expressions that should prove useful in the situations mentioned above:

What are the banking hours?	¿Cuál es el horario de trabajo?
I would like . . .	Quisiera . . .
to change some money	cambiar dinero
to make a deposit	hacer un depósito
to make a withdrawal	hacer un retiro
to take out a loan	pedir un préstamo
to cash a check	cobrar un cheque
to open an account	abrir una cuenta
to close an account	cerrar una cuenta

What is today's exchange rate?

Cuál es la tasa de cambio del dolár hoy?

What is the status of my acount?

¿Cuál es el estado de mi cuenta?

Is there a financial assistant who can help me?

¿Hay un especialista financiero que pueda ayudarme (aconsejarme)?

Do you have an automated teller machine?

¿Tiene Ud. un cajero automático?

Can I take out money twenty-four hours a day?

¿Puedo retirar (sacar) dinero las veinticuatro horas del día?

What is the transaction fee?

¿Cuál es la comisión por la transacción?

I'd like to get a personal loan.

Quisiera obtener un préstamo personal.

I'd like to take out a mortgage.

Quisiera obtener una hipoteca.

What is the time period of the loan?

¿Cuál es el plazo del préstamo?

How much are the monthly payments?

¿De cuánto son las mensualidades?

What is the interest rate?

¿Cuál es la tasa (el tipo) de interés?

Is it a fixed or variable rate?

¿Es una tasa (un tipo) fija (fijo) o variable?

What are the terms of payment?

¿Cuáles son las condiciones de pago?

Banking Terms

If your financial needs are more specific, consult the following list for the necessary banking terms:

TERM	SPANISH
account	la cuenta
automated teller	el cajero automático
balance	el saldo
bank	el banco
bill (money)	el billete
change (coins)	la moneda
change	el cambio

check	el cheque
checking account	la cuenta básica
credit	el crédito
customer	el cliente
debt	la deuda
deposit	el depósito, el ingreso
exchange rate	la tasa de cambio
interest rate	la tasa de interés
(to) invest	invertir
loan	el préstamo
payment	el pago
savings account	la cuenta de ahorros
signature	la firma
teller	el cajero
traveler's check	el cheque de viajero
window	la ventanilla
withdrawal	el retiro

THE STOCK MARKET

The words and phrases in this list could be useful if you like to dabble in foreign markets.

TERM	SPANISH
asset	el activo
business	el negocio
capital	el capital
dividend	el dividendo
fees	los gastos
foreign exchange	el mercado de divisas
fund	el fondo
growth	el crecimiento
investment	la inversión

market	la bolsa
market price	el precio de mercado (corriente)
mutual fund	el fondo mutualista
rate	el índice, la tasa
revenue	el ingreso
security	la acción
stock	la acción, el valor
stock broker	el (la) agente de bolsa

You're in the market. You watch the ticket tape every day and often place a call to your agent. Someday you might need these useful stock phrases:

Are my stocks going up?	¿Están avanzando mis acciones ?
Are my stocks going down?	¿Están bajando mis acciones?
What is the price per share?	¿Cuál es el precio por acción?
What is the commission rate?	¿Cuál es la tasa (el tipo) de comisión?
Do you have a prospectus?	¿Tiene Ud. un prospecto?
Do you know a good stockbroker?	¿Conoce Ud. a un buen agente de bolsa?
What is the status of my account?	¿Cuál es el estado de mi cuenta?
Are my investments secure?	¿Están aseguradas mis inversiones?

PRESENT PARTICIPLES

The present participle is not used in the same way in Spanish that it is in English. Refer to Chapter 22:00 for the formation of the present participle (*el gerundio*) in Spanish. Many English words ending in *-ing* are not equivalent to Spanish present participles (usually ending in *-ando* or *-iendo*):

Cashing this check is impossible.	Cobrar este cheque es imposible.
I love accounting.	Me gusta la contabilidad.

Present participles may be used as follows:

- With the verbs *estar*, *seguir*, *continuar*, and other verbs of motion to show that an action is currently taking place or continuing at the moment indicated:

We are looking for a bank.	Estamos buscando un banco.
Mr. López keeps on speaking.	El señor López sigue hablando.
I'll continue investing.	Continuaré invirtiendo.
She left, counting her money.	Ella salió contando su dinero.

- To express *by* + an English present participle: *Trabajando, ahorrará mucho.* (By working, you will save a lot.)
- As a verb:

Wanting to save money, I opened a bank account.

Deseando ahorrar dinero, abrí una cuenta en el banco.

You left, forgetting your bank book.

Ud. salió, olvidando su libreta de ahorros.

PERFECT PARTICIPLES

The perfect participle is formed with the present participle of the appropriate helping verb and the past participle, and is used to show that one action took place before another:

Having sold his stocks, he bought himself a new car.

Habiendo vendido sus valores, se compró un coche nuevo.

Having gone to the bank early, they avoided long lines.

Habiendo ido al banco temprano, evitaron largas filas.

Note that the present participles of *estar*, *ir*, and *venir* are not used to form the present progressive tense. Instead, use the correct simple tense:

You're being silly.	Eres ridículo.
He was going to the movies.	Iba al cine.
We're coming soon.	Venimos pronto.

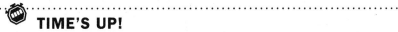

TIME'S UP!

Try to perform the following tasks without looking back in the lesson:

1. Say that you have to go to the bank.

2. Say that you would like to cash some traveler's checks.

3. Ask if they have an automated teller machine.

4. Ask if it's open twenty-four hours.

5. Say that you'd like to buy some stocks.

6. Ask if there's a financial assistant to help you.

7. Tell someone that one learns a lot by traveling.

8. Tell someone that you are going to the bank.

9. Say that they came in laughing.

10. Say that, having entered the bank, you went to the teller.

The Language
of Business

MASTER THESE SKILLS

. . . .

- Fulfilling your stationery, photocopying, and faxing needs

- Fulfilling your computer needs

- Conducting business

- Using prepositions before infinitives

. . . .

In this lesson you'll learn how to manage
in a business setting, using fax machines,
photocopiers, and computers. You'll also
learn about verbs that need and don't
need prepositions before other verbs.

STATIONERY NEEDS

The list that follows presents the necessary stationery supplies that can be purchased *en la papelería* (at the stationery store). You might begin by saying: *¿Dónde puedo comprar* . . . (Where can I buy . . .)

Supply	Spanish
ball-point pen	un bolígrafo
calculator (solar)	una calculadora (solar)
envelopes	los sobres
notebook	un cuaderno
paper	los papeles
paper clips	los sujetapapeles
pen (fountain)	una pluma
pencil	un lápiz
scotch tape	la cinta adhesiva
stationery	el papel de cartas

▽ **NOTE**

The file of information that is kept in a company regarding its accounts or customers is called *un expediente*.

PHOTOCOPIES

La fotocopiadora (copier) is an essential machine to any business. Many stationery stores also provide photocopying services, often at reasonable prices to students, travelers, and business people on the go. The phrases below will help you get the copy of the document, paper, or receipt you need:

I would like to make a photocopy of this paper (this document).

Quisiera hacer una fotocopia de este papel (este documento).

What is the cost per page?

¿Cuánto cuesta por página?

The verb *mandar* (conjugated) + *hacer* is used to express "to have something done." Use the indirect object *le* or *les* (for him, her, or them) or the preposition *para* + the name of the person for whom the work is being done, or the correct prepositional pronoun:

I'm having a photocopy made for them.	Yo les mando hacer una fotocopia.
I'm having a photocopy made for my boss.	Yo mando hacer una fotocopia para mi jefe.
I'm having a photocopy made for him.	Yo mando hacer una fotocopia para él.

FAXES

Being able to send a fax is a convenient service that allows for efficient, inexpensive, and rapid transmittal and receipt of important information. Therefore, fax service has become almost indispensable. The phrases below will help you with your fax needs:

Do you have a fax machine?	¿Tiene Ud. un fax?
What is your fax number?	¿Cuál es su número de fax?
I'd like to send a fax.	Quisiera mandar un fax.
Fax it to me.	Envíemelo por fax.
I didn't get your fax.	No recibí su fax.
Did you receive my fax?	¿Recibió Ud. mi fax?
Please send it again.	¿Puede Ud. enviármelo otra vez?
Please confirm receipt of the fax.	Favor de confirmar la recepción del fax.

COMPUTERS

A working knowledge of computers is a must in today's world. The phrases below will get you started if you need basic computer information from another individual.

The following computer terms are essential:

to computerize	informatizar
computer science	la informática
computer scientist	el (la) informático(a)

What kind of computer do you have?

¿Qué sistema (tipo, género) de computadora tiene Ud.?

What operating system are you using?

¿Qué sistema operador usa Ud. (está Ud. usando)?

What word processing program are you using?

¿Qué procesador de textos usa Ud. (está Ud. usando)?

Do you have . . . ?

¿Tiene Ud. . . . ?

Do you use . . .?

¿Usa Ud. (Está Ud. usando) . . . ?

What is your e-mail address?

¿Cuál es su dirección de correo electrónico?

The list below gives you the terms and phrases you need to speak about your computer and the field of computer science.

WORD	SPANISH
CD-ROM disk	el disco optinúmerico
CPU	la unidad central
database	la base de datos
desktop computer	el ordenador, el (la) computador(a)
diskette	el disquete
e-mail	el correo electrónico
file	el fichero
floppy disk	el disco flexible
hardware	el hardware
inkjet	(de) tinta
keyboard	el teclado
laptop computer	la computadora portátil
laser	(de) laser
modem	el modem
mouse	el ratón
network	la red
operating system	el sistema operador
scanner	el scanner

screen	la pantalla
search engine	el buscador, el navegador
software	el software

CONDUCTING BUSINESS

The following vocabulary is for those readers who are serious about conducting business in a Spanish-speaking country.

WORD	SPANISH
bill	la factura
business	los negocios
consumer	el consumidor
contract	el contrato
cost	el precio
discount	el descuento, la rebaja
expenditures	los gastos
(to) export	exportar
(to) import	importar
interest rates	la taza de interés
job	el trabajo
manager	el gerente
merchandise	la mercancía
office	la oficina
owner	el propietario
partner	el socio
(to) pay	pagar
product	el producto
property	la propiedad
raise	el aumento
salary	el sueldo
shipment	el envío
tax	el impuesto

Use the following terms to refer to businesspeople:

un hombre de negocios   a businessman

una mujer de negocios   a businesswoman

PREPOSITIONS BEFORE INFINITIVES

In Spanish, the verb form that follows a preposition is the infinitive.

Llega a hablar español.	He succeeds in speaking Spanish.
Se alegra de obtener un trabajo.	He is glad to get a job.
Tardan en llegar.	They are delayed in arriving.
Yo cuento con comprar esas acciones.	I am counting on buying those stocks.

This next list contains some of the more common verbs requiring *a* before the infinitive.

VERB	MEANING	VERB	MEANING
aprender	learn to	ir	go to
ayudar	help to	ponerse	begin to
comenzar	begin to	regresar	return to (again)
decidirse	decide to	salir	go out to
empezar	begin to	venir	come to
enseñar	teach to	volver (ue)	return to (again)

Some of the more common verbs requiring *de* before the infinitive are listed here:

VERB	MEANING	VERB	MEANING
acabar	have just	olvidarse	forget
acordarse (ue)	remember to	tratar	try to
alegrarse	be glad		

Some of the more common verbs requiring *en* before the infinitive are:

VERB	MEANING	VERB	MEANING
consentir	consent to	insistir	insist on
consistir	consist of	tardar	delay in

Some of the more common verbs requiring *con* before the infinitive are:

VERB	MEANING	VERB	MEANING
amenazar	threaten	soñar (ue)	dream of
contar (ue)	count on		

The following prepositions are used before infinitives:

PREPOSITION	MEANING	PREPOSITION	MEANING
a	at, to	después de	after
al	upon, on	en	in, on, of
antes de	before	en vez de	instead of
con	with	hasta	until
de	of, to, from	sin	without

Él descansa en lugar de trabajar.   He rests instead of working.

Ella telefonea antes de enviar un fax.   She phones before sending a fax.

A verb + preposition + infinitive must have the same subject. If there are different subjects, *que* is used and a conjugated verb form (often in the subjunctive) is used instead of the infinitive:

I insist on working.   I insist that you work.

Insisto en trabajar.   Insisto en que Ud. trabaje.

I'm leaving after eating.   I'm going after you eat.

Me voy después de comer.   Me voy después de que Ud. coma.

The verbs below are used without a preposition before the infinitive.

SPANISH	MEANING	SPANISH	MEANING
deber	must, have to	pensar	intend
dejar	allow	poder	be able to
esperar	hope	preferir (ie)	prefer
hacer	make, have something done	querer, desear	want, wish
necesitar	need	saber	know (how)
oír	hear	ver	see

El jefe los deja salir.   The boss allows them to leave.

Ella debe comprar una computadora.   She must buy a computer.

⏰ TIME'S UP!

Try not to look back at the tables, and fill in a preposition, if needed:

1. Lo ayudo ____ completar su trabajo.

2. Queremos ____ hacer negocios.

3. Nosotros acabamos ____ regresar.

4. Insisto ____ recibir un descuento.

5. Ellos sueñan ____ viajar.

6. Él aprende ____ hablar español.

7. Trato ____ resolver el problema.

8. Ellos cuentan ____ ganar mucho dinero.

9. ¿Sabes ____ utilizar una computadora?

10. Ella sale ____ comprar disquetes.

The Final Countdown

Here's your final opportunity to see if you've mastered enough Spanish to get by on your own. Imagine you are in a Spanish-speaking country and give an appropriate response to each situation.

1. You are at a party and strike up a conversation with an interesting person. What information do you give about yourself?

    _____

2. You are talking to someone who is speaking too fast. What might you say?

    _____

3. You call a friend on the phone. Someone else answers. How do you respond?

    _____

4. You want to invite a friend to go to a museum with you. What suggestions would you make?

    _____

5. You are lost in the streets of Spain. You stop a passerby and ask for directions. What might you ask?

    _____

6. You don't like your hotel room. Tell this to the concierge and express why.

    _____

7. You are in a gift shop looking for a gift for a friend. Ask a salesperson for help.

    _____

8. You realize you have lost your passport. What do you say to the police officer?

_____

9. Tell a friend about your favorite leisure activity and why you like it.

_____

10. You are interviewing for a job in a Spanish firm. What do you tell the head of personnel about yourself?

_____

11. You are in a park in Mexico. Convince some acquaintances to engage in a sport.

_____

12. You are in a clothing store. Tell the salesperson what you are looking for.

_____

13. You are going to the movies with a friend. You want to see a spy movie but your friend wants to see a comedy. Convince your friend to see the spy movie.

_____

14. You are at the airport and have learned that your flight is delayed. What do you say to the airline clerk?

_____

15. You want to change your money into the currency of the country you are visiting. What do you say to the bank teller?

   _____

16. A customs officer at the airport asks what you have purchased on your trip. How do you respond?

   _____

17. You are having dinner in a restaurant. Tell the waiter what you want.

   _____

18. A friend has invited you to a bullfight. Express your feelings about going.

   _____

19. You want to make a dinner reservation at a fine restaurant. What do you say to the person answering the phone?

   _____

20. You rented a car and are having problems with it. What do you say to the rental agent?

   _____

21. You want to go to a concert. What information do you ask for on the phone?

   _____

22. You have an appointment in town. When you realize you will be late, you phone your acquaintance. What do you say?

_____

23. You don't feel well. What do you tell the doctor?

_____

24. Your friend has a cousin for you to meet. What questions do you ask about this person?

_____

Answer Key

Since there is almost always more than one way to say something, the statements and questions given as responses are just suggestions.

dehs-pah-see-yoh pohr fah-bohr
4. keh dee-hoh rreh-pee-tah loh pohr fah-bohr
5. kee-see-yeh-rah kam-bee-yahr mees doh-lah-rehs ehn
   eh-yoo-rohs pohr fah-bohr
6. pehr-doh-neh-meh dohn-deh ehs-tah lah ehm-bah-hah-dah
   ah-meh-ree-kah-nah
7. noh meh see-yehn-toh bee-yehn dohn-deh ehs-tah lah
   oh-fee-see-nah dehl meh-dee-koh lah mahs sehr-kah-nah
8. poh-dree-yahs ah-yoo-dahr-meh pohr fah-bohr pehr-dee oon
   doh-koo-mehn-toh eem-pohr-tahn-teh
9. kwahn-toh kwehs-tahn ehs-tohs pahn-tah-loh-nehs neh-grohs
   ee ehs-tahs kah-mee-sahs rroh-hahs
10. neh-seh-see-toh oo-nah koo-chah-rah oon teh-neh-dohr ee oon
    koo-chee-yoh grah-see-yahs

23:00
. . . .

Part I
1. el banco
2. ese plato
3. esta catedral
4. la flor
5. aquel hombre

Part II
6. un amigo
7. este francés
8. el actor
9. este policía
10. aquel profesor

22:00

1. estoy
2. soy
3. tengo
4. quiero
5. puedo
6. busco
7. mido
8. sustituyo
9. viene
10. vamos

21:00

1. tenía
2. iba
3. era
4. prestaba
5. jugaba
6. pidió
7. quería
8. estaba
9. fuimos
10. conocí

20:00

Part I
1. seré
2. querré
3. tendré
4. viviré
5. conduciré

Part II
6. pondría
7. daría
8. haría
9. compraría
10. diría

19:00

1. Él piensa profundamente.
2. La señora López es una mujer alegre.
3. Es un buen hombre.
4. Hablan frecuentemente.
5. Ella compra demasiados vestidos.
6. Necesito más dinero.
7. Es la primera vez.
8. Ellos trabajan facilmente.
9. Necesito cien dólares.
10. Ellos escriben rápidamente.

18:00

1. Buenos días, señor López.
2. Mucho gusto en conocerle.
3. Me llamo John Smith.
4. Estoy bien, gracias.
5. Soy de los Estados Unidos.
6. Vivo en Nueva York.
7. Soy americano.
8. Voy a España.
9. Le presento a mi esposa, Marta.
10. Adiós. Hasta luego.

17:00

1. ¿Quiere ir al restaurante conmigo?
2. ¿Puedes ir al circo con mi familia y yo?
3. Deseo ir al club.
4. ¡Por supuesto! Quiero ir a la catedral.
5. Lo siento mucho. No puedo ir a la feria. Estoy muy cansado(a).
6. Es imposible. No tengo ganas de ir al centro comercial.
7. No puedo ir al zoológico porque estoy muy ocupado(a).
8. No puedo ir al jardín porque no estoy libre.
9. ¿Ir al cine? Quizás.
10. ¿Ir a la fuente? Lo que prefieras.

16:00

1. Tengo veinte años.
2. ¿Cuál es la fecha de hoy?
3. Mi cumpleaños es el once de julio de mil novecientos cuarenta y siete.
4. ¿Que días esta cerrado el museo?
5. Estamos en el verano.
6. Hoy es el diez de agosto.
7. ¿Cuándo quieres salir?
8. Son las dos y media.
9. ¿A qué hora nos vemos?
10. La película empieza a las ocho y cuarto.

15:00

1. Estoy mirando solamente.
2. Quisiera comprar un coche para mi familia.
3. Ud. tiene que escuchar.
4. Ud. debe ir a la panadería.
5. Debiera hacer las camas.
6. Ud. me debe cinco dólares.
7. Es necesario ir de compras.
8. Quiero que saque la basura.
9. Quiero ir a la librería.
10. ¡No vacile! Tiene que lavar el coche.

14:00

1. ¿Por qué no vamos al restaurante?
2. ¿Tiene(s) ganas de ir al cine?
3. ¿Quieres ir de compras?
4. Vayamos al Prado.
5. Continúe caminando tres cuadras.
6. No vaya todo derecho.
7. ¡Despiértate temprano!
8. El Morro es fenomenal.
9. En mi opinión, es estupendo.
10. Ir al teatro es aburrido.

13:00

1. ¿Cuál es su nombre?/¿Cómo se llama Ud.?
2. ¿Cuál es su dirección?
3. ¿Cuál es su número de teléfono?
4. ¿De dónde es?
5. ¿Cuántos años tiene?
6. ¿Hay un restaurante por aquí?
7. ¿Cuál de las películas prefiere Ud.?
8. ¿Cuál es su profésion?
9. ¿Cuánto cuesta el periódico?
10. Lo siento pero no comprendo.

12:00

1. Sí, quiero ir al cine esta noche.
2. No, no tengo ganas de comer en un restaurante.
3. No, no fumo.
4. Me llamo Juan.
5. Vivo en Pittsburgh.
6. Mi número de teléfono es cinco, cinco, cinco, nueve, dos, uno, tres.
7. Tengo treinta años.
8. Cuesta dos mil quinientos dólares.
9. Prefiero (name two movies).
10. Hay plumas y papeles en mi escritorio.

11:00

1. ¿Puede Ud. ayudarme, por favor?
2. ¿A qué hora abre Ud.?
3. ¿Puede darme un recibo?
4. ¿Cuánto cuesta un sello para una carta por correo aéreo?
5. ¿Puede Ud. darme un corte de pelo?
6. ¿Puede Ud. lavar en seco mi traje?
7. ¿Puede Ud. darme otra lentilla de contacto?
8. Necesito una película de treinta y seis exposiciones.
9. ¿Puede Ud. arreglar mi reloj?
10. ¿Dónde está la comisaría de policía más cercana?

10:00

1. ¿Te parece ir a la playa?
2. ¿Qué hay en la televisión?
3. ¿Qué tipo de película están pasando?
4. Quisiera ver una comedia.
5. ¿Le gustaría ir conmigo al campo hacer una gira campestre?
6. Te quiero.
7. A mí me gustan los regalos.
8. Me falta una pluma.
9. Muéstremelo, por favor.
10. Me encanta mucho esta obra de teatro.

09:00

1. Vamos a nadar.
2. ¿Juega Ud. al golf?
3. ¿Quiere Ud. jugar al tenis conmigo?
4. Me faltan patines.
5. ¿Podrías prestarme una bicicleta?
6. ¿Qué tiempo hace hoy?
7. Hoy hace mucho calor. Hay sol. No está nublado.
   Hay una temperatura de ochenta grados.
8. No me gusta jugar al tenis porque es demasiado difícil.
9. Dudo que mi amigo juegue al baloncesto.
10. Estoy seguro que va a hacer buen tiempo.

08:00

1. Un perro es más grande que un gato.
2. El español es más fácil que las matemáticas.
3. Mi hermana es menos grande que mi hermano.
4. Cristina es la más bonita de mis amigas.
5. Mi esposo corre menos rápidamente que mi hijo.
6. Julio trabaja lo más diligentemente.
7. Tengo más trabajo que Ud.
8. Mi madre es tan alta como yo.
9. Tengo tanta paciencia como mi amiga.
10. Pienso que este libro es el mejor que pueda comprar.

07:00

1. ¿Hay un garaje?
2. Quisiera una habitación con vista al mar.
3. Necesito otra almohada.
4. ¡Qué habitación tan magnífica!
5. ¡Que entren!
6. Me quedaré en este hotel con tal de que tenga una cancha de tenis.
7. Busco un hotel que sea lujoso.
8. Hay alguien que hable inglés.
9. Esa es la habitación que quiero.
10. Tengo todo lo que necesito.

06:00

1. Necesito quinientos gramos de carne, por favor.
2. Para empezar, quiero caracoles.
3. Me gustan las zanahorias.
4. Quiero mi rosbif a término medio.
5. Quisiera un flan, por favor.
6. Necesito otra copa porque la mía está sucia.
7. Quisiera reservar una mesa en la terraza para esta noche a las nueve y media para cuatro personas.
8. ¿Cuál es el plato del día?
9. No puedo tomar productos lácteos.
10. La cuenta, por favor.

05:00

1. ¿Podría Ud. preparar esta receta en seguida?
2. Busco aspirinas.
3. ¿Dónde hay pañuelos de papel?
4. Tengo un dolor de cabeza.
5. ¿Qué le pasa?
6. Me duelen los pies.
7. Tengo un dolor de muelas.
8. Tengo una gripe. Estoy tosiendo mucho. Me siento mal. No puedo dormir. Me duele todo el cuerpo.
9. Sufro del vértigo.
10. Hace dos semanas que yo sufro.

04:00

1. Llevo la talla treinta y dos.
2. Mi número es siete y medio.
3. Su traje está de moda.
4. ¿Dónde está el departamento de niños?
5. Llevo pantalones negros y una camisa azul.
6. ¿Dónde está el vestuario?
7. ¿Podría remendar mis pantalones, por favor?
8. ¿Puedo ver algo más?
9. Muéstréme por favor una camisa de cuadros rojas y blancas.
10. ¿Hay gangas hoy?

03:00

1. ¿Puede Ud. ayudarme, por favor?
2. ¿Cuándo sale mi vuelo?
3. ¿Está anulado este vuelo?
4. Necesito un billete de ida y vuelta.
5. Quisiera alquilar un Honda.
6. Mi coche se ha averiado.
7. ¿Dónde está el garaje más cercano?
8. Llénelo con normal.
9. Dos coches se chocaron.
10. Un perro fue chocado por un coche.

02:00

1. Tengo que ir al banco.
2. Quisiera cobrar algunos cheques de viajero.
3. ¿Tiene Ud. un cajero automático?
4. ¿Está abierto las veinticuatro horas al día?
5. Quisiera comprar algunos valores.
6. Hay un especialista financiero que pueda ayudarme?
7. Se aprende mucho viajando.
8. Voy al banco.
9. Entraron riendo.
10. Habiendo entrado en el banco, fui al cajero.

01:00

· ·

1. a
2. —
3. de
4. en
5. con
6. a
7. de
8. con
9. —
10. a

00:00

· ·

1. Buenos días. Me llamo John Smith. Soy americano. Mucho gusto en conocerle.
2. Por favor, hable Ud. más despacio. No comprendo nada.
3. Diga. Habla Ramón. ¿Está Isabel? ¿Puedo hablar con ella?
4. ¿No quieres ir conmigo al museo de arte moderno? Hay una exposición magnífica de las obras de Picasso.
5. Quiero ir a mi hotel y estoy perdido. ¿Sabe Ud. dónde está la Avenida Quince?
6. No me gusta mi habitación porque no hay vista al mar. ¿Podría Ud. cambiarla?
7. Busco un regalo para mi amigo(a). Puede Ud. recomendar algo. A él (ella) le gustan mucho los deportes.
8. ¿Puede Ud. ayudarme? He perdido mi pasaporte. ¿Dónde está el consulado americano?
9. Me gusta mucho jugar al tenis. Es un deporte muy divertido porque siempre juego con mis amigos.
10. Soy una persona muy diligente y trabajadora. Siempre llego temprano a la oficina y hago todo lo necesario.
11. ¿Por qué no jugamos al fútbol? Hace buen tiempo y tenemos bastante jugadores. Vamos a divertirnos mucho.
12. Busco pantalones negros en lana. Mi talla es cuarenta y seis. También busco una camisa azul de talla mediana con rayas blancas verticales en algodón.
13. No me gustan las comedias. Pienso que son ridículas. ¿Por qué no vamos a ver una película de espía que será mucho más divertida?

14. Tengo una cita muy importante. ¿Por qué hay un retraso? ¿Cuándo va a despegar el avión?

15. Quiero cambiar doscientos dólares americanos en euros. ¿Cuál es la tasa (el tipo) de cambio del dólar hoy?

16. Compré un reloj de plata, dos botellas de ron, y juguetes para mis niños.

17. Para empezar quiero gazpacho. Entonces quiero paella de mariscos y una ensalada. Voy a tomar vino blanco con mi comida.

18. No me gustaría ir a una corrida de toros. Pienso que es demasiado violenta.

19. Quisiera reservar una mesa para cuatro personas para esta noche a las ocho y media.

20. Tengo un problema con el coche que alquilé. Los frenos no funcionan bien y tengo miedo de conducir el coche.

21. Diga. Necesito información acerca del concierto de esta noche. ¿A qué hora empieza y cuánto cuestan los billetes?

22. Lo siento mucho. Voy a llegar tarde porque tengo una goma pinchada y tengo que repararla. Llegaré en una media hora.

23. Me siento mal. Tengo un dolor de estómago y no tengo ganas de comer. También tengo fiebre. ¿Puede Ud. ayudarme?

24. ¿Cuántos años tiene su primo(a)? ¿De dónde es? ¿Cómo es? ¿Cuál es su profesión?

Appendix A

*24 Important Words
and Phrases*

ENGLISH	SPANISH	PRONUNCIATION
1. Hello.	Buenos días.	boo-weh-nohs dee-yahs
2. Good-bye.	Adiós.	ah dee-yohs
3. Please.	Por favor.	pohr fah-bohr
4. Thank you very much.	Muchas gracias.	moo-chahs grah-see-yahs
5. You're welcome.	De nada.	deh nah-dah
6. Excuse me.	Perdón. Con permiso.	pehr-dohn kohn pehr-mee-soh
7. My name is . . .	Me llamo . . .	meh yah-moh
8. I would like . . .	Quisiera . . .	kee-see-yeh-rah
9. I need . . .	Necesito . . .	neh-seh-see-toh
10. Do you have . . .	¿Tiene Ud . . . ?	tee-yeh-neh oo-stehd
11. How do you say . . .	¿Cómo se dice . . .?	koh-moh seh dee-seh
12. Please give me . . .	Déme por favor . . .	deh-meh pohr fah-bohr
13. What does this mean?	¿Qué quiere decir esto?	keh kee-yeh-reh deh-seer ehs-toh
14. Can you help me please?	¿Puede Ud. ayudarme por favor?	poo-weh-deh oo-steh ah-yoo-dahr-meh pohr fah-bohr
15. Do you speak English?	¿Habla Ud. inglés?	ah-blah oo-stehd een-glehs
16. I speak a little Spanish.	Hablo un poco el español.	ah-bloh oon poh-koh ehl ehs-pah-nyohl
17. I don't understand	No comprendo.	noh kohm-prehn-doh
18. Please repeat.	Repita por favor.	rreh-pee-tah pohr fah-bohr
19. What did you say?	¿Qué dijó Ud.?	kee dee-hoh oo-stehd

20. I'm lost.	Estoy perdido(a).	ehs-toy pehr-dee-doh (dah)
21. I'm looking for . . .	Estoy buscando . . .	ehs-toy boos-kahn-doh
22. Where are the bathrooms?	¿Dónde está los baños?	dohn-deh ehs-tah lohs bah-nyohs
23. Where is the police station?	¿Dónde está la comisaria de de policía?	dohn-deh ehs-tah lah koh-mee-sah-ree-yeh deh poh-lee-see-yah
24. Where is the American Embassy?	¿Dónde está la embajada americana?	dohn-deh ehs-tah lah ehm- bah-hah-dah ah-meh-ree kah-nah

Appendix B

Verb Glossary

Present	Preterit	Imperfect	Future	Conditional
(do)	(did)	(was)	(will)	(would)
us**o**	us**é**	us**aba**	usar**é**	usar**ía**
us**as**	us**aste**	us**abas**	usar**ás**	usar**ías**
us**a**	us**ó**	us**aba**	usar**á**	usar**ía**
us**amos**	us**amos**	us**ábamos**	usar**emos**	usar**íamos**
us**áis**	us**asteis**	us**ábais**	usar**éis**	usar**íais**
us**an**	us**aron**	us**aban**	usar**án**	usar**ían**

-er Verbs

Comer, to eat
Gerund: comiendo **Past participle:** comido **Commands:** ¡Coma Ud.! ¡Coman Uds.! ¡Comamos!

Present	Preterit	Imperfect	Future	Conditional
com**o**	com**í**	com**ía**	comer**é**	comer**ía**
com**es**	com**iste**	com**ías**	comer**ás**	comer**ías**
com**e**	com**ió**	com**ía**	comer**á**	comer**ía**
com**emos**	com**imos**	com**íamos**	comer**emos**	comer**íamos**
com**éis**	com**isteis**	com**íais**	comer**éis**	comer**íais**
com**en**	com**ieron**	com**ían**	comer**án**	comer**ían**

-ir Verbs

Vivir, to live
Gerund: viviendo **Past participle:** vivido **Commands:** ¡Viva Ud.! ¡Vivan Uds.! ¡Vivamos!

Present	Preterit	Imperfect	Future	Conditional
viv**o**	viv**í**	viv**ía**	vivir**é**	vivir**ía**
viv**es**	viv**iste**	viv**ías**	vivir**ás**	vivir**ías**

vive	vivió	vivía	vivirá	viviría
viv**imos**	viv**imos**	viv**íamos**	vivir**emos**	vivir**íamos**
viv**ís**	viv**isteis**	viv**íais**	vivir**éis**	vivir**íais**
viv**en**	viv**ieron**	viv**ían**	vivir**án**	vivir**ían**

CONJUGATING STEM-CHANGING VERBS

-ar Verbs

Pensar (*e* to *ie*), to think
Present: pienso, piensas, piensa, pensamos, penséis, piensan

Other verbs like *pensar* include *cerrar* (to close), *comenzar* (to begin), and *empezar* (to begin).

Mostrar (*o* to *ue*), to show
Present: muestro, muestras, muestra, mostramos, mostráis, muestran

Other verbs like *mostrar* include *almorzar* (to eat lunch), *contar* (to tell), *costar* (to cost), *encontrar* (to find), and *recordar* (to remember).

Jugar (*u* to *ue*), to play (a sport or game)
Present: juego, juegas, juega, jugamos, jugáis, juegan
Preterit: jugué, jugaste, jugó, jugamos, jugasteis, jugaron

-er Verbs

Defender (*e* to *ie*), to defend, to forbid
Present: defiendo, defiendes, defiende, defendemos, defendéis, defienden

Other verbs like *defender* include *descender* (to descend), *entender* (to understand, to hear), *perder* (to lose), and *querer* (to want).

Volver (*o* to *ue*), to return
Present: vuelvo, vuelves, vuelve, volvemos, volvéis, vuelven

Another verb like *volver* is *poder* (to be able to, can).

-ir Verbs

Pedir (*e* to *i*), to ask for
Gerund: pidiendo
Present: pido, pides, pide, pedimos, pedís, piden
Preterit: pedí, pediste, pidió, pedimos, pedisteis, pidieron

Other verbs like *pedir* include *impedir* (to prevent), *medir* (to measure), *repetir* (to repeat), and *servir* (to serve).

Sentir (*e* to *ie*, *i*), to feel
Gerund: sintiendo
Present: siento, sientes, siente, sentimos, sentís, sienten
Preterit: sentí, sentiste, sintió, sentimos, sentisteis, sintieron

Other verbs like *sentir* include *advertir* (to warn, to notify), *consentir* (to consent), *mentir* (to lie), *preferir* (to prefer), and *referir* (to refer).

Dormir (*o* to *ue*, *u*), to sleep
Gerund: durmiendo
Present: duermo, duermes, duerme, dormimos, dormís, duermen
Preterit: dormí, dormiste, durmió, dormimos, dormisteis, durmieron

Another verb like *dormir* is *morir* (to die).

-*uir* Verbs (except -*guir*)

Incluir (*i* to *y*), to include
Gerund: incluyendo
Present: incluyo, incluyes, incluye, incluimos, incluís, incluyen
Preterit: incluí, incluiste, incluyó, incluimos, incluisteis, incluyeron

Other verbs like *incluir* include *concluir* (to conclude, to end), *construir* (to construct), *contribuir* (to contribute), *destruir* (to destroy), and *sustituir* (to substitue).

-*eer* Verbs

Leer (*e* to *y*), to read
Gerund: leyendo
Preterit: leí, leíste, leyó, leímos, leísteis, leyeron

Other verbs like *leer* include *creer* (to believe), *poseer* (to possess), and *proveer* (to provide).

-*iar* Verbs

Enviar (*i* to *í*), to send
Present: envío, envías, envía, enviamos, enviáis, envían

Other verbs like *enviar* include *confiar* + *en* (to confide in), *guiar* (to guide), and *variar* (to vary).

-uar Verbs

Actuar (*u* to *ú*), to act
Present: actúo, actúas, actúa, actuamos, actuáis, actúan

Another verb like *actuar* is *continuar* (to continue).

CONJUGATING SPELLING-CHANGE VERBS

-cer or -cir Verbs

Convencer (*c* to *z*), to convince
Present: convenzo, convences, convence, convencemos, convencéis, convencen

Conocer (*c* to *zc*), to know
Present: conozco, conoces, conoce, conocemos, conocéis, conocen

Conducir (*c* to *zc*), to drive, conduct
Present: conduzco, conduces, conduce, conducemos, conducéis, conducen
Preterit: conduje, condujiste, condujo, condujimos, condujisteis, condujieron

-ger or -gir Verbs

Exigir (*g* to *j*), to demand
Present: exijo, exiges, exige, exigimos, exigís, exigen

Escoger (*g* to *j*), to choose
Present: escojo, escoges, escoge, escogemos, escogéis, escogen

-guir Verbs

Distinguir (*gu* to *g*), to distinguish
Present: distingo, distingues, distingue, distinguimos, distinguís, distinguen

-car Verbs

Buscar (*c* to *qu*), to look for
Preterit: busqué, buscaste, buscó, buscamos, buscasteis, buscaron

-gar Verbs

Pagar (*g* to *gu*), to pay
Preterit: pagué, pagaste, pagó, pagamos, pagasteis, pagaron

-zar Verbs

Gozar (*z* to *c*), to enjoy
Preterit: gocé, gozaste, gozó, gozamos, gozasteis, gozaron

CONJUGATING IRREGULAR VERBS

Dar, to give
Present: doy, das, da, damos, dáis, dan
Preterit: di, diste, dio, dimos, disteis, dieron

Decir, to say
Gerund: diciendo Past participle: dicho
Present: digo dices dice decimos decís dicen
Preterit: dije dijiste dijó dijmos dijisteis dijeron
Future: diré dirás dirá diremos diréis dirán
Conditional: diría dirías diría diríamos diríais dirían

Estar, to be
Present: estoy, estás, está, estamos, estáis, están
Preterit: estuve, estuviste, estuvo, estuvimos, estuvisteis, estuvieron

Hacer, to make, to do
Past participle: hecho
Present: hago, haces, hace, hacemos, hacéis, hacen
Preterit: hice, hiciste, hizo, hicimos, hicisteis, hicieron
Future: haré, harás, hará, haremos, haréis, harán
Conditional: haría, harías, haría, haríamos, haríais, harían

Ir, to go
Gerund: yendo
Present: voy, vas, va, vamos, vais, van
Preterit: fui, fuiste, fue, fuimos, fuisteis, fueron
Conditional: iba, ibas, iba, íbamos, ibais, iban

Oír, to hear
Gerund: oyendo
Present: oigo, oyes,oye, oímos, oís, oyen
Preterit: oí, oíste, oyó, oímos, oísteis, oyeron

Poder (*o* to *ue*), to be able to, can
Gerund: pudiendo
Present: puedo, puedes, puede, podemos, podéis, pueden
Preterit: pude, pudiste, pudo, pudimos, pudisteis, pudieron
Future: podré, podrás, podrá, podremos, podréis, podrán
Conditional: podría, podrías, podría, podríamos, podríais, podrían

Poner, to put
Past participle: puesto
Present: **pongo,** pones, pone, ponemos, ponéis, ponen
Preterit: puse, pusiste, puso, pusimos, pusisteis, pusieron
Future: pondré, pondrás, pondrá, pondremos, pondréis, pondrán
Conditional: pondría, pondrías, pondría, pondríamos, pondríais, pondrían

Querer, to want
Present: quiero, quieres, quiere, queremos, queréis, quieren
Preterit: quise, quisiste, quiso, quisimos, quisisteis, quisieron
Future: querré, querrás, querrá, querremos, querréis, querrán
Conditional: querría, querrías, querría, querríamos, querríais, querrían

Saber, to know
Present: sé, sabes, sabe, sabemos, sabéis, saben
Preterit: supe, supiste, supo, supimos, supisteis, supieron
Future: sabré, sabrás, sabrá, sabremos, sabréis, sabrán
Conditional: sabría, sabrías, sabría, sabríamos, sabríais, sabrían

Salir, to go out, to leave
Present: **salgo,** sales, sale, salimos, saléis, salen
Future: saldré, saldrás, saldrá, saldremos, saldréis, saldrán
Conditional: saldría, saldrías, saldría, saldríamos, saldríais, saldrían

Ser, to be
Past participle: sido
Present: soy, eres, es, somos, sois, son
Preterit: fui, fuiste, fue, fuimos, fuisteis, fueron
Imperfect: era, eras, era, éramos, erais, eran

Tener, to have
Present: **tengo,** tienes, tiene, tenemos, tenéis, **tienen**
Preterit: tuve, tuviste, tuvo, tuvimos, tuvisteis, tuvieron
Future: tendré, tendrás, tendrá, tendremos, tendréis, tendrán
Conditional: tendría, tendrías, tendría, tendríamos, tendríais, tendrían

Traer, to bring
Past participle: traído
Present: **traigo,** traes, trae, traemos, traéis, traen
Preterit: traje, trajiste, trajo, trajimos, trajisteis, trajeron

Venir, to come
Gerund: viniendo
Present: vengo, vienes, viene, venimos, venís, vienen
Preterit: vine, viniste, vino, vinimos, vinisteis, vinieron
Future: vendré, vendrás, vendrá, vendremos, vendréis, vendrán
Conditional: vendría, vendrías, vendría, vendríamos, vendríais, vendrían

Ver, to see
Past participle: visto
Present: veo, ves, ve, vemos, veis, ven
Preterit: vi, viste, vio, vimos, visteis, vieron
Imperfect: veía, veías, veía, veíamos, veíais, veían

Index

Nouns, *continued*
    referring to groups of people, 22
    singular, 12
    subject, 28
    in superlative sentences, 202
Number (singular or plural)
    of comparative and superlative adjec-
        tives, 202
    of demonstrative pronouns, 176
    of nouns, 12
    of pronouns, 28
Numbers, 71
    cardinal, 108–10, 113
    ordinal, 110–11
    writing, 108
    writing date in, 113
Numerals, 14, 108
Nunca, 155
Nuts, 227

O

O, ó (vowel), pronunciation of, 4
Object pronouns, 178
    direct, 177, 179
    double, 182–83
    indirect, 178–81
    position of, 182–83
Objects of prepositions
    que as, 218
    quién as, 218–19
Obligations, expressing, 123–24
Ofrecer (to offer), 39
Oír (to hear), 41, 304
Opinions
    exclamations for, 213
    expressions of, 192–93
    negative, 191
    subjunctive after superlative for,
        208
Opposites, 202–3
Optician, seeking help from, 169
Ordinal numbers, 110–11
Os, 178
Outdoor activities, 188–89. *See also*
    Leisure activities
Outdoor eating stands, 224

P

Paella, 226
Para (for, to), 100, 147
Para + noun, 237–38
Para + verb, 238
¿Para qué?, 147
Participles
    past, 52–53
    perfect, 266
    present, 183, 265–66
Parts of the body, 13, 92, 238
Passive voice, 86, 260
Past participles
    of irregular verbs, 52–53
    of regular verbs, 52
Past tense (preterit)
    forming, 48–51
    imperfect vs., 54–57
Pastimes, 174–75
Patterns, fabric, 250
Pedir (to ask for), 100
Pensar (to think), 35
Peor, placement of, 202
Perdón, 152
Perdóneme, 152
Perfect cognates, 22–23
    of adjectives, 22
    of feminine nouns, 23
    of masculine nouns, 23
Perfect conditional mood, 64
Perfect participles, 266
Perfect subjunctive, 130–31, 194
Periods (in numbers), 108
Pero (but, however), 158
Person (of pronouns), 28
Personal *a*, 179
Personal hygiene items, 236–37
Persuasion, 131, 141, 192–93
Pharmacies, 236–37
Phone conversations, 162–64
Photocopying services, 270–71
Photographs, 169–70
Physical challenges, seeking help with, 171
Physical conditions, *hay* with, 149
Place names, 100, 166
    continents, 89
    countries, 87–89

About the Author

Gail Stein has an M.A. in French literature from New York University and has taught French and Spanish in New York City public junior and senior high schools for more than thirty-three years. She has authored numerous text and trade books in both languages. Mrs. Stein has also assisted in a revision project of the French curriculum for the New York City Board of Education and has served as an adjunct professor to St. John's University in its Early Admission Extension Program. She has given presentations and demonstration lessons at numerous foreign language conferences and has had her lessons videotaped by the New York City Board of Education for national distribution. Mrs. Stein has been recognized in the 2000 and 2002 editions of *Who's Who Among America's Teachers*.